Widowed Too Soon

SECOND EDITION

A Young Widow's Journey through Grief,

Healing, and Spiritual Transformation

By

Laura Hirsch

Published by Rainbow Books - 2006

Cover design by Eye Design Online

Widowed Too Soon - Second Edition
ISBN: 0-9776653-0-5

Table of Contents

Preface

"If you learn from your suffering,
and really come to understand the lessons you were taught,
you might be able to help someone else
who is now in the phase you may have just completed.
Maybe that's what it's all about after all."

—*Source Unknown*

I became a young widow on February 11, 1995. I was only 27-years-old. I had been with my beloved husband and best friend, Darren, for eight years, since my sophomore year in college. We had been married for just two years and had just moved into our new home two months earlier when he was tragically killed in an automobile accident with a friend at the wheel. Part of me died that day too, and I thought that my life was over.

During the early stages of my grief, I searched everywhere for a book written by another young widow. I wanted to know that someone else had walked the dark path of grief, and had made it out of this hell I was experiencing. I wanted to know if anyone else had ever felt the inner mental and emotional turmoil that totally consumed my existence. I needed to know for certain that my husband still existed in spirit somewhere. If he was no longer here, where was he? I felt I must have this unrelenting question answered.

Surely, I reasoned, some other woman had to have gone through this before me and had written about her experiences. The only books I found about widowhood were written by and for older widows. I found that they were filled with practical information which didn't relate to my situation. It definitely appeared that the younger widows were completely overlooked.

Also, none of these grief books answered the spiritual questions you inevitably face when you lose a loved one, such as "Is he in heaven now?" and "Is he okay?" I didn't want to believe that Darren had simply ceased to exist. It is a normal human desire to want to know what becomes of a loved one when they die. None of these grief books offered any information about life after death or spirit communication, which were topics I was now desperate to investigate. Before long, I realized that the book I so desperately sought did not exist.

Two years after Darren's death, I remarried and started a family, but the hole in my heart remained. After years of searching for answers and after many life-altering experiences, along with some gentle nudging from the other side, I decided to write the book I never found. I finished the draft for the book in February of 2000, the same time I found out I was pregnant with my second child, and I put the book on the back burner.

I was eight months pregnant on September 11, 2001 as I watched the agony of those who lost loved ones in the terrorist attacks. For me, the most heart wrenching stories were those of the expectant mothers who were widowed that day. Grieving the loss of my husband was the most difficult thing I had ever experienced. Pregnancy, childbirth, and new motherhood was second. I couldn't imagine having to face both at once. My heart ached for these women, and I wanted to reach out to them. The young widowed mothers of 9/11 were my inspiration to publish this book. I felt the need to share what had taken me years to discover in the hope that this sharing might ease someone else's pain.

While my story is written from the perspective of a young widow, this book offers hope and help to expedite healing for anyone who has ever grieved over the loss of a loved one and is looking for comfort and answers. If sharing my experiences can do this for just one person, then all of the pain that I relived during the writing process will have been worth it.

With Love and Blessings,
Laura Hirsch

Part One

<u>In the Beginning</u>

<u>Growing Up</u>

"Life can only be understood backwards, but it must be lived forwards."

—Soren Kierkegaard

I am starting at the beginning of my life to show that I was not raised by a band of gypsies, but rather had a very normal Midwestern upbringing. I was born on August 28th, 1967 in Milwaukee, Wisconsin, and grew up in Mukwonago, a small suburb of Milwaukee. As one would expect, I lived on a farm, and sat around all day watching the Green Bay Packers while drinking beer and eating cheese and bratwurst. (Just kidding- it's an inside Wisconsin joke.)

Actually, we lived in a tri-level home on an acre and a half lot in a subdivision out in the boonies. I was the second of my parents' five children. I have an older brother, a younger sister, and two younger brothers. My dad was an ex-Marine and ran his own architectural firm and my mom stayed at home to raise us. We had a big, close-knit, extended family; and spent most weekends and holidays together.

I was a very shy and obedient child, and apparently wouldn't do anything without my mom's permission. I'd even wake her up in the middle of the night to ask if I could go to the bathroom, or so the story goes. I idolized my older brother Joey, copied everything he did, and wouldn't do anything without him. We were only 16 months apart. I was a total tomboy growing up. I hated dresses and nightgowns, with the exception of my cool polyester "magic nightgown" which lit up when I turned over under the sheets. Static electricity is magic when you're a kid, I guess. I preferred wearing pants and pajamas, and I still do. I didn't like dolls, and I played with all of my brother's toys instead. I loved sports and collected baseball cards, watched baseball and football games on TV, and played with all the guys in neighborhood ball games.

My sister, Kim, and I shared a room and were best friends. She liked dresses, dolls, and all the frilly girl stuff. We had so much fun together in our room, building forts between our dressers with a sheet. We would entertain ourselves for hours. We had a huge collection of stuffed animals. I surrounded myself with my animals at night, like a fortress, to protect me from the evil clown who lived under my bed, waiting for my arm or leg to stray over the edge. One day, I decided that Kim's stuffed animals needed haircuts, and proceeded to shear them all. She's still mad at me for cutting off her Eeyore's mane and tail, leaving him looking like a hippo.

I was nine years old when my youngest brother, Tommy, was born. My sister and I loved taking care of him, until he pooped his pants. Then he became my mom's baby again. In fact, he didn't walk until he was 18-months-old because we carried him everywhere. I even carried him with me into our basement to protect me from the boogeyman that I was certain lived down there. We had this creepy crawlspace that you had to walk past to get to our spare refrigerator that my mom always needed me to get something out of for her. Either baby Tommy or one of our fearsome toy poodles accompanied me on each trip to the laundry room or the refrigerator in the basement. They'd protect me. We thought that Tommy was going to be a girl, so Kim and I thought it was fun to put a dress and my mom's makeup on him and pretend he was our little sister. Kim still has the blackmail pictures.

My siblings and I had all the cool toys of the time. Among the most memorable were: Easy Bake Oven, Lite Brite, Etch-a-Sketch, Shrinky Dinks, Rock-em Sock-em Robots, Stretch Armstrong, Slinky, Weebles, Hoppity Hop, Operation, and the Six Million Dollar Man and Bionic Woman action figures with removable bionic parts. Who could ask for anything more?

We grew up in the seventies, before cable TV and VCR's, so we watched whatever was on the four local TV channels. Some of our favorite shows included: *"Land of the Lost," "Dr. Shrinker," "H. R. PufnStuf," "Sigmund and the Sea Monsters," "Shazam," "Isis," "Speed Racer," "Fury," "Scooby Doo" "Superfriends," "Grape Ape," "Captain Caveman," "Underdog," "Hong Kong Phooey,"* and- best of all- was *"School House Rock;"* educational cartoon musicals placed between Saturday morning cartoons. To this day, in order to recite the Preamble to the Constitution, I have to sing the *"School House Rock"* version!

I had a great childhood and had everything a kid could want. We had an in-ground pool, and we spent our summers swimming and making up crazy dives. I also have fond memories of riding my bike around the subdivision with the neighbor kids, playing hide and seek and flashlight tag, picking wild raspberries and asparagus around the cornfields near our house and playing in the sandbox and on the swing set. Of course, there was also ice-skating, sledding, building snowmen, and snowball fights in the winter. And who could forget going out for Friday-night Fish Fry? Yeah, hey there!

I was also involved with Girl Scouts, and went on lots of camping and hiking outings, and trips to places like the museum, and the Milwaukee County Zoo. I also went roller-skating, and to drive-in movies for fun. I had many friends. We had slumber parties, and did all the typical stuff, like putting a sleeping person's hand in warm water to make them wet themselves, and the "light as a feather, stiff as a board" séance. Neither one ever worked.

Many weekends were spent with my family at our cottage on a lake in northern Wisconsin, near my dad's parents' house. I'll never forget the long 4½ hour drive in a cramped station wagon with two adults, five kids, and two panting dogs with bad breath, plus all of our luggage and pillows. Kim and I made our younger brother, Ricky, sit on the floor and our youngest brother, Tommy, sit in the back window with the luggage so we could lie down on the seats. We'd be arrested for that these days. We'd irritate our parents by saying "Stop touching me," or "Get off my pillow," the whole way there. The inevitable "Are we there yet?" and "I have to go to the bathroom," was repeated by someone every ten minutes. Ah, the good old days.

Four of my dad's five siblings also owned a place either on the same lake, or in the same town. We spent a lot of time with relatives, going fishing and waterskiing or tubing, and making great bonfires at night to roast marshmallows. We'd also visit my paternal grandparents at their house, one town away. We enjoyed helping them pick and can the fruit and vegetables they grew in their many gardens. Grandpa would take us to the local grocery store and buy us all the penny candy our hearts desired.

We spent time with my mom's parents too, as well as her only sister and her family. My maternal great-grandmother was also still living when I was young, and I remember going to visit her in the nursing home, and getting wheelchair rides down the halls from great grandma's friends.

As the family instigator, I was the mastermind behind all the mischief. Kim and Ricky helped me execute all my great ideas. Ricky would do anything we asked him to do, just to make us laugh; including running around the neighborhood in his Superman Underoos in the snow. I was always a practical joker. I enjoyed doing things like short-sheeting my parents' bed, tape-recording my dad's so-called singing in the shower, and making Ricky laugh at the dinner table by mimicking his eating pattern so that he had to go eat in the other room. I made up funny nicknames for everyone, some of which are still used to this day. We call my mom "Jell-O" more often than "mom." Don't ask.

My siblings and I loved to jump on the beds and got in trouble every time we did it, but it never stopped us. Kim and I liked to slide down the stairs in our sleeping bags, with Ricky at the bottom to cushion the landing. The one time we let him be on the top, he scraped his face up on the prickly textured wall, and screamed the whole way down. Kim and I still chuckle about that sometimes. We also had hand stand contests and made my mom panic by doing flips throughout the house. Obviously, there wasn't a lot to do in Mukwonago, so we found plenty of ways to entertain ourselves at home. There were no fast food restaurants, movie theaters, or any kind of entertainment in town. Now, there is plenty to do, but not when we lived there.

Growing up, I loved animals and had a lot of pets. I used to want to be a veterinarian until I found out I'd have to cut open the animals. My personal zoo included parakeets, gerbils, hamsters, and guinea pigs. Our family pets included dogs and stray cats, which I also had nicknames for. Even the frogs and tadpoles in our pond became pets. Much to the dismay of my mom, we'd also find salamanders and bring them into the house. Mom drew the line at salamanders.

Most of all, I loved gymnastics. It was my passion. My dad had been a gymnast when he was younger, and my sister and I followed in his footsteps. I started when I was eight-years-old and it soon took over my life. I was a natural. I'm pretty modest, but my success in gymnastics is something I'm very proud of and for which I worked very hard. I started competing in junior high as an "all around" (competing in all four events) and won or placed in all competitions. I also began teaching gymnastics at our local gymnastics club. In my freshman year of high school, I qualified for the state tournament as an all-around, individual, and team participant. I earned a varsity letter my freshman year; and my letter jacket was adorned with medals won at invitational meets. I qualified for state again during my junior and senior years. As team captain and Most Valuable Player, I broke many school records. Junior and senior years were great because Kim and I were on the team together. She was a freshman when I was a junior. My teammates were like a second family to me.

For the first two years of college, I competed on the gymnastics team. I broke the school record on balance beam, was voted Athlete of the Week, was an All-American, and competed in Nationals. I decided not to compete my junior year because I wanted to have a job listed on my resume when I graduated. So, I became the head gymnastics coach at a local high school. (What a stretch!) My friend Moe was the assistant coach. We were on rival teams in high school, but soon became like sisters. We coached the team to their first gymnastics win in the school's history. It was not only fun, but very rewarding as well! Moe and I were the biggest goof-balls, and used to coach using our "helium" voices. We both had a talent for being able to make our voices sound like we had just inhaled helium from a balloon. The kids dug it. Drive-through restaurant workers did not.

Ok, I'm getting ahead of myself here. Back to high school. Most of my close friends were also on the gymnastics team. We spent all of our study halls and lunch hours in the gym, where we'd mostly goof off on the trampoline instead of practicing our routines. I was still a practical joker in high school and got into my share of mischief with friends after school: toilet papering the girl's locker room, using our coach's keys to get free sodas from the teacher's lounge, and shooting off fire extinguishers in the hall: pretty innocent stuff. I was a good student, was on the honor roll and excelled in English and Science. I guess I would have been considered a jock in high school, and a bit of a goody-goody. I didn't smoke or do drugs and I tried alcohol for the first time on New Year's Eve my junior year.

Kim and I still shared a room; and like typical teenagers, we had our little schoolgirl crushes. Our room was wallpapered with posters of guys in bands, either British Pop or Hair Bands. On my side of the room were pictures and posters of Duran Duran, especially of John Taylor, their bass player. (We're talking *hundreds* of pictures here.) I was sure that I would marry him. On Kim's side were mainly pictures of David Lee Roth, the lead singer of Van Halen, including a very disturbing poster of him wearing nothing but chaps. How I loved waking up each morning to see Diamond Dave's bare ass (sarcasm). She also had pictures on her side of Jon Bon Jovi (on the ceiling) Tommy Lee, and other cute guys from bands. I used to torture Kim by playing my Duran Duran tapes (yes, I said tapes) over and over. I would write down all the lyrics, stopping often to rewind the tape so I could hear what they were saying. Kim learned all of the words too, but not by choice.

During summer vacation we always went to Milwaukee's giant festival on Lake Michigan called Summerfest. It was great. There were many different music stages that played every type of music imaginable. I, of course, hung out at the rock stage. There was also every type of food you could think of. I particularly remember the roasted corn that you dipped in the barrel of butter. Yummy! It was also a great place to people watch. I've never seen so many people testing the limits of how far spandex can stretch. Frightening.

The summer after high school I started dating my first "serious" boyfriend. In the fall, we both started college at the University of Wisconsin-Whitewater. Whitewater was relatively close to home; but it was in the middle of nowhere. You passed many cow, chicken, and pig farms on the 30-minute drive from home, always with the windows rolled up! I would come home on Saturdays to see my family, and drop off my laundry for my mom to do while I drove over to the high school to teach gymnastics. I'd return home and mooch food and money off of mom, grab my clean clothes, and head back to school. It was a beautiful thing.

Freshman year, I was living off campus with a girl who had been on my high school gymnastics team. We competed on Whitewater's team as well. Because we were underage, we couldn't go out to any of the college bars. However, a lot of our old high school crowd also ended up at Whitewater, and our apartment became "party central" because we didn't live in the dorms. My roommate and I would come home from gymnastics practice and our apartment would be full of my boyfriend's drunken friends playing card games. We had to go to the library to get any studying done.

I broke up with my boyfriend at the beginning of my sophomore year, after realizing that he was completely wrong for me. I had just turned 19, the legal drinking age in Wisconsin at the time. When I turned 18, the drinking age changed to 19; then when I turned 19, the drinking age changed to 21. I just made the cutoff date or Grandfather Clause as they called it, by three days. There were plenty of mornings I wish I hadn't made it. It was October 1995; and I'd just started going out to the college bars with Kimberly, one of my three roommates. Like many small college towns, Whitewater's main social scene was the bar scene. This is where I met Darren.

<u>Our Story</u>

*"And think not you can direct the course of love,
for love, if it finds you worthy, directs your course."*

—*Kahlil Gibran*

Darren and I met at a campus bar. I was instantly attracted to him because he looked like John Taylor from Duran Duran. He had the same hair, long on top and in the back, short on the sides, and dyed blond in the front. I now joke about this hair style, known as a "mullet" or as I like to call it, a "mud flap," "ape drape" or "Wisconsin waterfall." It was really hot at the time, though. If you had a mullet and lived in the Midwest at that time, you were cool.

I hate to admit it, but I had really bad hair myself; a perm, too many highlights, tons of mousse and hairspray, bangs as tall as my face. Just watch any music video from the late 1980's and you'll get the idea. My wardrobe was pretty special too. Typical 1980's attire: leggings, a big sweater with an even bigger belt, a few pairs of multi-colored socks that matched the outfit, high-top tennis shoes and giant earrings. Or my other favorite look was strategically ripped jeans and a black motorcycle jacket. It's pretty embarrassing now, but we thought we were cool then.

Darren's opening line was "Are these your keys?" (He had found them on the floor.) Thinking the keys were actually his and that it was a bad attempt at a pick-up line, I said "No, are they yours?" He said "No", and I suggested that he turn them in. He did. We talked for a while, and then played darts with my roommate Kimberly and his roommate Mike. Apparently, he already knew who I was because I was casually dating a friend of his and he had seen us out together.

Darren asked me about my relationship with his friend Brett, and I told him it was nothing serious. We went our separate ways that night, but I hoped to see him again. The next day, Darren wrote Brett a note in a class they had together asking about me. Brett wrote back that I was very cool; but that there was nothing serious between us. Darren soon asked me out on a date. We went to dinner and rented some movies that we watched at his apartment. We had the best time, laughing, talking, and smooching. I wished the night would never end. I knew that night that he was the one for me.

It was six months before we became exclusive. Each of us had recently ended a long-term relationship when we first met and didn't want to rush into things. I was ready sooner than he was. I guess it took me throwing a beer in his face one night, followed by the plastic cup, after catching him purposely kissing another girl in front of me, only to top it off by giving him the finger as his cab drove past me walking home that made him realize how much he loved me. We joked about that one for years.

Despite our rough beginning, Darren and I had a wonderful, loving relationship. He was my best friend, and we shared the same silly sense of humor and taste in music. He was almost like another brother to me, that's how close we were. We could just be idiots around one another, and loved to make each other laugh. We were very happy and very much in love. We knew that we'd get married some day, and talked about getting engaged after graduation.

Darren was a beautiful person, inside and out. He was tall, dark, and handsome; an Italian Stallion, as he liked to put it. He liked to stand out from the crowd, and had a unique look and wardrobe; a trendsetter. He had a healthy ego, but underneath the facade, he was very sensitive. He had a huge heart, and was very generous and honest. He loved to laugh, tease, and joke around. He loved sports, especially football. He was from a suburb of Chicago, Illinois, and attended the Chicago Bears training camp every year, and all of the home games. He was also an avid golfer and downhill skier. He had a special bond with his mom that was immediately apparent. I remember thinking that if a man treats a woman like he treats his mom, then I had it made. Although he was adopted, I had never seen a more loving mother-son relationship. When he first told me he was adopted, and I asked if he knew who his real parents were, he defensively responded, "These are my real parents." Darren was a friendly, outgoing, down-to-earth person that got along with everyone. I was absolutely smitten. I felt so blessed to have him in my life.

Darren went home for the summer the first year we dated. We only got to see each other on weekends. It was agony, and we each ran up quite a phone bill. We returned to Whitewater in the fall and lived in the same apartment building. We scheduled a lot of our classes at the same time so we could walk together; and we even took a few classes together. We wrote each other love notes, exchanging them between classes. Most of our free time was spent together; but we also did things with our friends, as we both valued our other friendships. We'd go out separately with our friends, and then meet up at the end of the night for some together time. We weren't the couple making out in the corner who were inseparable; in fact, he was always teasing me that I cramped his style by hanging out with him and his friends. He was always trying to set up his friends with girls, and I was like the fifth wheel. I didn't mind, I liked to have fun alone with my friends too. I hated it when a close friend got a new boyfriend and suddenly their friends were nonexistent.

I loved Darren's family from the beginning, especially his mother. She was one of the sweetest people I had ever met. I started calling her "mom" almost immediately, and I still do. She was like a mother to me and took me under her wing and treated me like one of her own. I not only considered her like a mother, but also a dear, trusted friend.

Darren and I stood up together at his sister's wedding, where I met his extended family. I couldn't wait to be a part of this wonderful group of people forever. We planned to get married ourselves right after graduation. Darren was going to take over his father's business one day, so I knew I would be moving to Illinois eventually.

Darren graduated in December of 1988. I still had another semester to go, plus summer school. After graduation, he moved back to Illinois, got his own condo, and began working for the family business. This was a horrible time for us. We saw each other only a few times a month. The only reason I didn't drop out of school and move in with him was that I wasn't a quitter. I had made it this far and was determined to finish what I started. I became the first person in my family to graduate from college. I was very proud of that accomplishment. Darren and I would have the rest of our lives to be together, so a few more months of my being in school wouldn't matter in the long run. Problems began to surface in our relationship as a result of being separated, but mainly because of Tyler.

Tyler was Darren's graduation present from me, a Siberian Husky puppy that he'd always wanted. Tyler would take my place until I moved to Illinois. Good theory, but Tyler turned out to be the dog from hell. He flunked out of puppy training classes, and was like a bull in a china shop living in Darren's condo, even digging his way through concrete. Darren worked all day, five days a week, so he couldn't spend much time with Tyler.

Eventually, Darren's mom ended up keeping Tyler at their house during the week. On the weekends, Darren felt guilty about leaving the dog with his mom again to come and visit me in Wisconsin; and because I was living in a crowded house with eight other girls, there was no room for Tyler. I drove an unreliable, beater car, and was afraid to drive it any distance, as it had failed me many times in the past. So, we saw each other less and less and we started growing apart. Darren enjoyed spending weekends going out with his single friends back home; and I spent them with friends at school. Eventually, Tyler was given to friends who lived on a farm; but by then our relationship had suffered and things were not the same between us.

When I did finally graduate, in the summer of 1989, Darren and I were certainly not ready to live together, much less get married. He came to visit me the weekend of my cousin's wedding. Instead of going to the wedding, we had a long talk, and tearfully decided that it would be best if we split up. We still loved each other, and we knew that if we were meant to be together, it would happen when the time was right. I had just taken a job as a retail salesperson at a clothing store in Milwaukee, and Darren was in Chicago. It just wouldn't work like this. Neither of us was happy.

I was heartbroken. In order to avoid the pain of the breakup, we both started dating other people right away. I dated only one guy, named Rick (I called him "Ricky" just like my brother.) I also met Rick in a bar in Whitewater, go figure. He was staying in Whitewater for a few months with his friend Mark, whom I knew. I was out with Moe and she grabbed my arm and said "cute boy alert." I turned to look and was not disappointed. He was one of the best looking guys I had ever seen, resembling a young Brad Pitt.

He was tall, with long dirty blond hair, blue eyes, chiseled features, and a tan muscular build. His only visible flaw was that he was smoking a cigarette. We met that night and became friends, and when Darren and I split up, Rick was there to comfort me and became my new boyfriend. Not only was he easy on the eyes, he was funny and fun to pick on.

One of my favorite memories of Rick is one day, after my last college class ever, I went over to his apartment to share my excitement with him, but he was sleeping and grouchy and would not wake up. I had some McDonald's French fries with me and decided to put all of the crispy ones in his cupped hand that was hanging over the edge of the couch he was sleeping on. When I finally got him to wake up, he noticed the handful of fries and mumbled "what the *%&#?" as I laughed hysterically. As I said, he was fun to pick on. Another time, he fell asleep sitting up on the couch at my parent's house and started drooling and "dancing" in his sleep. My sister and I decided to have a little fun and tore a bunch of pieces of string from my torn jeans and piled them on his face. When he woke up, he was covered in string and mumbled another "what the *%&#?"as Kim and I roared. He was a good sport.

Darren, on the other hand, went out every weekend and played the field during our separation. Even though we were broken up, Darren and I still talked and cried on the phone because we missed each other so much. After a few months of dating other people, we realized that we'd made a mistake, that we were still in love, and that we should do whatever it would take to make things work out.

He asked me to move in with him in October 1989, with a promise to get engaged soon. I broke up with Rick, passed up a promotion and quit my job, packed up my life, and moved to Illinois. It was truly blissful... for about a month, when Darren decided that he wasn't ready to take that big of a step. He suggested that I move back home, and that we should see each other on weekends only. I was furious, and embarrassed to have to move back home again. I told him that if I moved home, it would be over between us. This was ridiculous. In tears, I called my mom and told her I was moving home again. Both of our families were mad at Darren for doing this to me. I returned home with my tail between my legs and swore I would never speak to him again. In my mind, it was over- this time, for good.

I got my old job back and was immediately promoted to assistant manager. Rick and I started dating again. He made me laugh, which I really needed then; plus it made Darren jealous that I was seeing him again, an added bonus. Darren still called me all the time, sent me cards, told me he loved me and wanted to marry me. I was still mad and didn't trust him, but we decided to still see each other as friends. He would come to Wisconsin, and we would go to rock concerts together the way we used to, and always had a good time.

Even though we were just friends, Darren invited me to spend Christmas with his family in Illinois. It was magical: the snow, the warmth and the love I felt from his family. I knew I belonged there, but we still had a lot of things to work out. I got snowed in and had to stay the night. I was still dating Rick, and remained faithful to him, even though the old feelings for Darren came rushing back. Rick had also been talking about wanting to marry me, although I didn't think he was capable of that type of commitment. He had cheated on a former fiancée, and was a big flirt. Women adored him and he ate it up. But he and I still had something special. I told Darren I needed more time, and we'd have to see what happened. Darren continued to try to get me back for months. I was truly torn between the two of them.

That spring, Rick was a passenger in a car accident and was seriously injured and ended up staying in the hospital for a long time. He broke his pelvis, both ankles, and a lot of other bones. I brought him food and music, and even washed his hair for him. I spent all of my days off from work and all of my free time in the hospital. Once he was released, he was restricted to a wheelchair during his recovery. About a week later, he broke up with me, saying that he didn't want to put me through this. I didn't deserve it, he said. He said a lot of cruel and chauvinistic things to push me away. I felt helpless and crushed; but I respected his wishes and left him alone. He lived with his mom, so I knew she'd take good care of him. He eventually made a full recovery.

This twist of fate gave me an opportunity to see if Darren had finally grown up. Was he serious about wanting me back? It had been eight months since I moved back home. I called Darren and told him that Rick and I had broken up. He wanted to see me right away, and told me that he had changed, and that he'd spend the rest of his life making it up to me if I'd give him another chance. Third time is the charm, he said. We officially got back together and did the weekend commuting thing for about a month. Then, he finally asked me to marry him at an Aerosmith concert.

We were there with another couple, Daren and Karen, good friends of ours from Illinois. Darren was acting strange and nervous throughout the whole concert, and I kept asking what was wrong. Nothing was wrong, he repeatedly insisted. During the encore song, *"Love in an Elevator,"* he put his arm around me and said he had to ask me a question. "Okay" I said. "Do you want to marry me?" he asked as he reached into his front pocket and pulled out a small gray pouch. "Are you asking me?" I responded. He pulled out the ring he had picked out, got down on one knee and rephrased the question "Will you marry me?" "Yes, of course I will" I responded. We embraced as I looked over to see his two smiling accomplices. Darren had been waiting for them to play *our* song, *"Angel,"* so he could propose during it, but they never did. So, *"Love in an Elevator"* became our engagement song. How romantic! When we got back together, I told him that I wouldn't move back in with him without a ring on my finger. So now that we were officially engaged, I moved back to Illinois within a month.

We had a two-year engagement, because we wanted to get married in the spring. We got engaged during the summer and decided we needed longer than nine months to prepare for an out of state wedding. We decided to get married in Wisconsin and wanted to get married in the church, to please our Catholic families. Since Darren never had his confirmation, a prerequisite for marrying in the Catholic Church, he had to do that first; and there were pre-marital classes as well. Since I got only one weekend off a month from work, planning a big out of state wedding would be difficult. We were very excited, as were our families. I always knew in my heart that we'd end up together. My dreams were all starting to come true.

Darren sold his condo, and we moved in with his parents to save money to buy a house after the wedding. I was still working in retail; but I also began to do some modeling. I took a few jobs here and there. I was growing tired of all the late hours and weekends that I was required to work in retail. For a while, I had to do both, but my goal was to quit retail.

We did all the traditional pre-wedding things, like gift registry, numerous bridal showers, and bachelor and bachelorette parties. The day of our wedding came quickly, May 23, 1992. Both the church and the hotel where our reception was held had been designed by my architect father. It was the happiest day of my life. I was marrying my best friend, the love of my life... finally!

The ceremony was so beautiful, and my heart was overflowing with love and joy. The reception was a blast. We played a lot of unconventional wedding music, like Nirvana, Red Hot Chili Peppers and Smashing Pumpkins. Even the older folks danced- and moshed to our choice of songs. We paid the DJ to stay longer because we were all having such a good time. We were on top of the world, and didn't want the day to end.

Much to my disappointment, we didn't go on a honeymoon. Instead, we used the money we received as wedding gifts, along with money we had saved for a down payment on a house. Darren was the more practical of the two of us and he convinced me that we could take a honeymoon later. We bought a cute contemporary house that we loved; but after living there less than a year, we realized that we didn't like the area our house was in, and certainly wouldn't want to raise a family there. We decided to sell the house, move back in with his parents, and design and build our own home in the town where Darren attended high school.

A few months after our wedding, we got a puppy that we named Dakota, another Siberian Husky. We loved her, and treated her as if she were our baby. On a trip to visit Darren's grandfather in Georgia, we kept her picture on the dash of the car; and when we returned home, we pushed each other out of the way to be the first to hug her. The only thing we argued about was whose turn it was to take her for a walk. Life was sweet.

Shortly after our wedding, I had a vivid dream about my old boyfriend Rick and woke up with an overwhelming desire to drive to Wisconsin to see him. I quickly talked myself out of it because I was married now. I had recently seen him at Whitewater's graduation. He had me in tears telling me that he loved me and that it should have been his ring on my finger. I had also seen him at a mall in Milwaukee a few months before my wedding, and he called my parent's house looking for me that night. I was afraid he was going to crash my wedding. So, needless to say, this dream disturbed me.

The next day, I got a call from Rick's friend Mark. He told me that Rick had been stabbed to death by an angry customer in the bar where he bartended. Rick had kicked the guy out, but he had returned with a knife, stabbing Rick in the chest when Rick wouldn't allow him back in. Rick died shortly thereafter. Mark said that Rick always held a special place in his heart for me, and would have wanted me to know. I tried not to show any emotion in front of Darren as I hung up the phone, but as soon as I was alone, I lost it. I couldn't imagine what Rick must have gone through. I remember playing a song that had always reminded me of him, called *"Fly to the Angels,"* by Slaughter. I was crying hysterically as I listened to it and I fell to my knees, asking God "Why did this happen? Rick was a good person and didn't deserve to die!"

My friend Moe and my sister Kim, who both liked Rick a lot, went to the wake with me. I was touched that Darren not only sent me off with his blessing, but he also comforted me when I broke down and cried in front of him. When we got there, Rick's mom came over and embraced me, rocked me back and forth and repeated over and over "You should have been mine," which made me burst into tears. We'd always loved each other dearly. Her strength during the wake astounded me. I never saw her cry. She told me that shortly before he died, Rick told her that the biggest mistake he had ever made was letting me go. Another thing that shocked me was that she forgave the man who did this to her son. I didn't forgive him. I was furious and bitter. A few months later, I called her to see how she was doing, and she said that after the funeral she just cried and cried. I knew grief would hit her once the shock wore off. That was the last time I talked to her, but I think of her often.

I thought about my dream I had before I learned of Rick's death and wondered, "Was this some kind of premonition?" I was angry with myself for having dismissed it. Was I being warned? I felt as if I had missed my chance to say goodbye. I tried not to think about it too much, and was comforted by my happiness with Darren. Rick's murderer was caught and is serving a life sentence, by the way. I had my mom save all of the newspaper articles from the trial, and I still have them. I miss him and I am grateful for the good times we shared.

I was finally able to quit my retail job to pursue modeling. I didn't have time for both, so while I was still young I decided to give modeling a shot. Modeling wasn't something that I ever aspired to do, but a lot of people suggested that I should be a model, so I thought, why not? Making more money and working fewer hours made sense to me. I was doing a job as a movie extra and met two other extras who did a lot of local modeling and they shared a lot of information with me including some good agencies and photographers. I had some new pictures taken, registered with a few modeling agencies and I started getting booked right away for trade shows. Chicago's huge convention center, McCormick Place, hosts conventions and trade shows year round. Vendors hire local girls from modeling/talent agencies to help out with various tasks at their booths, but primarily as "eye candy." I did one or two shows per month, lasting from a few days to one week at a time. In between trade shows, I worked part-time at a theme restaurant, and did promotions for them as well.

One of the promotions I did for the restaurant was a golf outing that we sponsored for Darren's and my favorite talk radio personality, Kevin Matthews. At the promotion, I met the show's producer and jokingly told him I wanted to be an intern. Their current interns, he said, were leaving that week; and if I was serious, I should come to the studio on Tuesday. I jumped at the opportunity. Working there was a total blast. It was awesome! Kevin nicknamed me Judy Jetson, because I always came to work with my long blonde ponytail on top of my head.

I got to be on the air, meet celebrities and bands, attend live broadcasts and radio station events, and go to concerts for free. I worked two or three days a week, but unfortunately, interns don't get paid. In addition to doing trade shows, working at the restaurant, and interning, I did promotions for beer and liquor companies. My plate was full.

I worked at the radio station for only six months before I had to quit in order to coordinate all the details involved with building our new house. Something had to go, and the job that didn't bring in any money was the obvious choice. I actually had to pay for parking and gas, so I was paying to work there. I cried when I left, because even though I wasn't paid, it was the most fun I'd ever had in any job. It would have been worth it if I wanted to get a job in the radio business, but after seeing what really goes on, I decided that it wasn't for me.

Our new house was completed in December of 1994. We moved in shortly before Christmas. We couldn't have been happier. Our relationship had matured since our on-again off-again days and was built on honesty, respect, great friendship, and love. At the same time, Darren and I were like kids at heart. We were both practical jokers. He got a kick out of calling me at work; and if someone else answered, he'd say it was Kip Winger, or some other rock star that I thought was cute. Sometimes, if I answered, he used a fake voice saying he was Dick Fitzwell, or some other play-on-words name. We both had a juvenile sense of humor, and had lots of inside jokes between us.

I got a kick out of cutting pictures from magazines or the Sunday paper and

Laura Hirsch

placing them over Darren's picture on his driver's license. A geeky actor or a constipated-looking baby- he never knew who he was going to be next! One time, we went to a club with some friends, and I forgot that I had taped a picture of Doogie Howser on his I.D. Darren got carded; the bouncer looked at his I.D. and started laughing. As he handed it back to Darren, he said "Have a good time, Doogie." Darren looked at his picture and laughed, and then called me a jerk or something. I got him so good that time. We laughed about it all night.

We also liked to trip each other unexpectedly, flick each other's ears from behind, put an ice cube with a fake fly in it into each other's drinks, and hide fake dog poop around the house for the other one to discover. You know, silly childish pranks. Also, the animated TV show on MTV called *"Beavis and Butthead"* was new at the time, and we'd imitate their voices as we quoted lines from the show. We even used their voices while giving our speech during some friend's wedding video. Darren would often do his imitation of The Great Cornholio to make me laugh. Beavis became The Great Cornholio, usually after ingesting too much caffeine or candy, then he'd pull his shirt over his head so that his face was showing through the neck hole, hold his arms out like a football goalpost and then ramble on saying hilarious things. It was totally our kind of humor.

Once, for fun, we went to a karaoke recording studio, and recorded a duet of *"18 and Life"* by Skid Row. It was beyond horrible. Darren also did a solo of *"Light my Fire"* by The Doors, and I sang *"Edge of a Broken Heart"* by Vixen. We always threatened to send the other's tape to the radio station I worked at so they would play it on the air. That would have been humiliating, so it was a good bribery tool.

Darren's Grandpa was having some health problems at this time, and moved back to Illinois from Georgia to be closer to his family. Grandpa moved to the same town that we and Darren's sister lived in. Darren had always wanted to rebuild an old muscle car, and his Grandpa knew how to do it. Grandpa had rebuilt numerous classic cars. Darren bought a "jalopy," an old Dodge Charger, like the General Lee on *"The Dukes of Hazard."* He and his Grandpa had a great time rebuilding it together. He let me pick the color to paint it; I chose Plum Crazy, a cool metallic purple.

During this time, I met a woman (also named Laura), who owned her own modeling agency. I started out by doing some promotions for her and eventually worked as her assistant at the agency. I quit my job at the restaurant to work there exclusively. I had first pick of the trade shows and promotional jobs that came in, and also helped Laura with model interviews, bookings and paperwork.

Before I started working for Laura, Darren and I had felt that we were ready to have a baby, and I went off the pill. It was the end of 1994, and we had been together for a total of eight years, and married for two. The agency job, however, was a good opportunity, with the possibility to become part-owner, so we decided to wait another year to try to get pregnant. I would go back on the pill when I got my period again. This could be months away because my cycle was very irregular.

Darren and I were both independent in the sense that we had each other and loved spending time together, but respected the fact that our relationships with others needed to be nurtured as well. I visited family and friends in Wisconsin a few times a month, and Darren would use that time to see his friends. He was a born matchmaker, and always tried to set up his friends in Illinois with my Wisconsin friends when they came to visit. It never worked.

Together, we enjoyed going to concerts and movies, and having dinner alone or with friends. Darren's family also had season tickets to the Chicago Bears games, which we all went to together. If it was really cold, I'd wimp out and let one of his friends take my place. As a ritual, we'd always go out for ribs after the game. We vacationed in Florida at his parents' condo and we'd also visit my family and our Wisconsin friends together.

It was our dream to own a big, white, ultra-modern home, have a few kids, and take them to visit their grandparents at the condo in Florida in the winter. One day, Darren would take over his family's business, and I would stay home to raise the kids. Ours would be a simple life. Happily ever after.

Events Leading to the Accident

"You can't turn back the clock.
But you can wind it up again."

—Bonnie Prudden

Darren had two good friends whom he'd known since high school, Dave and Rico. I first met Dave in Whitewater, when he came to visit Darren. He was a really funny guy, and I liked him right away. In high school, he had been the class clown, and was always the life of the party. He had a cocaine problem for a while, but Darren still remained his friend even though he didn't approve of his drug use.

Dave lived in a trailer, partied a lot, and went from job to job- a stark contrast to the upper-class lifestyle Darren was accustomed to. Dave had no direction, and Darren was always trying to help him straighten up his act. Dave could get pretty out of control when he partied. It made me nervous when Darren went out with him, but you had to love the guy. He had a heart of gold, and was like a big teddy bear. He had an infectious laugh and was always cracking jokes. Dave and I always picked on each other and called each other names, like "Carnie" (carnival worker). Dave also had a bad habit of falling asleep at inappropriate times. During one of these times, while watching a movie, Darren and I put shaving cream in Dave's hand and then tickled his face. Dave instinctively went to scratch his face…you get the idea.

Darren and Dave would always wrestle and tease one another. Dave was like a brother to Darren, and few people understood their friendship. Darren enjoyed watching Dave attempt to hit on girls when we went out. He used the cheesiest pick-up lines and couldn't understand why they never worked. Darren tried his best to make Dave look foolish by egging him on to dance. Dave had this ear-piercing whistle that he made while dancing. It was quite entertaining. Darren just wanted to see Dave happy with the right girl. The two of them would come in to eat at the restaurant when I was working, and Dave would ask me the status of every girl who worked there. Darren thought my friend, Kristine, was perfect for Dave. They went out a few times, but it never went anywhere. Dave "fumbled the ball" according to Darren.

Darren's other good friend, Rico, went to college in Arkansas after high school, and later married, and moved there. We met up with him at Darren's ten year high school reunion. Rico had just moved back home to Illinois, and was in the process of getting a divorce. Darren and Rico rekindled their friendship and were like long-lost brothers from then on. Rico was Italian, and so was Darren; and Darren got a kick out of Rico's colorful Italian jargon. He nicknamed Darren Dino. Rico and his brother, Rocco, (real names) were into body-building, and when we moved into our new house, our basement soon became their gym. They got Darren interested in body-building as well. Soon, all three of them were working out in our basement every other day.

Now that Rico was divorced, Darren felt sorry for him. To cheer him up, Darren thought they should have a guys' night out. Dave and Rico were also friends, and the two of them together could get pretty out of hand. They were the loud goofballs everywhere they went; and they always managed to cause a scene. Darren was definitely the tame one in the bunch. When they went out, he rarely drank. Darren suffered from migraines, so he drank soda most of the time and let his friends have all the fun. He enjoyed their crazy antics. It made him feel like he was still one of the guys, not some married guy whose wife makes him stay home.

They planned a guys' night out for Friday, February 10, 1995, a little over two months after we moved into our new house. I remember Darren saying to me, "I don't care what you say; I'm going out on Friday." I felt that this was an odd thing to say, because he always asked for my permission first and besides, I never said he "couldn't" go out. I wasn't that way. I responded, "I don't care; I have a modeling job that night anyway."

We were both in our bathroom getting ready for our events. I had an uneasy feeling about him going out that night. I went over and hugged him. "Promise me you'll drive," I asked. "You know how crazy those two can get." He said "I know. Don't worry, I'll drive." Dave was a fast, reckless driver, as I had recently experienced on a trip home to Chicago from our vacation in Florida, which Darren invited Dave to join in on. I was scared for my life in the back seat screaming for him to slow down. After that, I asked Darren not to let Dave drive his car, and he assured me that he wouldn't.

Rico came over before I left. I remember Darren saying that the shower he took was the best shower of his life, and that the spaghetti I had made for dinner was the best spaghetti he'd ever had. I was getting ready to leave, and Darren and Rico were sitting on the couch. I asked Darren what time he thought he'd be home. Being a smart ass, he said "I'm going to say 5:00 a.m., because then you can't be mad at me if I'm late." I gave him a knowing look and said "OK, whatever you say." I kissed him goodbye and we both said, "I love you." Then he said something I'll never forget. "Don't forget to say goodbye to Dakota for me."

I gave him a strange look, and thought, "Why don't you tell her?" I went over to Dakota on my way out, scratched her belly, and said the last words he'd ever hear me say "Goodbye, Dakota." My modeling job lasted for two hours. I stayed a little later to talk to the other model I was working with, since I knew Darren wouldn't be home. I can remember almost bragging about how happily married I was, and what a great relationship we had. She was a little cynical about marriage, being in a bad one herself. But she was glad to hear about a happily married couple.

I went home and went to check our messages and noticed Darren's wedding ring was sitting on the counter. I wondered why he didn't have it on. I'd have to harass him about it when he got home. I turned on the TV and the *"Jon Stewart Show"* was on. A great new band called Sponge was singing my new favorite song, *"Plowed."* I had been asking Darren for weeks if he had heard this song yet. I even sang it for him: *"Say a prayer for me, say a prayer for me/ I'm buried by the sound...of a world of human wreckage."* Each time, he'd cut me off and say, "No, I've never heard it." Now it was on, and again he wasn't around to hear it. Darn it, I thought, it seemed he always missed it. I knew he'd love the song. I would tell him about it tomorrow. I tried to wait up for him, but I got too tired and I went to bed with Dakota curled up in her spot by my feet.

Part Two

Confusion and Chaos

Finding Out - The Nightmare Begins

*"It's not whether you get knocked down.
It's whether you get up again."*

—*Vince Lombardi*

I remember waking up around 2:30 a.m. with a sick feeling in the pit of my stomach. I was getting really worried. Darren should be home soon I reassured myself. The bars closed at 2:00 a.m., so he was probably on his way now. Rico had left his car in our driveway, and they all rode together in Darren's SUV. I decided to get up and see if Rico's car was still in the driveway. It wasn't. Maybe Darren had brought Rico here first to pick up his car, and then had driven Dave home. That had to be it, I reasoned.

I climbed back into bed, and was half asleep when the doorbell rang around 6:00 a.m. As I walked down the hallway toward the front door, I could see a police car in my driveway through the window. I knew something was dreadfully wrong. I slowly opened the door. The policeman asked me my name, and then handed me a piece of paper and told me that I needed to call the number that was written on it, regarding my husband, Darren. I asked the policeman, "Why? What is this about?" All that he would tell me was that it was about my husband. My heart was racing a mile a minute. I thought that maybe he had been arrested on a DUI and I had to pick him up. The policeman said he couldn't tell me anything, but he asked if I wanted him to stay while I made the call. I was getting very scared now, and asked "Why?" But he just repeated the question, and I knew he wasn't going to tell me anything, so I answered "If you want to."

He followed me into the kitchen where I went to make the call. With my hands trembling, I dialed the number from the piece of paper. A male voice answered "Will County Morgue." In a panicked voice, I managed to tell him who I was and that I had been told to call regarding my husband, Darren. In a cold monotone he told me that Darren had been involved in a car accident around 2:30 a.m., and he was pronounced dead at the scene. I screamed "Nooo!" and shouted "What about Dave and Rico?" He said that there was no Rico involved and that Dave was in the hospital, under suicide watch. He said that Dave had been driving.

Was he sure of that? I asked. "Yes," he replied. My thoughts were racing all over the place as I hung up the phone. With the receiver still in my hand, I remember collapsing to the floor and feeling as though I had just imploded. This couldn't be happening! And although I thought, "Why am I not crying? Shouldn't I be crying?" "What kind of wife doesn't cry when she just finds out her husband is dead?" I simply couldn't do anything but sit on the floor.

The policeman, who was still there, asked if I knew anyone who lived nearby, anyone who could come over. His voice brought me back to the moment. I struggled to stand up and tried to think. Darren's sister lived five minutes away. My hand was shaking as I dialed her number. She answered immediately. With no time to prepare what to say, I told her in a strained voice, "Come over… now. Darren is dead." She didn't recognize my trembling voice, and asked in disbelief "Who is this?" I said "It's Laura, hurry." She said that she and her husband would be right over.

I hung up and started pacing and asking the policeman "What am I supposed to do? I don't know what to do!" No one prepares you for something like this. I was clearly in shock. I sat down. I tried to cry. I paced some more. I repeated over and over "What am I supposed to do?" The policeman asked if I wanted him to wait until they arrived. "No, you can go," I told him. He apologized for the way I had to find out. He also said they'd had a hard time finding our house, because Darren's driver's license still had our old address on it. I felt numb as I locked the door behind him as he left.

When Darren's sister and her husband came over, I told them what little I knew. She had her husband call her parents in Florida to break the devastating news, she couldn't bear to. They would come home immediately, they said. I couldn't imagine how they were going to get through that flight. Darren's mom even called me from the plane hysterically asking where her Darren was. I couldn't tell if she was in denial of the news, or if she just wanted to know where his body was. I told her he was in the morgue. I hung up the phone, crying for her pain as well as my own.

I decided to call Rico to tell him what happened, and to find out what he knew. When I told him that Darren was dead, he didn't believe me. He thought that I was joking and kept repeating "Come on Laura, put him on the phone." Finally, I screamed at him "He's in the fucking morgue!" (Honestly, I don't use the "f" word very often.) That made it pretty clear. I told him that Dave was in the hospital, under suicide watch. Apparently, Rico had driven in another car with a friend they'd met up with

28

at the bar, and that's why he hadn't been driving with them. That friend drove Rico to my house to pick up his car when Darren and Dave didn't show up. Rico said he was going to the hospital to see Dave.

Next, I called Dave at the hospital to find out what had happened. He said that he didn't remember exactly. They were about to leave the bar they were at and Darren had slipped him the keys, saying "You're driving." They were on their way to meet up with Rico at another bar; driving on a winding country road that Dave claimed he knew like the back of his hand. The last thing he remembered was hearing Darren's voice yelling "Dave, no!" as Darren grabbed for control of the steering wheel. Dave pulled the steering wheel back the other way to regain control, and the next thing he knew, the SUV was off the road and in the trees, on the opposite side. Dave was very confused about what had happened. Did they flip? Was Darren thrown from the truck? Did he fall asleep at the wheel? He wasn't sure. He said something about Darren's head hitting a tree. He said he got out of the SUV and walked around to the other side to check on Darren. There was blood on his head. He knew that Darren hadn't survived the crash. He kept yelling at Darren: "What am I going to tell Laura?" He ran up the street to a friend's house and called 911. "Why were you driving?" I asked, and again, he said he didn't know. "Were you drunk?" I asked. He claimed that he'd had only four beers. I found that hard to believe, knowing him. He could put away a case by himself.

I got more answers from the copy of the death certificate that I received later than from Dave's foggy recollection of what had happened. It said that the cause of death was massive head injury and multiple traumas due to being a passenger in an automobile mishap. It also stated that the vehicle hit a guardrail, left the roadway and flipped, ending up in the woods. Another thing I learned from the death certificate was the time of the accident. It was at 2:30 in the morning, which was the same time I woke up feeling sick to my stomach. I thought that was strange, or was it?

I was so angry at Dave *and* Darren. Why hadn't Darren listened to me? Why had he let Dave drive? I remember angrily telling Darren's sister that I was going to sue Dave for everything he had, and everything he would ever have. I wanted to take everything from him because he took everything from me. I never did, or would, but in that moment it made perfect sense. Someone had to take the blame. I felt that Darren lied to me and betrayed me by letting Dave drive his car. My worst fear had come true.

While we waited for Darren's parents to arrive, I thought I should call everyone that Darren and I knew to tell them the devastating news myself. I remember calling my promotions coordinator to tell her I couldn't work the job I was booked for that night because my husband had died in a car accident. She couldn't believe that I'd had the where-with-all to call her, considering what had happened. I was on auto pilot; it hadn't sunk in yet. I started the conversation with everyone I called by asking "Are you sitting down?"

The next person I called was my mom. "The worst thing that could happen to me happened to me today!" I cried. From the sadness in my voice, she understood that Darren had died, but she didn't know how. After I told her what had happened, I started crying and asked her "Why does everyone I love die? First Rick, now Darren. Why does this keep happening to me? What did I do that was so wrong that God keeps taking the people I love away from me?" "It's not your fault" she tearfully assured me.

I remembered thinking after Rick died that I made the right decision by choosing Darren, because if I had married Rick instead, I would have been a widow. Now, I thought, I must be destined to be a young widow, because the two men in my life who'd wanted to marry me were both dead. Darren was supposed to be my protector. He was supposed to make sure no one ever hurt me. I didn't know that this much hurt was possible. Where was he now, when I needed him the most?

His parents finally arrived from Florida, and my heart sank when I saw the look on their faces. I remember hugging his mom, crying, and saying "Why didn't he listen to me? I just wanted him to be safe. He'd be here right now if he'd just listened to me. He promised me that he would drive." She said, "He would have done what he wanted anyway." We just held each other, sobbing hysterically. Nothing anybody said from this moment on could change what happened. Nothing could ever bring him back.

Darren didn't even get to see his rebuilt "jalopy" finished. It had just been painted and he was supposed to pick it up that day. I don't remember who eventually went to pick it up, but I cried when I saw it because it had turned out beautifully. I hoped that somehow, he could see it.

My brother-in-law handled a lot of the arrangements because he was the most composed among us. He was a local paramedic and knew what needed to be done. The rest of us were in such a state of shock, we couldn't think clearly. Arrangements had to be made for the wake and funeral. No one prepares you for a task like this-especially not a 27-year-old who's been married for only two years!

I didn't know what to do, so I just did as I was told, like a robot. We had to go to the funeral home to see his body the day before the wake. This was so horrible;

and I had flashbacks of that image for a long time. My in-laws, sister-in-law, and I were all holding each other up and clinging on to one another for dear life when they wheeled him out on the gurney. It was Darren! There was no mix-up. A towel had been placed over half of his face because there had been extensive injuries to one side of his head. When I first heard that he'd suffered a head injury, I was at home. It was a factor in deciding whether or not to have an open casket. I got so upset that I ran into my bedroom, threw myself on the bed, and sobbed inconsolably. I couldn't imagine what Darren must have gone through. He was all alone, out in the cold. I wondered if he was scared, or in pain? Did he suffer? Where was he now? Was he in heaven? Could he see me, and know how much pain I was in?

In an instant, all my plans and dreams were gone. The person who I thought I would share the rest of my life with, the person who knew me better and loved me more than anyone else in the world, the father of my future children, was gone forever. The center of my universe had been yanked out of my life with no warning. How could he just disappear? I couldn't bear the thought of never seeing him again. Darren had played so many roles in my life: husband, best friend, confidant, lover, advisor, protector, and provider. I lost all these people at once.

The Funeral

"To live in hearts we leave behind is not to die."

—*Clyde Campbell*

There were a lot of decisions involved with planning Darren's wake and funeral. Ironically, the wake was held on Valentine's Day, the funeral the following day. I couldn't believe that I would never be Darren's Valentine ever again. We decided to have an open casket, mainly upon my request. My decision was based on going to Rick's wake where they had a closed casket. Because I didn't see his body, I had a hard time accepting that he was dead, so I figured others may have the same reaction if they didn't see Darren's body.

I had to pick out the clothes that Darren was to be buried in. I had recently bought him a shirt that he wanted for Valentine's Day. It was the last present I ever bought for him. So he wore that shirt and his favorite pair of dress pants and dress shoes. I also had to pick out floral arrangements for the casket and the ceremony. The last time I had done something like this was for our wedding. "This isn't fair!" I told my mom. "My husband is supposed to be buying flowers for *me* on Valentine's Day, not me buying flowers for his funeral!" It seemed so pointless, because the flowers were just going to die too, but in my delirium I chose calla lilies, my favorite flower, just like the ones I had chosen for my bridal bouquet.

Darren's parents and I were in the funeral parlor with the funeral director looking at caskets and prayer cards. I remember sitting there in a daze, wondering how people in this much pain could make such important decisions? Was it just *my* brain that wasn't functioning anymore? My husband was dead, and I had to comparison shop for a stupid casket and read through all these lame prayer cards and make a logical choice… what a joke! I was so preoccupied with my own thoughts that I interrupted the conversation and blurted out, "I didn't think that 'till death do us part' would happen this soon." We all started to cry. I wasn't ready for this. I just wanted to go home, hide under my covers and go to sleep, never to wake up.

The events of the wake are somewhat of a blur. I remember bits and pieces. I remember being obsessed with delivering Darren's baseball glove to his friend Mike.

Mike was one of Darren's college roommates, the one he was with when we first met. They had played baseball together on a team that past summer. And here I was, carrying around this stupid glove at the wake because I knew Darren would want Mike to have it. Why did I feel the need to bring it to the wake? I don't know. Maybe because it was a distraction.

Before the wake started, I wanted to be alone with Darren one last time. As I walked into the viewing room alone, I was overwhelmed by the scent of flowers from the floral arrangements. As I knelt next to the casket, I cried hysterically, begging God for help. As I sobbed, with my face buried in my hands, I felt a sudden wash of calm come over me and I suddenly caught my breath and stopped crying. I felt that this was God trying to help me. I composed myself and walked back out into the lobby to join the others and felt peaceful for the first time in days.

A huge crowd of people showed up for the wake, yet I still felt alone. I must have been in some sort of denial, the way I was showing people around as though I were hosting a party. We had put together a photo collage of Darren at different moments of his life. I was showing it to people as though they were vacation photos, then escorting them up to see him in the casket. What was I doing?

I remember saying things to people like, "He's in a better place," and "He's still with me." I don't know where this was coming from, the words just spilled out of my mouth. I was still unsure of my beliefs about life after death. It was a nice idea, but I wondered if heaven was just a big lie that churches told so that we would keep giving them money. I know Darren didn't believe in life after death. He believed that dead was dead. Death was the one thing he was afraid of. We had recently seen a bumper sticker on a car that read "Live fast, die young, leave a good-looking corpse." Darren was amused and I thought it was tasteless. He said, "You work your ass off your whole life, for what? You just die anyway." That was when he told me of his fear of death and that he didn't believe in an afterlife. At that moment, I needed to believe that life after death was possible. It gave me comfort to believe that he was still alive in some other form, watching over me.

I remember writing Darren a letter, and putting it along with a recent picture of me and Dakota into the casket so he would never forget us. During the wake, I also remember sitting alone in a chair a few rows back from the casket, watching friends and family members go up to Darren and pay their respects. I was thinking, "This person lost a friend, this person lost a brother or brother-in law, this person lost a son, and so on." My husband was someone different to everyone there. In each person's mind, a different relationship had ended. I sat there looking on and cried for each of their losses.

I wasn't quite sure how I felt about Dave at this point. Mostly, I think I felt sorry for him. He was going to have to live with the guilt of killing his friend, and with the scrutiny and blame of everyone else. I did blame him for his bad judgment, for drinking and driving, but to be honest, most of the people in the room that day had all done the same thing at one time or another. Or they had been a passenger in a car driven by someone who had been drinking. Who were we to judge Dave? This sort of thing happened to other people, I kept thinking. We thought we were invincible. Darren and Dave were just out having a good time like they always did. How could this have happened? Why did Dave walk away and Darren die? Darren was one of the good guys. Or is it true that the good die young?

I asked Dave to come to the funeral and the wake, and even asked him to be a pallbearer. He said he'd be honored. At this time, I thought I could forgive Dave, because I knew he hadn't killed Darren on purpose. I asked myself which friends and family members Darren would have wanted as his pallbearers, and Dave was certainly one of them. I also thought it would be good for Dave. Later, I regretted this decision; but for now, in my clouded judgment, I thought it was what Darren would have wanted.

In addition to Darren's many friends and family members, a lot of people I didn't know came to the wake and the funeral: business associates who flew in from all over the country, old high school friends, and office friends. I remember looking around at all of the people in attendance and thinking how much he was loved. The girl I did the modeling job with the night of the accident came, along with my promotions coordinator. She said that when she heard the news, all she could think about was me talking about how much I loved my husband, and how happy we were, and she just had to come.

My high school gymnastics coach and some of my former teammates drove from Wisconsin to show support for me. I was so touched. I even remember laughing with them for a moment. It felt good to laugh, but afterward I felt guilty. I looked around to see if anyone had seen me laughing and wondered if they thought that I was acting inappropriately. My sister said it was good to see me laugh, and not to worry about what other people thought.

It's funny; it is the odd things I remember so vividly. I remember that one of my old college roommates said to me, "Even in your darkest hour, your hair still looks good." We were in the bathroom at the time. I used to spend a lot of time fussing with my appearance, but it just didn't matter anymore. I looked at myself in the mirror and thought, "Who gives a crap what my hair looks like? I don't care about anything any more. My life is over too. Who do I have to impress?"

There is no etiquette on death. I found it strange how people had such a hard time knowing what to say to me. Even friends and family who had known me my whole life didn't know what to say. Their presence alone would have said it all. Everyone had unsolicited advice for me. Everyone wanted to fix me. At the funeral and afterwards, I heard so many supposed words of consolation from well-meaning people. The one that bothered me the most was "It's God's will." I kept thinking, "And this is supposed to make me feel better? Why? Is God my enemy? What did I do to deserve God's will?" I didn't have the energy to argue.

Another favorite was, "You're still young and pretty, you'll find someone else." I didn't want someone else. This comment totally invalidated my relationship with Darren. I thought it was such a heartless thing to say. People tried to find something positive to say like, "At least he didn't suffer." How could they know that? They weren't there. I heard other comments such as, "The body is just a shell," "Now you have a guardian angel," "It was his time to go," and "God needed him in heaven." But my personal favorite had to be, "Thank God you didn't have any children." That was a real charmer. Yes, I thought, let's thank God that the other dream I've had for the past eight years didn't come true either. Nothing anyone said seemed to help or comfort me in any way. I just dismissed their insensitive comments because I knew they didn't know what to say; and that they were hurting too.

I went home to a cold and empty bed the night of the wake. I cried myself to sleep, knowing that the next day would be difficult. I would have to bury my husband. I didn't even want to go. I just wanted to run away and find somewhere to curl up and die. My dog, Dakota, who usually slept by my feet, instinctively slept in Darren's spot that night. She knew something was wrong. I remember feeling grateful for Dakota because she still depended on me for survival, and forced me to keep going.

The morning of the funeral, I got my period. It was like another death. There had been the possibility that I was pregnant. I had taken a pregnancy test a few weeks earlier, which was negative, but I hadn't had my period in months, and was secretly hoping that I was carrying Darren's child. The day before, at the wake, I had to force myself not to say anything about it when a friend of the family had commented, "Wouldn't it be wonderful if Laura was pregnant?" Now, all hope of having a child with my husband was dead too.

On the morning of the funeral, we started with a service at the funeral home, then moved to the church, and then to the burial grounds. There were few memorable things that the priest said during the service at the funeral home, both good and bad. On the good side, he made me feel secure in his belief that Darren was in heaven. He ought to know these things, right? Also, he talked about the symbolism of rainbows. "I have put the rainbow in the sky as a sign of my everlasting love for you," he read. I liked that. He was referring to God, of course, but I felt like he was talking about Darren. I kept praying and asking God for a sign that Darren was with Him, and that he was all right. That would be the sign I would look for I told God in my prayers; a rainbow. I needed to know that Darren's spirit was somewhere and that this whole idea of life after death wasn't just wishful thinking on my part. I would look for a rainbow.

I hung on the priest's every word, thinking he must have all the answers. But one thing he said rubbed me the wrong way and he lost a lot of credibility in my eyes: because Darren was baptized, the priest said, he was "stamped" and therefore went to heaven. I was raised as a Catholic; but I never believed that having a priest pour water on your head as an infant gave you the exclusive privilege of going to heaven. I didn't believe that God played favorites depending on if your parents raised you in the "correct" religion; I believed that he loved all of His children equally. I believed Darren was in heaven, if there was a heaven, because he was a good person not because he was "stamped" by being baptized in a Catholic Church.

Even at this early stage, I realized that I was beginning to search for answers to spiritual questions. I was forced to question all my former beliefs. Darren's death, this single devastating event, stopped me in my tracks and derailed my life. Nothing could be the same from this day forward. Part of me had died with Darren. He took part of me with him and left a part of himself with me, and that would never die.

Before driving to the church for the service, we all got to walk up to the casket to say goodbye one final time before they sealed it. Darren's mother went before me, and I saw her kiss him on the cheek. Even though I thought it was creepy to kiss a dead body, I thought it must have been customary so I followed her lead and also kissed his cheek. It was ice cold. My whole body shuddered. I knew then that Darren was truly gone.

The funeral service was held in the small Catholic Church to which Darren's family belonged, and in which his sister had been married. There was standing room only during the service. I remember looking around the church while walking up the aisle behind the casket. Everyone whose eyes met mine started crying. I had to look down before I completely fell apart. I was pretty much a zombie throughout the entire service. While sitting there, I felt guilty that I hadn't requested any special songs for Darren or said any special words for him; but I simply couldn't. I was so shocked. It had happened so fast. I wasn't equipped to do these things, and neither was anyone else in his family.

We had a short service at the cemetery in a building on the grounds. It was so cold and rainy that we couldn't have it at the gravesite. I felt so lightheaded that I was afraid I was going to pass out. I remember looking around at all my friends and family and feeling their support. But I also felt like I was an outsider, observing everything that was happening in a detached way. It is some sort of defense mechanism I'm sure, but I was actually more concerned with everyone else's loss than my own. I thought, how will his mom ever go on without him? He was her baby. I knew and loved him for eight years; she raised him and loved him for 28 years. Who would take over the family business now? They were counting on Darren. How could Dave live with himself knowing that he was responsible for killing his best friend? All of this was too much to handle. In my head I repeated, "I can't believe this is happening" over and over. It was surreal.

While the immediate family- Darren's parents, his sister and her husband and I- stayed for the burial, everyone else went on to a luncheon. I tried not to look as the casket was lowered into the ground. I just wanted to go home. Darren wasn't in that casket anyway, I told myself: only his body. My husband was still alive somewhere. He had to be. This couldn't be the end. Darren was probably watching us right now. Thoughts like these got me though the moment.

Darren was in a better place. We were in hell. I recall Darren's father saying that this was probably harder for me because I'd never lost someone I loved. He then mentioned how he had lost both of his parents, so he knew what to expect. I didn't want to get into the fact that I had lost Rick and a few other friends and family members in the past. It wouldn't have mattered because no amount of previous losses could have prepared me for what I was now going through.

I felt so sick and dizzy at the luncheon that I couldn't stay. I couldn't eat and couldn't bear to talk to anyone, so I left early. Darren's uncle drove my mom and me back to my house. My dad, who had just driven from North Carolina, was waiting for us. I barely even acknowledged him. Instead, I took Dakota into my room and went to sleep. Maybe I'd wake up with Darren by my side, and find that this had all been just a horrible nightmare.

Friends and Family

"In prosperity our friends know us; in adversity we know our friends."
—*John Churton Collins*

The world outside was just as frozen as my heart and my life. There had been an ice storm the week that Darren died and all of the trees were immobilized in a layer of thick ice, twinkling like diamonds in the sunlight. The snow on the ground was also topped with a blanket of ice. It was as if all forms of life were frozen in time. What a perfect metaphor for my situation. I felt trapped in a dark void, with no way out, and I could barely function.

It's funny how life around you goes on while your own life is standing still. The world doesn't stop because you're in pain. Luckily, I didn't have to go back to work right away, and quite honestly, I don't see how people can go right back to work after the death of a loved one. Something as basic as getting out of bed and getting dressed just seemed utterly pointless. I was blessed with wonderful family members and friends who supported me during this time of crisis. At this stage of my grief, they were instrumental in my healing. It was important to lean on other people. Part of what helped me was letting people help me. This trait didn't come naturally. I was pretty independent. I started accepting people's offers to help, and even asked for it.

I remember people bringing all kinds of food in casserole dishes over to my house beginning the day we found out that Darren had died. I thought that was a bit odd. I wondered, who thinks about food at a time like this? The very thought of food made me want to vomit. I didn't eat a bite of any of it, although I truly appreciated the gesture.

My mom stayed with me for the first two weeks following Darren's death. She said the first night was the worst. She heard me wailing from my bedroom all night long, a cry that comes from the depths of your soul. She told me later that this was the hardest thing she has ever had to do, because she knew that she could not do anything to comfort her own child. This was the one pain she couldn't make go away.

During those first two weeks, my mom basically did everything for me. She cleaned my house, did the laundry, tried to make me eat, and provided endless emotional support. I don't know what I would have done without her. I could barely remember to feed Dakota. A good day became one in which I actually got out of my pajamas and got dressed. Makeup was a waste of time because I just cried it all off anyways. I slept until noon every day, and then moved to the couch where I watched a lot of mindless talk shows with guests that made my life look good by comparison. Emotionally paralyzed, I would stare mindlessly at the TV for hours. I didn't know what to do, so I did nothing, while everyone around me walked on eggshells.

I remember not wanting to wash Darren's laundry or his pillowcase, because they still smelled like him. Trying to hold on to something, I curled up and cried on his pillow every night because it smelled like his hair products and cologne. I would also go into his closet and bury my face in the shirt he had worn to work the morning of the accident and just sob. How could he be gone? I could still smell him. This was one of the last remaining parts of him. So, my mom had to wash his clothes and my sheets for me. I was too much of a wreck. I kept waiting for him to walk through the doorway every night at his usual time, but he never did.

My mom said I took a lot of baths and showers and cranked the music, but she could still hear me crying over the music from other parts of the house. The first time I cried in the shower after Darren died, it was a cry I'd never cried before. I stood there wailing so hard that I could barely breathe and I felt like my insides were withering up. I felt so weak that I slowly slid down to the shower floor, melting like the Wicked Witch in "*The Wizard of Oz.*" I curled up in the fetal position, sobbing for what seemed like hours, as the water pelted me from above, becoming one with my tears. Sad lyrics filled the room, making me cry harder. I had no idea how I was going to get through this. I just wanted the pain in my heart to stop, or my heart to stop.

Already petite to begin with, I lost about 10 pounds after my mom left. You could now see my collarbone and ribs through my skin. All my size 3 clothes were big on me. This is where Rico stepped in. He grew up in a big Italian family and was an excellent cook. He came over almost every day to cook for me, and to talk. He was grieving too. He felt guilty that he hadn't driven that night, and couldn't make sense of what had happened. He had just gotten his friend back and now he was gone. One day I showed Rico all of our pictures from the time that Darren and I first met until then, and he felt like he had gotten a glimpse of what he had missed out on all of those years apart. Rico even got a tattoo honoring Darren, so that he would never forget. Rico's brother Rocco, who went to culinary school, also came over and helped with the cooking. I never ate so well in my life! Soon, I was no longer looking like a skeleton.

Rico's twin sister, Kathy, is a massage therapist. I met her for the first time at the funeral where she volunteered her massage services to me. She came over two or three times a week, and we became fast friends. My muscles had become so tensed up from crying all the time. Her massages really helped me relieve some of my stress and to relax. I always felt great when she was done. They were such a compassionate family, and I will be forever grateful for their kindness and generosity.

Some of my friends took turns staying overnight at my house because I didn't want to be alone. My friend Kimberly from college drove two hours from Wisconsin to stay with me on her days off from work, from Monday night until early Thursday morning. My friend Kristine, who lived close by, stayed on Thursday night. Moe and Brenda, also from Wisconsin, stayed with me on the weekends. There were also frequent visits from my sister, Kim, who had recently moved to Illinois to live with her future husband, Pat; as well as my mom, my brother Joey, my in-laws, and friends Daren and Karen.

Many of my old friends, as well as people who knew Darren, called with condolences and support. Even complete strangers sent cards and letters to show they cared. Another friend made a beautiful painting for me to express his sorrow. I wondered how all these people had found out about my tragedy. I had two large shopping bags overflowing with condolence cards, letters, and prayer cards. I remember crying and saying "There really are good people in this world." There was no shortage of loving people in my life.

The only thing I was disappointed in was lack of support from our church. We had requested that people donate money in Darren's name to the church, which they generously did. Yet, no one from the church ever called me or my in-laws who were long-time members, to offer any kind of support or counseling during our time of need, which I mistakenly expected. I felt very bitter afterward. Complete strangers had shown more compassion. One letter sent to my house anonymously particularly touched me. It said, "You don't know me, or I you. I heard of your recent tragedy and it touched my soul. Hope this poem can bring you some comfort. God Bless."

<u>What is death?</u> - By Harry Scott Holland
Death is nothing at all. I have only slipped away into the next room.
I am me and you are you. Whatever we were to each other, that we are still.
Call me by my old familiar name.
Speak to me in the easy way which you always used to.
Put no difference in your tone. Wear no forced air of solemnity or sorrow.
Laugh as we always laughed together at little jokes we enjoyed together.
Play, smile, laugh, think of me, pray for me.
Let my name be ever the household word that it always was.
Let it be spoken without effect, without the trace of a shadow on it.
Life means all it ever meant. It is the same as it ever was.
There is absolutely unbroken continuity.
Why should I be out of mind, because I am out of sight?
I am waiting for you, for an interval.
Somewhere very near, just around the corner.
All is well!

As I read this letter, my tears were falling all over the paper. It was so beautiful, and it blew me away that a stranger would take the time to send this to comfort me. For the first time, I believed that maybe Darren did still exist somewhere, and that whoever had sent it knew something that I needed to find out.

Believe it or not, even Dave tried to help me. He brought me groceries and cleaned out Dakota's pen for me. He felt somewhat responsible for me. This didn't last very long, because I soon started to blame him for what happened. Plus, he couldn't seem to comprehend the fact that his drinking and driving had led to the accident. He and Kristine had started dating again and went out to a bar one night, and he got drunk. Kristine didn't drink, but Dave refused to let her drive. When she told me this, I was furious. Dave came over and I yelled at him: "How many more people do you have to kill before you realize that it was your drinking and driving that killed Darren!" He said that he didn't see the connection. Drinking and driving had become normal behavior for him. He had done enough for me, I told him. I didn't want to see or talk to him anymore. I was afraid of what I might do or say. My pity for him was being replaced by anger and blame.

Kristine was a very compassionate person, and she wanted to be there for Dave too. They became inseparable and a few months later, I was shocked to learn that they had become engaged. She even asked me to stand up at their wedding. I felt that Dave had destroyed my marriage, so why would I want to celebrate theirs? At the time, I felt that Kristine had betrayed me. Instead of being there for her grieving friend, she was there for the man who killed her friend's husband. I couldn't even find it in my heart to attend her wedding. If she were marrying anyone else, I told her, there wouldn't be a question- I'd be there; but under the circumstances, how could I?

I thought that since the church didn't make any attempt to approach me to offer support, I would make the first move. Maybe just going to church might help me cope, I thought, so I started going on Sundays with Darren's parents. It was a month before Easter, and they kept talking about how Jesus died on the cross, was buried, went to heaven and returned three days later. This always made me cry because I thought about Darren coming back. The priest who did the Sunday mass was the same priest who did the services at Darren's funeral. Each time I went up to receive communion, the priest would say, "God loves you." I would cry on my walk back to the pew thinking, "If God loved me, how could he do this to me?" I stopped going to church after a few months because it only reminded me of the funeral which was held there, and I always felt foolish crying in front of strangers every week. They probably wondered what was wrong with me.

After a few months, I finally felt strong enough to spend the night alone in my house. I had to get used to it sooner or later. I still had Dakota there to protect me, so I didn't feel completely alone. This time alone was good for me and gave me time to grieve in private. I could cry or scream as loud as I wanted to. After a while, the cards stopped coming, people stopped calling, and I suddenly felt all alone. Some of Darren's best friends, even people who stood up to our wedding, never spoke to me again. I represented their pain and their worst fear, and they couldn't face me. I knew that I had to find my own identity. Now that I wasn't Darren's wife, who was I?

Part Three

<u>Grief</u>

About The Stages of Grief

"Never to suffer would have been never to have been blessed."

—Edgar Allan Poe

I would like to mention the stages of grief, and how I went through each of them. I had first learned of the five stages of grief during a class in high school. After Darren's death, I was reading some books about grief that Moe had given me, and again, they discussed the five stages of grief.

Originally, during her work with terminally ill patients in the 1960's, Dr. Elisabeth Kübler-Ross identified the now famous five stages of death; describing what a person went through when they learned that they were dying. Now, the same five stages are commonly used to describe the stages of grief; describing what a person goes through during the grief process. They are: shock and denial, anger, bargaining, depression, and acceptance.

In my logical mind, I reasoned "Well, if I get to the acceptance stage right away, I won't have to go through all the other crap. Besides, I've already felt all of those other things, so I just need to accept it, move past this, and get on with my life. Darren's gone, and nothing can bring him back. I accept that." Wrong! Reality check. That's not how it works. You can't just skip to the end. There is no detour through grief. The only way out of it is to go through it.

Grief doesn't necessarily happen in chronological order, as the stages suggest. You don't start at stage 1 and neatly work up to stage 5, where you're healed. Oh no... you go back and forth, and you might even get stuck, usually in anger or depression. Then, you may think you've accepted the death and moved on; but then something out of the blue brings you right back. You take two steps forward and one step back. I could have been having a perfectly good day, then I'd hear a song on the radio that reminded me of Darren, and I'd completely lose it. My day and my makeup were both ruined. I know now that grieving is a process, and it must be felt emotionally, not logically worked out.

Sometimes, you may experience more than one stage at a time. You might feel both angry and depressed. There are so many emotions to work through that *they fight for dominance in your mind. I never knew how I was going to feel from day to day. So, I just had to take it a day at a time and to honor what I was feeling each day. Now I can look back on the stages and understand the part each one played in my healing. This experience will always be a part of you, like it or not. You can't change what happened, but with time and a lot of work, you will hopefully realize that this experience brings its own gifts.*

Shock and Denial

"Every life has a measure of sorrow, and sometimes this is what awakens us."

—*Steven Tyler (lead singer of Aerosmith)*

My immediate reaction after learning about Darren's death was shock, along with panic. I didn't want to believe it; and until I saw his lifeless body on the gurney in the funeral home, I thought it was a cruel joke or a bad dream. Your body reacts this way as a protective mechanism, so you don't feel all the pain at once.

Shock is also a physical reaction, not just a mental one. I felt numb, paralyzed, on auto pilot. I felt dizzy, disoriented, and nauseous. I was breathing so fast I was almost hyperventilating, and I felt like my heart was going to beat out of my chest. Then later, I felt like I had been drugged. Everything slowed down. Detached from myself, I felt like I was watching this nightmare happen to someone else. Like a broken record, I kept saying, "I can't believe this is happening." This desensitized feeling lasted for months after the funeral. Then it all hit me. It was real. My husband was dead.

An example of how desensitization affected me came shortly after Darren's death. My wonderful friend Brenda became engaged. I should have been very happy for her, but I couldn't feel joy. I just felt dead inside, and couldn't share her happiness the way a friend should. The old me would have squealed with glee upon hearing this news and would have started discussing wedding plans; but the desensitized me was completely indifferent, showing no emotion when I congratulated her. I couldn't feel anything but my own pain, and I felt like I let her down.

Another aspect of shock was that I was in my own world. People talked to me, but I neither heard nor remembered what they were saying. Not a good thing when there are lots of important things going on around you. I asked people the same questions over and over; but right after I'd ask a question, I was off in my own world again and didn't hear the answer.

Another emotion I felt strongly in the beginning was fear. I was paralyzed with fear. The world I felt safe in wasn't safe any longer. I was afraid to leave the house, afraid to drive, afraid to be in a car with someone else driving, and afraid

49

when anyone I knew went out to a bar. I felt panic and anxiety about everyday experiences. My entire world came crashing down on me, and I was absolutely terrified of what my future held. I had to take baby steps to re-enter my scary new world.

One thing I learned about grief is that people do what they have to do to get through it. Others may perceive this as denial, when it is actually that person's way of trying to cope. Burying yourself in work, moving away, going on with your life like nothing has changed; these are all ways to try to forget about the pain. It's hard for your brain to process all the ways in which a death changes your life, so it's done slowly. There is no right or wrong. We grieve in our own way, and in our own time.

Of course, there are unhealthy outlets like drugs or alcohol, and it was easy for me to see why a grieving person would choose to do these things. I'll admit that there were more than a few times that I drank too much alcohol, hoping that it would make me feel better. It didn't. Since alcohol is a depressant, I ended up more depressed, I still cried all night, and ended up feeling worse in the morning. My problems were still there when I woke up, and I'd have a terrible headache and stomachache on top of it. This was definitely not the answer. I had always prided myself on the fact that I had never tried drugs; but for a fleeting moment, I thought that maybe I should. I might be missing something that would take away the pain I felt inside. I never did… but I sure thought about it. I thought that feeling sedated would be better than feeling the pain. Not for long. If you don't deal with your grief, it deals with you. Buried grief will come out, one way or another.

One thing that I did shortly after Darren died was to get rid of everything that was his. Maybe this was a form of denial, and there was definitely anger involved; but in my mind, the house we had built, and everything in it that we had bought together represented all my dreams that were never going to come true. I felt as if everything was just sitting there, mocking me. I had all this stuff, and no husband to share it with. I gave away some personal items to Darren's friends and family. Then I sold back all of his CD's to the used CD store, gave most of his clothes to his mom, and threw away all of his toiletries. I was making "our home" into "my home." Darren wouldn't need any of his personal things now, and it just upset me to see them. I even got rid of a lot of my own clothing; things that he or his parents had bought for me or things I had worn on special occasions that reminded me of him. It was just too painful, and I thought I would never want to wear them again.

I kept pictures, letters, and cards from him in a box, so that whenever I wanted to, I could reminisce; but I didn't want "his" stuff all over "my" house. For my own sanity, "our" house became "my" house when he died. For some reason, it made me feel better not to have Darren's things around anymore. I already knew how pathetic my life was. I didn't need constant reminders that he was no longer here. I wasn't in denial of my reality; I was just trying to survive in it. Later, I wished I hadn't been so hasty in getting rid of everything, but at the time I felt it was the right thing to do. When I really start to miss him, I just have to go into a department store that sells the men's cologne Drakkar, which was my favorite on him. I close my eyes as I smell the bottle and just for a moment I am curled up next to him again.

I think that the word denial is overused when discussing grief reactions. To me, denial is burying your head in the sand and pretending that nothing has changed. Some people are just more reality-based. They move on quicker, not out of lack of love or respect, but out of necessity. It is easy to sit back and judge other people's actions. I felt that Dave was in denial. He continued to party like a rock star and continued to drive, even after his license was revoked. He had jumped into a relationship with Kristine just a week after Darren died. A few months later they were engaged. To me, this was denial; but I'm sure that to him, he was just trying to get by the only way he knew how.

Another thing I did that certain people in my life viewed as denial was to begin dating again. I understand why people would think this way. I met Matt only three-and-a-half months after Darren died. Traditionally, you're supposed to wait a year after the death of a spouse before you start dating again, right? Who made that rule? Obviously, someone who's never gone through it. I find it funny that people who get divorced or end a long-term relationship are encouraged to move on and get back into the dating scene right away. In fact, the night that Darren died, they were out celebrating Rico's recent divorce. Heck, who needs the divorce? Just being separated gives you permission to date someone else. That's perfectly acceptable in our society. But if you are widowed, that's another story. You will be chastised, or at least the subject of gossip if you *ever* decide to date again. Give me a break! I see this as a cruel double standard.

Just because the relationship didn't end intentionally, doesn't mean widows want to spend the rest of their lives alone. We all get lonely, we're all human. Everyone needs to be loved, and deserves to be happy- with someone else if they so choose, when they choose to do it. Dating again is part of the recovery process after losing a spouse, especially if you're young. Recovery is not an act of disloyalty.

I had a stark realization when Darren died: I had never been without a man in my life since I began dating. I had always jumped from relationship to relationship with no down time. There was always someone waiting in the wings. So, being alone was new for me, and I didn't like it one bit. There was always that euphoric feeling of being infatuated with a new person, that it made the breakup more bearable. I didn't have that this time around, and the 100 days I spent alone seemed like an eternity.

The man I started dating after Darren died, I later married. When Matt and I met, I was not looking for a new husband. In fact, I had sworn off men all together and I had built up an emotional wall around myself so that I would never get hurt again. In my mind, I'd had the best years of my life, and I would never let myself fall in love again. It wasn't worth it. The emotional risk was too great. I even told my sister that no one would want to go out with me anyway with all my baggage, I was damaged goods. Everyone I love dies, I told her. I must be cursed. Kim just laughed and said that I had so much to offer, and that any man would be lucky to have me. Sisters are good that way.

The point is that I didn't feel like I was in denial by starting to date Matt, although others did. I had decided that the time was right for me to move on with my life. It was a conflict, certainly, because I didn't want to hurt Darren's family; but first and foremost, I needed to be true to myself. Dating Matt wasn't an easy decision to make; but after what had happened, I knew that life was short and that I couldn't let other people decide what was right for me.

Besides, I figured I would probably be grieving for a long time- perhaps the rest of my life- whether there was someone else in my life or not. So, if I could have a little fun and happiness while I was still grieving, darn it, I deserved it. Waiting longer to date wouldn't prove that I loved Darren any more or any less. Living in denial would have been pretending he'd be coming back. I had to face the fact that I was single now. Matt made me laugh, and gave me hope that I could have some happiness in spite of what had happened. The wall that I had built up around myself slowly crumbled. He was a Godsend, and I don't know how I would have gotten by without him.

Now, I'm not saying that starting to date is the answer for everyone. Let's face it; there are a lot of insensitive jerks out there. I didn't think that there were any gentlemen left in this world. I truly believed that someone "up there" as I call it, sent Matt to me, because I couldn't have found a more perfect person for myself at that time if I had tried. When the time is right for you, you'll know it.

Six months after meeting Matt, I sold my house and we moved to California, where he'd grown up. As much as I denied it at the time, I just wanted to get the hell out of Illinois and escape my old life. My mother-in-law thought I was making a mistake by moving away, but I knew this was what I needed to do. I wasn't so much running *from* something, as she suggested, as I was running *to* something- a new life. Illinois was Darren's state, this was his family and these were his friends. I felt like I didn't belong any more. I was beginning to hate it there. I certainly couldn't live in our house without him. I could start over, but not there.

Darren's absence was a constant presence in my life. Everywhere I went I was reminded of Darren and our life together. Memories flooded back to me when I saw the restaurants we ate at, places we went, and the people "we" knew. Worst of all, every time I drove out of town, I had to drive past the road where he had been killed. Whenever I did, I would crank up the radio and sing very loud to try to block out the memories of what happened on that road. Other times, I would just drive past it and give the road the middle finger. I'm sure it was horribly offended.

When I first met Matt, I thought he was safe to date because he was from California and I thought that he would be returning home soon. I decided to go out with him because I wanted to test the waters, get out of the house, and make a new friend who didn't know my circumstances. I never expected to fall in love and move across the country, but it was the best thing that could have happened to me. I could get away from this hell that was my life and start over. I didn't want to be a slave to my past. I needed to believe that I had a future. Besides, I knew that I could always move home if things didn't work out.

Another reason I was glad to move away was that I didn't want to be known as the pitiful young widow. I was strong. I made it through this, and I didn't want anyone's pity. Also, we lived in a small town where Darren had gone to high school. People noticed Matt and me together, and I learned that they were gossiping about us. I didn't need people judging me. What I did was none of anyone else's business. My real friends were happy for me, and that's all that mattered. Staying in Chicago would have held me back, and I would have been stuck living in the past. I needed a new start, so I gave myself permission to enjoy life. Darren would have wanted that for me. I know he wouldn't have wanted me to live my life alone. In honor of him, I had to live my life the way he would want me to, and that would be with someone who made me happy.

I don't know why, but Darren used to always ask me these crazy hypothetical questions like, "What would you do if I was disfigured in a car accident and would be a vegetable the rest of my life? Would you stay with me, or move on and be with someone else?" My answer was that I would stay with him no matter what. Then he said, "I would want you to move on, you deserve to be with someone who could make you happy." I asked him why he was thinking this way, and he said he didn't know. I thought about this after he died, and knew that in his heart he would not be mad if I was with someone else, and in fact wished it for me.

I will admit that having someone new to love may have kept me from fully feeling the impact of my loss, and a lot of my feelings were repressed. Eventually, I realized that I still had "issues." How could I not? But I needed Matt in my life to give me a reason to go on. I would grieve in my own time. Why couldn't I do both? Time alone wouldn't heal all of the wounds. I still had a lot to work through in my healing. With Matt's support, however, it was a lot easier. I didn't feel the hopelessness I had felt when I was alone.

It felt scary to be alone when Darren first died, but after a while, I actually came to enjoy the independence, and was even content to be on my own for a short time. I set new standards for myself, just in case I ever did date again. I wouldn't put up with any crap; things would be on my terms. I found a confidence and a maturity within myself that I didn't know I had. In the past, I was a "pleaser," always doing things to make everyone else happy. Now, partly out of fear, I was going to take control of my life. As much as I could control, that is. I told myself that if anyone treated me badly in any way, it would be over, no looking back.

Luckily for me, Matt turned out to be an angel who bent over backwards to make me happy. He understood what I was going through and respected me. I couldn't have asked for a more compassionate, patient, or loving man. I didn't know such men existed until he came along. He was not jealous and he never felt like he was playing second fiddle. He was mature beyond his years in this sense, and immature and funny at the same time, a quality I adore.

So, maybe I'm in denial that I was ever in denial; but I considered my actions to be *re*-actions to my new reality. I was just trying to get on with my life the best way I knew how. Although it crossed my mind that I was somehow "cheating" on Darren, or "disrespecting" him by dating Matt, I had to continually remind myself that Darren would rather have me happy with someone else than to see me give up on life and love. Also, because I was happily married once, I knew I wanted that again. I also wanted children. Both of these things required a husband. So even though Darren was gone, I still had the same dreams for myself that I had growing up: to be happily married with children.

As a young widow with no children, I wasn't about to get seriously involved with a man who didn't want children himself. I knew without a doubt that I was meant to be a mother, and I didn't want to waste my time with someone who didn't have the same dreams. I felt that I had blown my chance once, and I wasn't going to do it again. I wasn't getting any younger either. I even bluntly told Matt that if he didn't want to have children, I wouldn't want to date him anymore. Most guys would have run for the hills. He said "I don't want them right now, but when the time is right, definitely." I needed to test him to be sure we were compatible in all areas before getting too involved.

When someone is taken from you without warning, your own mortality becomes very apparent. I thought "Wow, I could die tomorrow." Until someone close to you dies young, you believe everybody around you is going to live to a ripe old age. Children aren't supposed to die before their parents; it's just not the way it should be. So, after considering the possibility that I could be the next to go, I decided that I wasn't about to put my life on hold any longer. I was going to live it, and be as happy as I could be. If some people weren't ready for me to move on, that was their problem, not mine. Darren and I thought that we had all the time in the world to start a family. Look where waiting had gotten me, back to square one.

After what I went through, I thought I deserved to do whatever I wanted with my life. There were many reasons why I wanted to move far away. I didn't feel as if I could truly start over in Darren's home town, the town that Dave still lived in. It took a lot of courage for me to move away from family and friends to face an unknown future in an unfamiliar place with unfamiliar people; but I knew it was what I needed to do, and I have never regretted my decision. Besides, home is where the heart is.

<u>Anger</u>

"An eye for an eye only leads to more blindness."

-Margaret Atwood

I was stuck in the anger stage for a very long time. It started out subtly, like obsessively reading the obituaries in the newspaper, and feeling angry that most of the people who died got to live a long life and have a family, while I didn't. I felt that Darren had been cheated too. Then, during one very dark period, my anger escalated to the point of plotting revenge on Dave for killing my husband.

I'm a little embarrassed now to admit that I felt the way I felt, and thought the things I thought; but I believe that as long as I didn't act on my anger, this was a normal part of my grieving process. Most of my anger was directed at Dave, whom I soon blamed entirely for Darren's death. I asked "Why didn't Dave die? Why did he walk away with only a scratch?" I felt like I was being punished for something Dave had done. It had been irresponsible and negligent of him to take the wheel, and as far as I was concerned, he was a murderer. He deserved the death penalty. An eye for an eye. I remember thinking that televised executions sounded like a good idea. Maybe it would deter some other drunken jerk from getting behind the wheel and killing someone else's loved one. When he took the wheel, Dave took Darren's life in his hands, and I felt that he should be held accountable whether he meant to do it or not. Darren was still dead.

I also had this fear of running into Dave in the grocery store; literally. In my recurring vision, I mowed him down with my shopping cart, and repeatedly ran him over with it. I was afraid to go grocery shopping in town and started shopping elsewhere because I was sure it would come to that if I did see him there. For some time I had myself convinced that Darren would want me to get back at Dave for what he had done to his family, and to him. I remember Darren saying many times, "If anyone ever hurt you or anyone in my family, I'd kill them and worry about the consequences later." At the time, I thought that was harsh. Now, I thought that it was reasonable. Darren would want me to get even for him, I reasoned. I was so angry with Dave, so full of rage that I fantasized about getting revenge. This rage frightened me because I had never thought that I had the capacity to hate someone, and now I felt that I did.

Now, how should I go about getting revenge? Blow up Dave's house? Shoot him? Hire someone else to shoot him? Or should I kill someone he loved, so he would have to suffer like I was suffering? No, I thought, Dave doesn't love anyone as much as I love Darren, so losing them wouldn't hurt him as much as losing Darren has hurt me. Of course, I would never have told anyone that I was contemplating payback. I knew I couldn't actually go through with any of these things, but I did think about it. I am one of the most docile, laid back, easy-going people, so for me to be thinking this way, I knew I was in some serious emotional pain.

About six months after the accident, just before moving to California, I was visiting my family in Wisconsin and I remember my brother Ricky asking me if I still talked to Dave. I got so angry and I went off on a tangent about how Dave was a murderer and how he deserved to die for killing Darren. Ricky's eyes just about popped out of his head looking at this stranger pretending to be his sister. He was stunned that I felt that way, and frankly, so was I. This wasn't like me at all.

I was mad at Dave for not taking responsibility for the accident. He pled *not guilty* to the initial charge of vehicular manslaughter and instead pled guilty to a lesser charge to avoid doing jail time. To me, this was like adding salt to the wound. By doing this, in my eyes, he was basically saying that he hadn't done anything wrong. What an insult! At least he should accept the consequences of his actions.

I was still stuck in the anger phase when Dave finally went to trial. I had been to a preliminary trial; but Dave's sentencing had been pushed pack so many times that I had already moved to California, and just couldn't make myself come back for the actual sentencing. I was so angry that I feared I'd be one of those grieving relatives you see on TV, going ballistic in the courtroom and having to be dragged away in handcuffs. I now understand where the term "blinded by rage" comes from. I remember seeing video footage on television of a guy who decided to take the law into his own hands and snuck a gun into a courthouse where the man who killed his son was about to be tried. The father was pretending he was talking on the telephone and when his son's murderer walked past him, he shot and killed the man. During this time when I was "blinded by rage" I thought that was pretty clever. He was subsequently arrested and put in prison, but he felt vindicated.

Regarding Dave's trial, I felt that there was nothing I could have done to change things even if I had been there. No sentence would have been severe enough in my eyes, and I didn't want to put myself through any more mental anguish. I certainly didn't feel strong enough to have to be face to face with Dave. I felt that I was the one who got the life sentence. I was a bit confused about the whole legal process, and didn't know if I needed to be there or not. However, once I found out that I was the only one in Darren's family not in attendance, I felt a little guilty about not being there for the sentencing. I didn't want Darren's family to think that because I had moved away that I didn't care anymore, or that I didn't want to be involved; but I just couldn't go through with it. I needed to heal, not to be pulled back into more torment.

I was also angry at the legal system for giving Dave a slap on the wrist for killing someone. He got no jail time, which I felt he deserved; only community service, fines, a revoked driver's license, and a felony conviction on his record. White collar criminals got more severe sentences than this! In my mind, the punishment didn't fit the crime. He probably felt like he was above the law in getting such a lenient sentence. I just wished that he'd be dumb enough to violate his probation by driving, get caught, and have to do some jail time. Maybe then he would understand the severity of his actions.

After Dave's driver's license was suspended, I heard through the grapevine that he was driving. I was so mad that I seriously thought about waiting in my car outside his house and when he got in his car, following him and calling the police on my cell phone for them to come and arrest him. Then Dave would have to go to jail for driving after a felony revocation. But, after thinking about it rationally, I realized that this wouldn't bring Darren back or change anything. Plus, all this energy I was spending on anger and planning revenge was exhausting and keeping me from healing. There's an ancient Chinese saying that says "When you seek revenge, you might as well dig two graves; one for the other person and one for yourself." I had enough sense to recognize that any act of revenge on my part would be worse than what Dave had done because mine would be premeditated.

As it turned out, Dave did eventually get caught driving after his license was revoked without any intervention on my part. I was living in California at the time, but my secret wish had come true. He did some minor jail time, and I can't say that I wasn't happy when I first heard about it. But then I felt disappointed because it really didn't make me feel any better about my loss, as I had expected it to. I actually felt bad for Kristine. I hoped that this would at least give him time to think about the seriousness of the judge's orders. Dave did not seem to realize that driving is a privilege, and when you kill someone in a car, you get that privilege revoked.

59

Eventually I forgave Dave, but it would take me five years to find it in my heart to do so. Dave received a life sentence too, I later realized, regardless of how the courts punished him for his actions. He had to live with the recurring image in his mind of Darren's dead body, knowing that it was his fault, and the guilt that goes with it.

For a while, I felt angry at Darren's dad for setting a bad example by drinking and driving himself on many occasions. Even shortly before his death, Darren and I were at his parent's house, and his dad drove himself home totally drunk. The next day, he didn't even remember talking to his wife on the phone from Florida when he got home. I remember Darren was mad at his dad for his poor judgment. Somehow I felt that if his dad would have taught him not to drink and drive, or drive with someone who had been, Darren would still be here with us.

As strange as this may sound, I was angry at Darren too, for many things. In my grief-stricken mind, it didn't matter whether his absence was voluntary or not. He abandoned me. I was angry at him for leaving me all alone. I felt like I had just wasted eight years of my life. A lot of my friends already had children, and here I was childless, husbandless, and starting over at age 27. I felt cheated and maybe mad at myself for choosing the wrong guy. What if I ended up never finding another man and never having children? It might sound stupid to someone who hasn't been there, but when your biological clock is ticking, and one of your dreams is to have children, and suddenly the man you have been with for eight years, the future father of your children is gone, a bit of panic sets in.

Now, of course, I don't feel like I wasted eight years of my life. In fact, I can honestly say that even if I knew in advance what the outcome of our relationship was going to be, I wouldn't have changed a thing. The years I spent with Darren were some of the most cherished times of my life. But I do remember feeling angry and cheated for a while, and saying that I wasted eight years of my life. They were certainly not wasted.

Also adding to my anger with Darren; he was the one who had taken care of the finances in our family. I didn't know or care when bills were due, or how much we owed each month. He always took care of that stuff so I didn't have to worry about it. Now Darren was gone and I was left behind in a new house without his income to pay for it. I didn't know how I was going to handle these financial burdens on top of my devastating emotional burden. For that, I felt resentful and angry. How could he have done this to me?

I was especially angry that he had broken his promise to me and allowed Dave to drive. I was furious that his poor judgment had ruined the future we had planned together. How could he have been so stupid to let Dave drive his SUV, after promising me he wouldn't; knowing that Dave had been drinking heavily and (I found out from Dave's blood test) smoking pot. I also learned (and I don't know if Darren was aware of it) that Dave had cocaine in his system the night of the accident. We knew that Dave used to do cocaine; but we thought that was all over years ago. We were wrong. I was also mad because I learned that Darren hadn't been wearing his seatbelt. Would he be here now if he had been? I eventually got over my anger with Darren, because I knew in my heart that he was the real victim here- not me.

At one point, instead of putting Darren on a pedestal, and thinking he was eligible for sainthood like people sometimes do when a loved one dies; I did just the opposite. Although it wasn't true, I convinced myself that our relationship hadn't been that great. I fixated on all the mean things Darren had ever said or done, and all the things I hadn't liked but just accepted. I told myself that we were doomed from the start. It was easier to move forward with my life if I was mad at him. On a much smaller scale, I guess you could compare it with breaking off a relationship. You tend to forget about all their good qualities and all the good times you shared; and you fixate on the breakup itself, and how much of a jerk they were in the end. Doing this helps you move on in your mind; instead of becoming a stalker because you can't let it go.

Another aspect of anger that I went through was intentional cruelty to people I loved. I took my anger out on them. I used words as a way to lash out because my anger had turned inward. I had no tolerance for other people's stupidity, and I let them know it. I didn't want to get involved with other people's problems; I had enough of my own. I was especially mean and vicious to my brother Ricky, and to my dad. All of the things from the past that had upset me suddenly seemed fresh, and my words felt like venom spewing out.

Even as harsh words spilled out of my mouth, I knew this wasn't the real me talking. It was as if someone else had taken over my body. Then I would feel guilty. Later, I'd apologize and explain why I was acting like I was possessed. They understood. My dad even said that our blowout was the best thing that could have happened because I had told him things he needed to hear. I acted like the fabled lion with the thorn in its paw: I hurt, so I felt it was okay to lash out and hurt someone else. I know now that this is a symptom of post-traumatic stress. I thought that I was doing fine, but my grief was finding other outlets.

I would get angry when I heard other people complaining about petty things that their husband or boyfriend had done. I had to force myself to keep from screaming, "At least you have a husband!" When your husband is suddenly gone, you realize what is important in life. We all waste so much time bitching and moaning about things that are so insignificant in the grand scheme of things. When you would do anything in the world to turn back the hands of time and erase this huge mistake, other people's petty complaints are even more magnified.

I was also angry with God. Why would He take my husband from me when I was so young? Why me? What had I done to deserve this? I didn't understand. I had always done my best to be a good person and to help others. Why was I being punished? What had Darren done to deserve this? He was a good person, too. My anger with God was short-lived, because I knew in my heart that God didn't just decide to screw up my life one day and take my husband. I think it is just a part of the grieving process to question why, and God is an easy target to cast the blame upon.

My feelings of anger with God changed when I visited Darren's Grandpa shortly after Darren's death. He told me that he was still mad at God for taking his wife, who had died of cancer many years earlier. I felt so sorry for him because he still carried around all of this anger. I was sad that this dear old man was still tormenting himself after all these years. I decided then that I never wanted to be like that. I realized that death is not God's way of punishing the living.

I received a poem from a friend that sums up my feelings about God's role in the tragic events in our lives:

> *My Life is but a Weaving*- *Author Unknown*
> *My life is but a weaving between my God and me.*
> *I do not choose the colors, he worketh steadily.*
> *Often times he weaveth sorrow and I in foolish pride*
> *Forget he sees the upper and I the underside.*
> *Not 'til the loom is silent and the shuttles cease to fly*
> *Will God unroll the canvas and explain the reason why*
> *The dark threads are as needful in the skillful weaver's hand*
> *As the threads of gold and silver in the pattern He has planned.*

Maybe we simply are not supposed to have all of the answers now. I believe that everything happens for a reason, and that when it is our time to leave this life, the reasons for everything will be made clear.

<u>Bargaining</u>

"For of all sad words of tongue or pen,
the saddest are these:
'It might have been!'"

—*John Greenleaf Whittier*

This is the "Why me?" stage. This is also the stage where you say "If only I had (fill in the blank) this tragedy could have been prevented." "Why didn't he listen to me? I told him to drive," I kept telling myself repeatedly. I also thought, "If only I hadn't done that modeling job that night maybe I would have been there and this wouldn't have happened because I would have driven." I felt guilty because I hadn't been there to protect him.

All of Darren's friends and immediate family thought they might have been able to change what happened, if only they had done something differently. *Everyone* wanted to take the blame. His mom blamed herself for being in Florida. If she had been home, maybe he wouldn't have gone out that night, and would have been with her. Rico blamed himself for not driving. He also felt that if he never came back to town, this wouldn't have happened. Darren's friend Daren (Shaggy) blamed himself for not being out with them. Maybe he would have been driving had he been out with them. If only…. Thoughts like these must be worked through before you can accept the loss. Nothing could change what had already happened, and that was a hard pill to swallow.

Along with bargaining comes guilt. The one thing I felt most guilty about was accepting life insurance money. Darren was very practical. Not many 28-year-olds have a life insurance policy, but he did. We actually had a conversation about it a week before his death. Darren wanted to get a policy for me and increase his own, because our new house cost more than his old policy was worth. This haunted me for a long time after he died, because it seemed almost prophetic. We needed this insurance policy, he said, in case something happened to either of us. I didn't want to talk about it. I said, "I'm not going to die, and you're not going to die, so let's stop talking about it." But Darren was insistent. "Seriously, he said, if something happened to me, I'd want to be sure you would be taken care of. You could do whatever you wanted with the money." I thought this was a morbid conversation and said, "Let's talk about it later." Later never came.

Nevertheless, I received the life insurance money that there was, along with some money from the automobile insurance company because we had an uninsured motorist policy, which Dave was, and I felt horribly guilty about it. I felt as though I had just traded my husband's life for blood money. It was a burden for me. I put it in the bank and didn't touch it for a long time because of this guilt. Later on, I knew that it was a blessing and that this was Darren's way of still taking care of me. Things could have been much worse; but it's hard to feel grateful for something you didn't work for and don't feel like you deserve.

I also received money from people at the funeral. I remember feeling guilty about that too. I thought, "I don't want your money, I just want Darren back!" Just two short years earlier, some of these same people were giving us money at our wedding as we started our lives together. Now, they were giving me money as I started my life again…alone.

Another thing I felt very guilty about was dating Matt. I worried about what other people would think, especially my in-laws. I didn't want to keep it from them; but at the same time, I didn't want to hurt them. I was afraid they would look upon it as a betrayal, which I knew it wasn't. It was one of those "your head tells you one thing, but your heart tells you another," situations. Their heads told them that I would eventually find someone else, but in their hearts, I would always be Darren's wife.

I felt like I was cheating on the family more than on Darren, because they were still here. I knew I wasn't technically "cheating," but I felt like I was betraying someone. I still felt loyalty to Darren, even though I knew he was gone forever. We had a once-in-a-lifetime love, one that couldn't be "replaced." I treasured our time we had together, but I knew he was never coming back. We hadn't divorced. There was no chance for reconciliation. No, this was it. Our relationship (in the physical sense) was over. These guilty feelings didn't last too long, because I repeatedly told myself that this was my life and I needed to do what made me happy. The time was right for me to move on, even if it wasn't the right time for others.

I also felt guilty that I never had a chance to say goodbye to Darren or to let him know how much he meant to me. It wasn't supposed to happen this way. It was unnatural. To relieve this guilt, I just talked to him in my mind, and hoped that he heard me. I told him I was sorry for all our dreams that wouldn't come true. We had always envisioned ourselves growing old together, teasing and calling each other silly nicknames. Now, we would never do this. We would never have children together. I could still do these things, but Darren couldn't. He had been cheated and I felt sad for him, and guilty for still being here. Survivor's guilt, they call it. With a sudden death, there are no goodbyes, no time to do all the things you always wanted to do, no time to make things right.

Shortly after Darren's death, Rico learned that his mother was dying. I encouraged him to spend as much time with her as possible. I urged him to tell her how much she meant to him, how much he loved her. Reminisce about the good times you shared, I told him, so you won't have to live with regret and guilt. He took my advice, and thanked me for it after she passed. I was glad that he was able to do with his mother what I wished I had the chance to do with Darren- say goodbye.

Depression

"Being defeated is often a temporary condition.
Giving up is what makes it permanent."

—*Marlene vos Savant*

It is hard to pinpoint exactly when I was depressed. I feel like I've had moderate to severe depression since the day Darren died. I'd read that the symptoms of depression include: loss of interest in life, irritability, withdrawal, lack of energy, inability to eat, inability to sleep or excessive sleeping, and inability to function. I thought "How about all of the above?" At least it felt this way in the beginning.

Soon after Darren died, I actually contemplated suicide. I wasn't the only one; his parents felt the same way, but they had a daughter to think about. I felt as though I no longer had anything to live for, and that my life was over. I would never be happy again. I thought about driving my car off a bridge or into a tree, so I could be with Darren again in the afterlife- if there was one. Then I realized that I might not be successful in the attempt. I might end up a paraplegic compounding my grief and suffering. Probably not a good plan. Plus, I was unsure of the consequences of suicide in the afterlife, and didn't want to chance not being able to be with Darren after resorting to such a desperate act.

One night, I had a very vivid dream about trying to kill myself by lying on a railroad track and waiting for a train to come by and kill me. I saw the train approaching in the distance. At that moment, Darren appeared, walked over to me and lifted me up off of the tracks, saying "You can't come yet. It's not your time. You have more to do here." I was crying as he held me in his arms and I told him that I didn't want to live without him. I could smell him, hear his voice, and feel his body against mine. I woke up, wet with tears. I had actually been crying in my sleep. I cried even harder then, because I realized that Darren wasn't really there with me, even though it felt so real. I knew then that I could never kill myself, because I would never want the people I loved to feel the way I felt now. I knew that when it came right down to it, I could never really end my own life. Still, I wanted to end this emotional pain, and there was no end in sight. I so desperately wanted to be with

Darren again, and death seemed to be the only way we could be together.

I recall one moment when I had lost the will to live. A few months after his death, Darren's mom and I were on a very bumpy plane ride, returning home from a trip to Florida in a failed attempt to return our lives to some state of normalcy. I fantasized about the plane crashing, and almost hoped it would. I was holding my mother-in-law's hand, and we were both very scared. "I wouldn't care if this plane crashed," I said. She finished my thought: "Because then we'd be with Darren." We both started to cry and squeezed each other's hand harder. Then on the drive home from the airport, I was alone in the back seat with my in-laws up front, and I sobbed quietly because I didn't feel like I had anything to come home to. Even sadder, I didn't feel like I even had a home anymore.

Definitely, there were times at the beginning of my loss that I was clinically depressed. I couldn't eat, wanted to sleep all day, and got no pleasure out of anything. I saw no way out. A big part of me had died with Darren, and I couldn't imagine my life being good again. But I think I had an underlying depression that lasted for years. On the surface I looked happy. I had moved on with my life, and had a lot to be grateful for. However, a sadness remained that could surface at any time and emotionally cripple me.

I saw a psychologist for a little while because you are "supposed to" get help when you go through this kind of trauma. Honestly, I still don't think it did me any good. Here I was telling a stranger the same things I told my friends and family, but I didn't get any relief or any answers. Not to mention, it's expensive too! I desperately wanted to know when I was going to feel like myself again. When would this agony go away? The psychologist told me that I might *never* feel like myself again. She said that it would probably be a year before I would even feel better. I didn't want to feel this bad for a year! Besides, I realized that I was telling her what she wanted to hear, not the whole truth, because I believed that she would think I was a threat to myself and to others if I told her my real feelings, and then she'd have me committed!

I realized that I needed to do everything I could to get past my despair. I saw the psychologist for a couple of months and then decided I could do fine on my own. I would spend the whole hour with her, rehashing what I'd already told my family and friends, who genuinely cared about me. I felt like I was just paying the psychologist to listen. I decided that I no longer needed a professional. I wasn't mentally ill. There was no "cure" for what ailed me, and I decided that I had to get through it myself.

Now, don't get me wrong. I'm sure there are plenty of people who don't have anyone they can talk to about their loss and would be lost without their counselor or support group. I really admire these brave people who provide grief support. It's got to be heart-wrenching to hear about the pain people are in on a day-to-day basis. It's hard enough comforting a bereaved friend or relative; but to comfort a complete stranger must be extremely challenging.

I had thought about joining a widow's support group, but there were none that I could find in my area for young widows. I couldn't see myself sitting around with a bunch of seniors whose concerns were completely different than mine. I didn't get to spend a lifetime with my husband and raise children and grandchildren with him. Besides losing a husband, there was no common ground. No offense to older widows, I just wanted to talk to someone my age that had been through what I was going through. I felt that I was the only one.

Personally, I got more comfort and healing out of reading self-help books, and books on spirit communication than seeing the psychologist. Instead of an hour of counseling, I sometimes spent all day reading and healing my heart. I was on a crash course, determined to find all the answers and get past the pain. I would go to the bookstore and buy numerous grief related books at a time. The clerk would look at me strangely as if to say "Are all of those for you?" I guess I didn't look like a grieving widow. I wore my Happy Mask out in public.

It was such a strange and uncomfortable feeling for me to go into a bookstore and buy books about grief and widowhood at my young age. I almost felt ashamed to have to be buying these types of books. I didn't want to admit that they were for me. I remember telling a checker at a chain bookstore that the grief books I was buying were for a friend who had lost a spouse. Why did I feel the need to do that? Maybe it has something to do with the fact that young women are conditioned their whole lives to believe that once they get married, their lives are now complete and they will live happily ever after. What happens when your spouse dies? Your life is now incomplete and you will live unhappily ever after?

Since this chapter is about depression, I thought it would be appropriate to mention a few thoughts about antidepressants. The psychologist I saw had suggested that I go see my doctor to prescribe an antidepressant for me, as she was unable to write prescriptions. I told her that I didn't want to take any. She felt that I needed them. I told her that I didn't want to be dependent on an artificial means of coping; and just delaying the inevitable: hard-core grief. How would I learn coping skills on my own if I was doped up on happy pills? I am glad I didn't take them to get through my grief. I wanted to feel every emotion as much as possible, because I felt that this would to be the only way I would truly heal.

Years later, after each of my children were born; I had pretty bad postpartum depression. I didn't take antidepressants after my first son was born, although those who lived with me probably wished I had. However, after my second son was born, I was rocking him one day, and began sobbing for no reason whatsoever. I decided it was time to call my doctor. I thought I would give them a try. I stayed on them for a few months, and boy, what a difference. I felt as if a light switch had been turned on in my brain. I was much calmer and wasn't upset or angered by the smallest things like I had been prior to taking them. To me, this was different than taking antidepressants for grief because my post-partum depression was caused by hormonal fluctuations that occur after childbirth. After my menstrual cycle returned to normal, so did my emotions, and I went off of the antidepressants.

So, in hindsight, having had some experience with antidepressants, would I recommend them for others going through grief? Yes, if you feel you can't cope on your own, and you need to take the edge off, they can be tremendously helpful. However, you will inevitably have to go through the grief process. They don't erase your memory, or take away the need to grieve. For some, the initial shock of learning of a loved ones death is so overwhelming they need to be hospitalized, or worse! I've heard of people dying of a heart attack after learning the news of a loved ones death. So, who am I to give advice on what is best for everyone? I remember feeling that I would be weak if I gave in and took antidepressants, but after taking them for post-partum depression,

I realized that they didn't make me unable to feel or unable to cry anymore. My second son, Damon, was born a month after the terrorist attacks of September 11th, and even though I was taking antidepressants at the time, I often cried while watching the news of the aftermath. They didn't make me unable to feel emotions, as I thought they might. So, I guess I'm saying it is a personal choice. I didn't take them for my depression during the grief process, but I did take them for post-partum depression, and they were helpful. So, you make the call.

If I had know then what I know now, I would have turned to homeopathic grief remedies after losing Darren. They are safe with no side effects. I had an allergic reaction to one of the antidepressants I had tried, and they killed my sex drive; definite negative side effects. Eight years after Darren's death, I still had some residual side effects of grief, and had started seeing a homeopathic doctor for various things. I was prescribed a homeopathic remedy for a month called *Ignatia Amara* which is used for healing grief caused by the loss of a loved one as well as post-partum depression. After I began taking it, I had a few days where I went through what is known in homeopathy as a "healing crisis," where I relived some of the anger and sadness I felt during the grief process, followed by the feeling that something had definitely lifted from my spirit. Homeopathy has helped me and my family in so many ways, but that is another story.

I think of my depression as a constant feeling rather than a phase. I had good days and bad days, or a string of good days, followed by one really bad day. I would do things I enjoyed to avoid feeling depressed. It was easy to sit around and do nothing, to feel sorry for myself. But, I realized I had a choice. I could sink or swim, so to speak, and I had always been a fighter. Feeling depressed, giving up, and clinging to anger was the easy short-term solution. Or, I decided, I could do some hard work now, and there would be a payoff.

During my 13 years in gymnastics, I was taught not to quit, not to give up. Gymnastics is a sport where you train hard for months, even years for one day of competition. You have to do conditioning, weight training, and endless repetitions of your routines to be prepared for competition. I had to take the same approach with grief. I was now dealing with the biggest challenge of my lifetime. I had been trained to believe that quitting is not an option. You fall off the beam; you get back up and try again. You fall off the high bar onto your head and scare yourself silly; you get right back up and find the courage to finish your routine. You might fail at a new trick one hundred times before getting it right once. To succeed, you needed determination and stamina. It was a way of life. This ingrained mentality was proving to be very helpful in my grief. I knew I couldn't give up now.

A few years after Darren died; the gymnasts from my high school threw a retirement party for our coach. I pulled him aside at the party and thanked him for giving me this wonderful gift. I told him that I credited a lot of my resilience to him, and that he taught me so much more than just gymnastics. We were both crying, and he told me how proud he was of me. It was a beautiful moment. It's a strange parallel, perhaps, but I believe that all those years of training and competing prepared me in some way for this part of my life. From my gymnastics coach that I had since I was eight-years-old, I learned how to be strong and brave, and not to give up. Without realizing it, he taught me how to survive a devastating loss.

One last thing that I noticed about depression is that it can be recurring. My initial intense feelings of losing Darren came back years later with a vengeance while I was pregnant with each of my children and again afterward, during the post-partum period. During these times, when I was "hormonally-challenged," I sank into depression again, crying constantly, feeling as if I had just had a relapse. You never really know the profound emptiness that loss creates until you experience it firsthand, and that emptiness never really goes away completely, no matter how full the rest of your life becomes. It was as if a scab had been ripped from my heart, re-opening a wound that had finally been healing.

Acceptance

"You will not grow if you sit in a beautiful flower garden.
but you will grow if you are sick, if you are in pain, if you experience losses,
and if you do not put your head in the sand, but take the pain as a gift to you
with a very, very specific purpose."

—*Elizabeth Kübler Ross*

I tried to convince myself many times that I had accepted my loss and I could therefore move on with my life. By saying that I had accepted Darren's death, I reasoned, I would be done grieving. Unfortunately, that's not the way it works. Acceptance comes a little bit at a time. I honestly don't believe that we ever accept it, but that we learn to live with it.

Also, I feel that the word acceptance is a bit misleading. It connotes an ending. I think that in the context of grief, acceptance means that you are no longer in denial and you can think about a future without your loved one. It does not mean that you are happy about it. It doesn't mean that you will not have a setback occasionally, even after you think you've accepted it. That's the nature of the beast. It is okay to relapse, it doesn't mean failure.

Simply put, there were just too many things to accept. I had to accept the fact that Darren was never coming back. I had to accept the fact that the future we had planned was never going to happen. I had to accept the fact that Darren's wonderful family and I were no longer related. I had to accept the fact that I had to find someone else to love. But the hardest thing for me to accept was the idea that Darren himself no longer existed. I needed to find proof that part of us continues to exist after our physical body dies. You see, until I got a handle on the spiritual aspects of loss, I could not be at peace with it.

Grief changes over time, although it has a lifelong impact. I knew that because I was widowed so young, I could potentially have decades of pain and suffering ahead of myself if I did not find a way to deal with it. For me, that meant finding real answers, and accepting grief as part of my life. Just because you have moved on with your life and found happiness in other people and other things, doesn't mean you never miss your loved one anymore, or that you never think about them with sadness. The emotional wounds may heal, but the scar remains forever. I finally felt like I had accepted the loss (if you want to call it that) when more often than not, I found pleasure and comfort in remembering Darren, rather than pain or sadness.

Talking about the person you've lost is a healthy thing. Pretending like they never existed is not! The old way of dealing with grief- not thinking or talking about it- doesn't work. I truly believe that a lot of illness and diseases are caused by suppressed and unresolved grief. The mind and body are connected. That which poisons the mind manifests itself in the body. There are many books out there that are devoted to this topic. My favorite is *You Can Heal Your Life* by Louise L. Hay. Her key message is this: "If we are willing to do the mental work, almost anything can be healed." I couldn't agree more; and believe me, it does take work. The back of the book is kind of fun. You can look up various ailments or diseases, along with their possible mental cause, and affirmations to overcome them. It is amazingly accurate.

Your past is part of who you are today. During the early stages of my grief, I wished for amnesia to blot out the pain of my memories. There was nothing I could do, no place I could go, that didn't remind me of Darren, and it made me upset. Now, I cherish those very memories I wanted to forget. I'm grateful for the wonderful times we shared. Those memories are mine to treasure, and I hope that they never fade.

Over time I've learned that just because your loved one is no longer physically here, doesn't mean that your relationship with them has to end. The hope is that you can let go of the pain, while continuing to have a spiritual connection to them. But until I had the proof that I was searching for; that the spirit does indeed survive physical death, it was still only wishful thinking at first that I could continue that type of relationship with Darren. (More on this later.) I came across this beautiful poem and thought it would be an appropriate end to this chapter. Although I don't believe that grief ever fully ends, this poem touches on some real issues.

When Does Grief End?
Grief hits us like a ton of bricks,
Flattens us like a steamroller,
Hurls us into the depths of despair.
We know in a flash when grief hits,
But when does it end?

Like the month of March,
Grief rushes in like a lion,
And tiptoes out like a lamb.
Sometimes, we don't know when grief leaves,
Because we don't let go of the lion's tail.
Why do we hold on so long?
Grief offers us safety,
Protection from the world.
We don't want to let go
Because we secretly fear
That we'll forget our loved ones,
And we don't want to forget- ever.
We don't want to let go
Because we fear the future
And having to face life without our loved ones.
We don't want to let go
Because we make the mistake
Of measuring our grief with the depth of our love-
When neither has anything to do with the other.
How do we know when grief has run its course?
How do we know when we've grieved enough?
Cried enough?
"Died" enough?
How do we know when it's time to let go of the tail?
We know when we feel joy again, in something or someone.
Joy in living. Joy in life.
We know when we wake up in the morning
And our first thought is on something other than our loss.
We know when we look ahead with a smile
And back with fond memories,
And when we no longer dread the nights.
We know when our life starts filling up with new interests and people,
And we start reaching for the stars.
Grief ends when we let go of the tail.
—Margaret Brownley, Bereavement Magazine, Jan/Feb 2002

Part Four

<u>Healing</u>

About Healing

"When one door of happiness closes, another opens,
but often we look so long at the closed door that we
do not see the one which has been opened for us."

—*Helen Keller*

It's hard to separate grief and healing, because when you are grieving, you are also healing. But you make a conscious choice about how you grieve. Unfortunately, there is no cure for it. The old saying, "Time heals all wounds" does not apply here. Time may take away some of grief's intensity and make it more tolerable; but until you face it and deal with it head on, unexpressed grief will stay inside of you, and keep on resurfacing. You alone have to do the work.

I decided that this tragedy could either make me a bitter person or a better person; the choice was mine. I chose to find a way to learn from it, to grow from it, and to try to become a better person in spite of it. I refused to let grief kill me, too. One morning, I woke up and realized that I was still here. I had to go on living, like it or not. I looked inside myself and asked "What am I going to do now? What will make me happy now?"

Self-pity was getting me nowhere; but every day I survived became a small victory. Taking one day at a time, I resolved to do the things that I wanted to do, and to try to find new meaning and purpose in life. I decided to work through the pain, knowing that the pain was healing, and that I could get to the other side of grief.

This section contains some of the coping mechanisms and tools that have worked for me. This is not a quick fix; grief takes years to work through. There are no guidelines to follow, no one-size-fits-all formula. You can't follow steps a, b, and c, and then your grief will be over. You have to find your own way, as I did. Your grief is as personal as your relationship to your loved one was. There are many different issues surrounding each relationship and each death, which need to be worked out internally.

It was mainly trial and error that led me to know what worked for me, and *what didn't. In hindsight, it is easier to identify the things that were helpful. For instance, listening to certain music was healing; drinking too much wine to numb the pain was not healing. I'm not suggesting that what worked for me will necessarily work for you, but it might give you some ideas. That is my hope in writing this personal journey; that it helps guide someone else down the long, dark path of grief. This path has no map to follow, no road signs telling you which way to go. So, follow your own instincts, as I followed mine, and do what feels right for you.*

Please bear with me as I skip around my life over many years along the path toward healing. My healing didn't happen in a particular order; and it sure didn't happen at once, like a flash of insight or understanding. It took many years of one day at a time.

Little Things

"Pain nourishes courage. You can't be brave if you've only had wonderful things happen to you."

—*Mary Tyler Moore*

The title of this chapter was inspired by the Bush song of the same name. Part of the chorus is *"It's the little things that kill/ tearing at my brains again."* After losing Darren, there were so many unexpected little things that I had to go through that did indeed "kill." Each situation felt like another knife in the heart.

Having to face all of these changes that his death brought about was part of the healing process, and even though they were painful to go through, they made my reality more believable and helped me accept things as they were. Here are some of the more difficult situations I had to overcome:

- Seeing Darren's name on his headstone. Besides the usual stuff, we also had "Forever In Our Hearts" engraved on the headstone. Seeing his name and death date on a headstone made Darren's death more real, but going to the cemetery did nothing for me. For a while, I went to visit Darren's grave and brought flowers, like I thought I was supposed to; but I just didn't feel his presence there. The cemetery was a cold, depressing place. There was no privacy with other mourners wandering about and traffic rushing by on the nearby busy street. I felt stupid sitting there staring at a stone and the thought of Darren's body decaying in a box underneath me was also quite disturbing, so I stopped going. I talked to him from home, or wherever I was, and felt certain that he heard me. I felt better about this decision after coming across the following poem:

Do not stand at my grave and weep
I am not there, I do not sleep.
I am a thousand winds that blow
I am the diamond glint on snow.

I am the sunlight on ripened grain
I am the gentle autumn rain.
When you wake in the morning hush
I am the swift uplifting rush
Of quiet birds in circling flight.
I am the soft stars that shine at night.
Do not stand at my grave and cry
I am not there, I did not die.
—*Mary Frye*

- <u>Deciding if I wanted to be buried next to Darren.</u> My mother-in-law called to ask if I wanted them to buy me a plot next to his, because they had to decide how many they needed. This was not a decision I felt prepared to make. After thinking about it, I told her that I was honored they had asked me, but that being so young, I didn't know what was going to happen in my life. If I were to die tomorrow, I said, then yes, absolutely! However, I knew that one day I would probably remarry and have a family. In that case, I might choose to be buried elsewhere, or maybe I'd want to be cremated. I didn't want to think about these kinds of things, but suddenly I had to. Ultimately, I turned down their generous offer.

- <u>Referring to myself as "me," not "we," or saying "mine," instead of "ours."</u> This was a hard habit to break, but each time I had to correct myself, my reality became clearer.

- <u>Filling out paperwork and checking the box marked "widowed" in the marital status section.</u> I didn't want to be a widow. I felt as though people would judge me when they saw it, or think I had checked the wrong box.

- <u>Removing Darren's name from our checking account.</u> I started bawling at the bank when I had to do this. It seemed so final. The poor teller didn't know what to do, except to get me a box of Kleenex and get me out of there as fast as she could. I guess I was making a scene… bad for business.

- <u>Erasing Darren's voice from our answering machine.</u> I must have listened to our recording 20 times before I found the nerve to re-record the message. I worried about upsetting Darren's family if they heard his voice on the machine.

82

- <u>Referring to Darren as my "late" husband.</u> People actually asked me, "Late for what?" Duh!

- <u>Calling Darren at work.</u> Darren was always the first person I called when I had any news. When I heard things during the week on television, like celebrity news that he'd be interested in, I'd pick up the phone and call him. After he died, I had to break that habit. The year Darren died, Michael Jordan came out of retirement to play basketball for the Chicago Bulls again, and I picked up the phone and habitually started dialing, excited to tell Darren the news, then reality hit me. He was no longer a phone call away. It was sort of a knee-jerk reaction. Even after I had moved to California with Matt, we were walking Dakota on the beach in Malibu one day, and we saw a pregnant Pamela Anderson in a bikini tanning and Tommy Lee playing with their dogs in the ocean. Dakota even sniffed their dog's butts. It was a great ice-breaker to say hello. Darren loved Pamela and we were both big Mötley Crüe fans. My first instinct was that I couldn't wait to call Darren and tell him. Then, I came to my senses, and hoped that maybe he was there in spirit, and was jealous.

- <u>Getting rid of Darren's things.</u> I knew he didn't need them anymore, and I didn't want them around, reminding me of my loss. I cried while doing it; but I knew it needed to be done. My anger fueled my abrupt desire to get everything that was his out of my sight. Don't get me wrong, I'm not completely heartless- I kept some things for sentimental reasons, and I will treasure them as long as I live. Luckily, when my sister and I were clearing out Darren's closet, an old friend called me, so Kim, along with my mother-in-law and brother-in-law finished this most difficult task for me.

- <u>Deciding what to do with our wedding rings.</u> At the suggestion of Darren's mom, I had our wedding rings melted together and the stones re-mounted into a new design. This way, I could still wear it when I wanted to. For me, it was symbolic of love that didn't end, but simply just changed its form.

- <u>Going grocery shopping.</u> When I finally got my appetite back, I went to the grocery store; and when I reached the soda aisle, I automatically started to grab a case of Mountain Dew for me and Pepsi for Darren. As I put my hand on the Pepsi, my eyes filled with tears. I didn't need to buy this anymore. As I proceeded through the rest of the store, I realized that I no longer had to buy Darren's favorite foods. I was only cooking for one now. I struggled not to cry the whole time I was there. I made it out in record time, and sobbed as I put away groceries for one.

- <u>How to speak of his death.</u> Saying that "he died" was too final, and sounded harsh. I prefer to say he "passed on." It implied there was another place to go. I also like "made his transition." At home I use these, but in the context of this book I use lots of terms; death, loss, died, crossed over, etc.

- <u>Saying Darren's name.</u> For a while this made me feel uncomfortable. You may remember that one of his best friends was also named Daren (different spelling). I began using his nickname, Shaggy, to refer to him. Also, Darren's sister named her son Darrin (another different spelling). I understood the honor she intended by naming him after Darren, but the name itself was now sacred to me. For a long time, whenever I heard it, I felt pain in my heart.

- <u>Knowing whom to tell my story to, and when.</u> I learned the hard way not to tell new acquaintances too much, too soon. Many people are afraid of the topic of death; and some began to avoid me as though I had the plague or some other contagious disease that they might catch. Once I understood this, I allowed myself to get to know someone before I dumped my tragic story on them. It worked: once new acquaintances became friends, they also became more comfortable hearing that I had survived such a trauma. People's reactions sometimes made me feel guarded; but I learned quickly with whom I could share things. Sometimes, I'd even find myself diverting a conversation to avoid talking about my past. To open up that can of worms, I had to be in the right mood.

- <u>Holidays, birthdays, and anniversaries.</u> Each occasion was bittersweet. The anticipation of these special days was always worse than the actual day itself. I'd worry about it for weeks or months ahead of time, but when the actual day came, I found that by keeping myself busy, I wouldn't fall apart. Sometimes, on certain days, I would look at old cards, letters, and pictures in the morning, just to acknowledge the day, get the crying out of the way, and be done with it. Valentine's Day was particularly rough. I thought I'd never celebrate it again. I couldn't let Matt down by boycotting the holiday altogether, so I did my best to be grateful for having a Valentine to celebrate it with instead of feeling sorry for myself.

- <u>Changing my name.</u> I kept my married name for two years after Darren died. It was a reminder of my connection to him; but when I wanted to find a new identity for myself, it became uncomfortable. The name tag I wore at work had my married- and very Polish- last name on it. People would invariably ask if I was Polish, and then look at me strangely when I said no. I just got tired of explaining.

- <u>My new relationship to Darren's family and friends.</u> The one thing we all had in common was gone. Who were we to each other now? Relatives? Friends? It's hard to know if it is okay to talk openly abut the deceased with others who loved him. It's impossible to predict how they will react from day to day. Will talking about him bring comfort or pain to that person? Sometimes people didn't know what to say to me, so they said nothing. Sometimes they talked about everything *but* Darren when they talked to me. It hurt my feelings that a lot of his friends (who I also considered to be my friends) simply disappeared from my life. I felt shunned by some people with whom I had felt very close. Either it was too hard for them to talk to me, or I reminded them too much of their loss. Or maybe they felt that they were intruding on my life. Either way, it was another loss for me and added to my grief. Even Darren's dad, who had been a father figure to me for eight years, found it too difficult to see me after a while, which hurt me deeply. Darren's inner circle was shattered and separated due to each person's ability or inability to come to terms with his death. I know I can't expect people to act the way I want them to; but I now understand the meaning of the phrase "You find out who your friends are." There's nothing like a tragedy to make this painfully clear. I have a plaque in my kitchen that says "A true friend is one who walks in…when the rest of the world walks out." I couldn't have said it better myself.

- <u>Going to the site of the accident.</u> A few weeks after Darren's death, even though I dreaded going, I asked Rico to drive me up to the spot where Darren died. I remember getting out of the car and screaming to Rico, "This is it? This is where he died? Where is the dangerous curve? This is totally flat!" I searched the area in the woods for bloodstains or any other evidence of the accident, but saw nothing. I picked up a stick, threw it into the woods, and screamed at the top of my lungs. I was so angry. I expected something else, I guess; like a dangerous curve, perhaps. I cried most of the way home, and never had any desire to return.

- <u>Knowing if I should continue to give gifts and cards to Darren's family and friends.</u> I sent birthday cards and gave Christmas gifts to Darren's parents and his sister the first year, then just cards for a few years. Then I felt that my gifts to Darren's dad and sister were a painful reminder of their loss. Now, I just send his mom flowers or cards on Christmas, Mother's Day and her birthday. We have always had a special friendship, and Darren's death hasn't changed that. She does the same for me, and sends my boys gifts for Christmas and their birthdays as well. I sent Christmas cards to some of Darren's friends for a few years, but then I got the feeling that they were not comforting, but rather a painful reminder of their loss that they hadn't healed from, so those stopped also.

- <u>Receiving phone calls and mail for Darren after his death.</u> Phone calls from telemarketers upset me terribly. I would yell at these poor people, telling them that Darren was dead, and never to call back. I even had my lawyer call some of the more persistent callers because it was so upsetting for me. For many years, I received offers for pre-approved credit cards addressed to Darren. I usually wrote on the envelope "Return to sender, recipient deceased." Now, I can laugh about the idiocy these companies pre-approving credit cards for dead people. Then again, how would they know? Darren is just a name on a mailing list to them.

The rest of the chapters in this section are broken down into specific topics that were helpful in my healing process. I don't like to think of it as advice, but rather as "suggestions." I feel that everyone grieves in their own way, but maybe something that helped me, may help someone else. So, here are my suggestions of things that may help process your grief, and help you move through your loss, based on my experience.

Exercise

"Adversity causes some people to break; others to break records."

-William A. Ward

All those years in gymnastics made me crave exercise. I didn't feel good about myself if I wasn't doing some form of exercise a few times a week. You get a natural high from physical activity and you can't help but feel better. Exercise boosts endorphins (mood-elevating chemicals) in the brain. Exercise also helps you sleep better. If muscles are worked during the day, they will be more relaxed when they are at rest. Doing something outdoors, or just being out in nature, was especially therapeutic for me. Darren's mom said that she would have gone crazy if she hadn't gone on her walk every day. She would wear Darren's jacket and walk for an hour, no matter how cold it was outside.

Darren died in February, and anyone who has lived in the Midwest knows how "non-user-friendly" the weather can be in winter. It was so easy for me to do absolutely nothing. I was the thinnest I had been in years. In my warped mind, I thought my skeletal form looked nice. As soon as the weather started warming up a bit though, I decided to get off my butt and do something. Lethargy didn't feel right and I longed for that good feeling that exercise brought out in me. I'd recently started mountain biking, so I bought a new bike and rode every day. It helped boost my self-esteem. I felt empowered after a long ride. Feeling my heart beating actually made me realize that it was still functioning, and not shattered into a million pieces.

On my bike rides, I would wear headphones and listen to rock music, and ride until I was exhausted. Within months, I was riding between 10 and 20 miles a day. Being in the sun brought some color to my pasty skin, and I started to look alive again. My muscle tone returned, and I had the biggest calves ever, even bigger than in the peak of my gymnastics training. I actually felt good about myself again.

I also took Dakota on a long walk every day. Darren and I had moved into our house during the cold month of December, and were one of the first houses in the area, so I didn't know any of my new neighbors. Everywhere I went with Dakota, people asked me about her. She's a beautiful dog, black and white with ice blue eyes and beautiful markings. She gets a lot of attention, and little kids always want to pet her. Sometimes, however, on our walks, I would see a mother with her baby in a stroller, and got very sad. I was coming back to life again, but I still felt that pain in my heart that I'd been robbed of my chance to have a baby.

Skipping ahead now, after I moved to California with Matt, I got into other physical activities that I had never tried before. We arrived in California on Christmas Eve day. Matt's youngest brother, Jordan, got new roller blades for Christmas and taught me how to use them. It was much easier than the roller skates of my childhood. At the time, we had the same size feet. I thought it was *so cool* to be able to do this- outside, mind you, on Christmas Day! Instead of a Midwestern blizzard, I had 75- degree weather to play around in. I bought my own pair of roller blades and found it very calming to skate on the boardwalk next to the ocean. Being near the ocean brought me a sense of peace and a perfect environment in which to reflect on my life.

I also tried some ocean sports, like snorkeling and body boarding. Seeing all the sea life while snorkeling was magical, but the undertow made me feel seasick. I confess; I'm also afraid of sharks. I credit this fear to watching the movie *"Jaws"* as a child, and from watching too many episodes of *"Shark Week"* on the Discovery Channel. When the water visibility was poor, I'd panic, certain that a Great White shark was lurking underneath me, waiting to strike. I'd swim as fast as I could back to the safety of the beach. Body boarding is thrilling. You sit on your board, waiting for a wave and dolphins and seals come right up to you. The first time I caught a wave, I screamed the whole ride in because I didn't know how to slow down or stop. It was a lot of fun, but I felt too much like shark bait. Take it from me, trying new things and facing new fears can make you feel alive again.

I also became interested in Yoga, and bought a lot of videotapes to follow along with at home. Because of my background in gymnastics, I was naturally flexible and caught on easily. *Yoga* means "union": physical relaxation, feeling at peace within yourself, and above all, the union of the soul with God. Yoga is good for strength, flexibility, and the spirit. It is also a great stress reliever. As you focus on your breathing and the mind/body connection, you forget about your troubles for a while. I would always feel peaceful and relaxed, yet strong after I finished one of my Yoga tapes. Certain types of Yoga can also be used as a powerful spiritual practice, not merely an exercise regime. It can be an aid to deep meditation and a way to commune with the divine within. I haven't gotten to that level yet, but I hope to someday.

There is one exercise that I didn't do, but I think would be great if you were in the anger stage of grief: kickboxing (into a punching bag). If I had the chance, I would have done it and imagined Dave's face on the bag and just beaten the thing silly. Pillows would also be a safe alternative to beat the snot out of, rather than a person. And, I must confess, my pillows took a few blows.

Another form of exercise that I have taken up is Pilates. There are different forms of Pilates, but the one I use is done on a machine, called a reformer, that uses numerous springs for resistance, and you can work every body part in an hour workout. There are over 500 exercises you can do on the machine, and it is the best workout I've ever done. You see really quick results, as far as muscle definition goes, but it is easier on the joints than weight training, and is low impact. I am actually now a Certified Reformer Pilates Instructor, and love teaching it almost as much as I enjoy doing it.

There is something about strengthening your body physically that is empowering mentally. Pushing your body to its physical limits is a good, healthy way to release anger and frustration, and keep it from settling into your tissues. Whatever form of exercise you enjoy, get out there and move! It will help your body, mind, and spirit.

Music

"Music is the shorthand of emotion"

—*Leo Tolstoy*

I have loved music as long as I can remember. As shallow as it sounds, a person's musical preference was a very big factor in my choice of friends and people I dated. Their coolness factor was influenced heavily by which bands they liked. I was one of those people who had to buy the new releases on the day they came out, and learned all of the lyrics to the songs before I saw my favorite bands in concert so I could sing along. Music was also an important part of my healing process, and certain songs became anthems for my grief.

Coming of age in the late eighties and early nineties, Darren and I loved rock music- especially the "hair bands," as well as alternative music. We had an unspoken bond because we liked the same music. We went to lots of concerts together, I can't even begin to estimate how many. We saw some bands as many as five times. We would go to see those mega-concerts, like the "Monsters of Rock," with up to 10 bands playing. It was awesome! This was also the time when rock bands had "power ballads," and a lot of these ballads had special meaning for us. Bands like Motley Crüe, Guns-n-Roses, Tesla, Poison, Ratt, Winger, Whitesnake, Skid Row, Scorpions, and Aerosmith were some of our favorites.

We also liked a lot of the new British Pop bands like Depeche Mode, Gene Loves Jezebel, The Cult, and especially Duran Duran. By the early nineties our tastes had shifted and we loved the new grunge music scene, including bands like Nirvana, Alice in Chains, Pearl Jam, and Stone Temple Pilots. We also liked more mellow stuff, like Sade, Whitney Houston, and especially Seal. So, needless to say, after Darren died, I couldn't very easily listen to the radio without feeling nostalgic and breaking out in tears when one of "our songs" came on. So, for a while, I only listened to upbeat CD's in the car so I controlled what I heard.

It is amazing how certain songs define a period in your life, and bring you back there as though it were yesterday. Every time I hear the song *"Plowed"* by Sponge, it brings me back to the night Darren died. I went to bed singing that song in my head. Also, the lyrics to the song include the words *"human wreckage"* and *"a head that's broken"* which is pretty disturbing. After a while it became a song I raged to because of the upbeat tempo, the lyrics, and the personal meaning behind it. It helped me release anger by feeling the emotions and screaming the lyrics.

There is tremendous healing power in music. It touches the depths of our emotions like nothing else can. Certain songs became the soundtrack of my grief. The music that Darren and I had enjoyed took on new meaning. Lyrics "spoke" to me in a new way, and somehow fit my current situation. A song that I had liked before may have been about a breakup, or something unrelated to losing a loved one to death, but now it became about losing Darren. I tailored the messages in the songs to fit my new circumstances. Sometimes, it may have been just one particular line from a song that would get to me, other times, the whole song seemed like it was written either by me or for me.

I would play certain songs over and over, cranked up loud, and I would sing along at the top of my lungs, cry, and just let it all out. Waves of sadness came over me as I felt the music. Sometimes, I would watch myself sing in the mirror (come on, everyone does it!) while I screamed out the lyrics that touched my soul. I would have felt like a complete idiot if anyone had seen me doing this, but it was a great release. Other times, I would dance around my living room to certain songs as if I were choreographing a dance routine. It really helped me to release stress and pent-up emotions.

Different songs bring out different emotions: sadness, anger, longing, encouragement, or faith. I'd choose songs that reflected what I was feeling at the time. Singing along helped me purge my emotions. Music is a healthy outlet for grief. Hearing someone else singing about the things you're feeling inside somehow gives you permission to feel them as well. This is especially true with anger. Sometimes it wouldn't even be that the lyrics were especially angry, but that a song just rocked, and let me scream at all of the chaos in my life. I loved the CD *"Operation Mindcrime"* by Queensrÿche before Darren died, but afterward, I put it on just so I could scream and try to reach some of the high notes that Geoff Tate reaches, which is no easy feat. I felt so much better after belting out these songs at the top of my lungs for an hour.

One of my favorite places to sing and cry was in the bathtub or the shower. I felt like all of my sadness and grief was being cleansed away. My other favorite place was my car. Sometimes, I'd be so into a song and my own thoughts that I wouldn't know how I arrived at my destination. I would just be a blubbering mess, and could barely see the road through all of the tears. Driving under the influence of grief can be pretty dangerous, and I don't recommend it.

Sometimes, out of the blue, I would be out in public and hear one of my grief songs or a song containing sad lyrics over the sound system. This would catch me off guard, and I would totally lose it. Once, shortly after Darren died I was visiting Moe in Atlanta. I really needed to escape and be anonymous for a few days. We were out with a group of friends at a bar, and they were playing *"Only the Good Die Young"* by Billy Joel. This wasn't a song that I associated with Darren, and it is pretty upbeat, but hearing that title over and over was upsetting. I remember struggling to hold back tears while everyone else was singing along, having a good old time. Moe could tell that it bothered me, and put her hand on mine and asked me if I was okay. Not wanting to cause a big scene, I toughened up and said, "Yeah, I am fine." But I really just wanted to crawl under the table and sob.

The most influential and helpful CD for me after Darren's death was Seal's self-titled second CD. Not only did the lyrics speak to me, but I also felt that Darren *himself* was speaking to me through the lyrics. The CD had come out shortly before Darren died, and we had gone to see Seal in concert for Darren's birthday in November, three months before he died. It was the best concert I'd ever been to. We were both mesmerized. After Darren died, I opened up the sleeve of the CD and read what Seal said about the lyrics. It felt like he had written it for me.

The part that touched me most deeply was this: "One of the most popular questions people seem to ask is, 'Why don't you print your lyrics on the album?' Well, the answer to that is that quite often, my songs mean one thing to me and another to the listener. But that's okay because I think it's the general vibe of what I'm saying that is important and not the exact literal translation. I guess what I am saying is that the song is always larger in the listeners' mind because they attach imagery which is relative to their own personal experience. So it is your perception of what I'm saying rather than what I actually say that is the key." The last sentence reads, "So if ever you feel you can't go on, rest assured that you are not alone and that fast changes are arriving." That really choked me up.

Every song on the CD had messages for me: *"Prayer for the Dying," "Don't Cry," "Fast Changes," "Kiss from a Rose," "People Asking Why," "If I Could,"* and *"I'm Alive."* I listened to it over and over, and I felt that through the music, Darren was trying to comfort me and give me answers. When I told Darren's mom about this, I think she thought I was cracking up.

Even some of my friends associated certain songs with Darren, and cried or thought of him every time they heard them. Moe told me that years after Darren's death, she was in church one Sunday and they played a song that they had played at Darren's funeral, and she broke down crying, and couldn't contain herself. Brenda associates the song *"Ordinary World"* by Duran Duran with Darren. She told me that on numerous occasions while driving, that song came on when she was cut off by another driver. Before road rage took over, she noticed this song was playing on the radio and thought of Darren, and it calmed her down. Even Dave has shared with me that he believes that Darren is messing with him from beyond by playing certain songs when he is not expecting it, like when he's in a store. He said that he looks up and swears at Darren whenever this happens. But it also makes him smile.

This does not sound crazy to me, because after Darren died, I kept hearing certain songs on the radio that reminded me of him during times when I was thinking about him, or had been asking him for assistance with something, or just plain missed him. It is comforting to think that he is aware of my thoughts, and that these songs are his way of validating what is happening. There are two songs in particular.

The first song is called *"The Boys are Back in Town"* by Thin Lizzy. Darren liked it because it reminded him of his rekindled camaraderie with Dave and Rico, and he turned it up each time it came on the radio shortly before he died. He loved that they used Rico's nickname for him, "Dino," in the song a few times, as in the lyrics, *"Down at Dino's Bar and Grill."* It wasn't a song that I particularly liked, but it always made me think of Darren when I heard it. After Darren died, I couldn't get away from this song. It was as if it were a new song, for the amount of times I heard it on the radio, even though it was classic rock. Even seven years later, when we moved to Reno, NV, I was wondering if Darren followed us there, and I began hearing this song on the radio every time I got in the car. I took it as a sign that he was still around.

The second song I heard a lot and took as a sign that Darren is around is *"Love in an Elevator"* by Aerosmith. This was the song we became engaged to during their concert, and also the first song Darren chose to play in our first home. Many times, I have been driving and either talking to my mom about Darren or thinking about him, when this song comes on the radio. One time, my mom and I noticed that every day for a week straight, no matter what time of day it was, or what station was on, *"Love in an Elevator"* was the song on the radio when we got in the car. Coincidence? I think not.

The following lists are some of the songs that speak to my heart in some way, along with the emotions they have helped me confront and work through. Some of them are personally meaningful, while others are more universally meaningful. Some of them I listened to over and over at the beginning of my loss and they helped me through my darkest times, and some are more recent songs that touched my soul just the same. Everyone has different tastes in music, and I'm sure there are some great ones in other genres that I'm missing, but here are my grief anthems. (See my website for an updated list and where to find these songs at www.widowedtoosoon.com)

SADNESS/ DEPRESSION
- *"Always" by Bon Jovi*
- *"I Remember You" by Skid Row*
- *"Alone Again" by Dokken*
- *"Angel" by Aerosmith*
- *"What It Takes" by Aerosmith*
- *"Every Rose Has It's Thorn" by Poison*
- *"I Won't Forget You" by Poison*
- *"Don't Know What You've Got (Till It's Gone)" by Cinderella*
- *"No Ordinary Love" by Sade*
- *"Do What You Have To Do" by Sarah McLachlan*
- *"Gloomy Sunday" by Sarah McLachlan*
- *"Fade To Black" by Metallica*
- *"Headed For A Heartbreak" by Winger*
- *"Didn't We Almost Have It All" by Whitney Houston*
- *"It's All Coming Back To Me Now" by Celine Dion*
- *"My Immortal" by Evanescence*

ANGER
- *"I Don't Believe In Love" by Queensrÿche*
- *"Breaking The Silence" by Queensrÿche*
- *"You Oughta Know" by Alanis Morissette*
- *"Rearviewmirror" by Pearl Jam*
- *"Plowed" by Sponge*
- *"One" by Metallica*
- *"One Step Closer" by Linkin Park*

LONGING

- *"Paradise" by Tesla*
- *"I'll Never Let You Go (Angel Eyes)" by Steelheart*
- *"Still Loving You" by The Scorpions*
- *"All At Once" by Whitney Houston*
- *"I Have Nothing" by Whitney Houston*
- *"Fly To The Angels" by Slaughter*
- *"I Will Remember You" by Sarah McLachlan*
- *"Here Without You" by Three Doors Down*
- *"In Loving Memory" by Alterbridge*
- *"I Miss My Friend" by Diamond Rio*

ENCOURAGEMENT/ FAITH

- *"Love Song" by Tesla*
- *"Ordinary World" by Duran Duran*
- *"Don't Cry" by Seal*
- *"Kiss From A Rose" by Seal*
- *"Prayer For The Dying" by Seal*
- *"Hold On" by Sarah McLachlan*
- *"Angel" by Sarah McLachlan*
- *"My Heart Will Go On" by Celine Dion*
- *"It Can't Rain All The Time" by Jane Siberry*
- *"One Sweet Day" by Mariah Carey with Boys II Men*
- *"To Where You Are" by Josh Groban*
- *"I'm Already There" by Lonestar*
- *"There You'll Be" by Faith Hill*
- *"When I Look To The Sky" by Train*
- *"I Believe" by Diamond Rio*

<u>Writing</u>

"Adversity has the effect of eliciting talents,
which, in prosperous circumstances,
would have lain dormant."

—*Horace*

I always kept a diary growing up, and in high school, my favorite class was creative writing. This is where I started keeping a daily journal, which I continued for years. So, I already knew that writing was a powerful outlet for me to express my feelings. But I hadn't been writing when Darren died. There were a lot of pent-up feelings that I needed to release, so after he died, I started writing again. I wrote free verse poetry about whatever emotions I was feeling. I also resumed writing in a journal before I went to bed each night. It was very helpful for me to get out all the things I was afraid or ashamed to tell people about; like my rage and thoughts of suicide.

I even wrote some letters to Darren, and I believed he somehow read them. I told him everything I never got to say to him- my regrets about not having his baby, and my sorrow that our dreams would never come true. Remember the letter I put in his casket? I don't remember what it said exactly, but I felt the need to do it at the time and felt much better afterward.

I also wrote, but never sent, a letter to Dave. It was full of blame, anger, and frustration. I never sent it because I knew I was venting my grief and despair. Perhaps my feelings would change. They seemed to change as frequently as the weather in those days. Once I met Matt, however, I stopped writing. I wanted to concentrate on this new relationship, and a new life. In fact, when I was packing up to move to California, I threw away everything I didn't think I'd need, including my poetry and my journal. I thought they had served their purpose. (Little did I know then, that I would write a book on my experience. Oops!)

A huge part of my healing and closure came about through the process of writing about my journey through loss. As I wrote, I realized how many issues were still painful for me to recall. I had a lot of unresolved grief to confront. I cried while

I wrote it by hand with bright metallic gel pens on black paper, symbolizing bringing light to darkness. Both my mom and I cried while I read my handwritten notes aloud for her to type them into the computer. (She types faster than I do.) Some chapters were particularly rough on us, and we went through quite a few boxes of tissue. I highly recommend that you write about your own journey. Even if my book never gets published, it has already helped bring someone through grief to healing; me.

<u>Reading</u>

"The book to read is not the one which thinks for you,
but the one which makes you think"

—*James McCosh*

When Darren first died, some friends of mine gave me a lot of books to read on topics including grief, death and dying, and spirituality- all of which I devoured. I wanted answers fast so that I could get past this pain. But there was something missing in all of these books; I needed to find a personal story written by another young widow who had gone through a similar experience, and had found proof to answer my most urgent question "Where is Darren now?" Faith alone was not enough for me; I wanted tangible proof that there was indeed life after death. I searched high and low for this book I desperately needed to find, but to no avail. To the best of my knowledge, and the knowledge of every local bookstore, this book didn't exist. Was I the only one out there who wondered about this kind of stuff?

There was only one book for young widows that I found. However, it was written by a professional grief counselor with experience counseling young widows, not by the widow herself. I read it, but I wanted the widow's story, not the counselor's story. As for the other kind of widow books I found, most were focused on older women, possibly with one short chapter for young widows. They were very practical, and they didn't address my main concerns. Other grief books I found tried to give comfort through scriptures. This may be helpful for the devout, but at that point, I was mad at God. I felt isolated in my experience, an absolute freak. Widowhood wasn't supposed to happen to a girl my age.

I did get a little something out of each book I read; but the books that gave me the most comfort and hope were the books about life after death and spirit communication. This was one area about which I was clueless. It was also the one topic that other widow books didn't touch. How can you lose a loved one and not think about heaven? Losing Darren made me question all my beliefs about the afterlife. I needed to know for sure that there was a heaven, that he was there, and that he was okay. I couldn't rest until I knew for sure.

During my internship at the radio station in Chicago, we had a guest on the show named Betty Eadie, who was promoting her book *Embraced by the Light*. It was her personal story of near-death experiences, in which she recalls what happened during the time that she was clinically dead. I was intimidated by her, as if she knew too much. But now, newly widowed, I was desperate for answers. I drove for the first time since Darren's death- straight to the bookstore. Since Darren died in a car accident, I was afraid to drive, but my drive for answers was greater. My mom was staying with me, and I remember reading passages to her that seemed incredible to me. I was floored by her story.

Embraced by the Light was the first of many books that changed my views about life after death and guided me on my spiritual journey. The book gave me some idea of what Darren may have experienced when he died; and it gave me some comfort I so desperately yearned for. I knew Betty Eadie was a real person, not some weirdo, because I'd met her at the radio station. Her account gave me such a sense of peace. I became more certain that Darren was safe with God in heaven, and that he was watching over me, now and forever, and that we'd be together again. I felt that I now had some evidence that there was indeed life after death. It was the first of many books I read that helped me accept my loss. I still needed to grieve and find peace with all the aspects of my tragedy, but reading about Betty Eadie's experience made me feel less alone.

I didn't get as much help from the practical grief books, because everyone's situation is different, and everyone grieves differently, and they offered a one-size-fits-all solution to grief. Whenever I'd read the more practical books, I'd find myself skipping through the parts that I didn't need, which was the majority of the book. The practical things had all been taken care of; now what about the answers to the big questions that losing a loved one forces you to face?

The books I found which answered these questions for me were written by spiritual mediums, describing their experiences contacting departed loved ones, and reuniting them with the living. A medium is a person with the ability to talk to the dead. This was a concept I was unfamiliar with, and very skeptical of. But what if? Who doesn't want to know for certain that their loved one survived death, and that life after death is real? It seems to me that the books that explain what happens when we die, especially those books that discuss after-death communication, in which people actually have contact with their loved ones on the other side, are meaningful to everyone.

The way I discovered my first book on this subject was quite unexpected. I was living in California about three years after Darren's death, working as a makeup artist at a cosmetics counter in a department store. A woman came in looking for a new lipstick. She said she was going to appear on the *"Oprah Winfrey Show"* and needed a lipstick to match the outfit she would be wearing. I normally don't pry, but for some reason, I asked her about the topic of the show. She told me that her son had died in a mountain climbing accident, and that she and her husband had gone to see a medium that was able to contact their son on the other side. The medium, James Van Praagh, gave them messages from their son. He told them things that only their son would have known, as well as things that were validated after the reading. The reading had brought the couple so much peace and comfort, and the certainty that they would all be together again someday.

James was to be Oprah's guest promoting his new book, *Talking to Heaven*, in which this woman's story was featured. As she talked, my eyes welled up with tears. I told her about Darren, and that I was very interested in reading the book and watching the show. She didn't know when the show was going to air; but the book was already available in bookstores. She gave me her name and phone number, said I could call her, and promised to find out when the show would be aired. We talked a while longer, picked out her lipstick, and she was on her way. I knew that meeting her was no coincidence.

On my break, I went to the bookstore in the mall, found the book, and started reading it that night. One of the stories sounded like my customer's story. The woman's name in the book was the same name that was on the card my customer had given me. Wow, this was another real person! I read her story and was deeply touched and inspired. As I read all of the details, I cried. Here was another person who had lost a loved one, just as I had, and was able to come to a place of peace in her heart through the help of a spiritual medium.

I felt that I had finally found some answers. This had to be legitimate, I reasoned, otherwise how could James, a complete stranger, know such personal things that only the deceased or their loved ones would know? This book also expanded my vocabulary. I learned the differences between the physical body and the etheric (spirit) body; as well as the differences in a psychic or medium's sensitivities. For example, clairvoyant is clear seeing, clairaudient is clear hearing, and clairsentient is clear sensing, or feeling a spirit's emotions. Not only were the readings featured in the book amazing, his insights and his description of what happens when a person "dies," were just what I needed to know. Now, I needed more. I was on a mission.

When I got home, I looked up Oprah's website and found out when the show was going to air. I not only watched it, I also taped it to watch again later. My customer and her husband appeared briefly, and seeing her made her experience that much more meaningful for me. Oprah seemed pretty skeptical, but I felt like I was really on to something here. I was on a quest for knowledge, and I felt that this was a big step in the right direction.

Shortly after seeing this Oprah show, I was listening to a DJ on a talk radio program who used to be on the station I interned at in Chicago and was now in Los Angeles. His guest that day was none other than James Van Praagh. I cried as he did readings for listeners who called in. James even blew away the DJ by the particulars of a personal message for him. Here was another person I knew having a reading with a medium, and believing in the validity of the messages.

After that, I read every book I could get my hands on about spirit communication. I watched talk shows with mediums as guests. I saw Sylvia Browne on the *"Montel Williams Show"* numerous times, and was blown away by her gift. I kept asking, "How does she know all this stuff?" Then, I saw Rosemary Altea on the now cancelled *"Leeza."* Rosemary gave Leeza a personal message from a friend who had died, and Leeza was in tears, and obviously deeply moved. Rosemary Altea was promoting her book *The Eagle and the Rose*, which I immediately went out and bought. It was very uplifting and healing.

Years later, I saw an HBO special where group of mediums (including the well-respected George Anderson and John Edward) did scientific experiments to try to find where the messages were coming from that the mediums received. I thought that HBO did a poor job putting it together by trying to remain impartial, when the evidence of legitimacy was overwhelming. The results were conclusive enough to me that the messages were coming from another source. Again, another validation that contacting the dead was possible. (The results from this study are discussed in detail in the book, *The Afterlife Experiments* by Gary E. Schwartz, Ph.D.) I was now becoming a believer, but I wanted to have my own experience with a medium. If I could personally contact Darren, I could eliminate any doubts that remained.

By that time, I was happily remarried to Matt and we had our first child, a beautiful baby boy named Trevor. I was content with my life, but something was driving me to take my interest in spirit communication to the next level. How would I tell Matt that I wanted to see a medium to help me talk to Darren? I didn't want him to think that I was still wishing that I was with Darren, but hoped that he would understand my need to heal my internal wounds. We had started dating so soon after my loss that I was still grieving to some extent the entire time we had been together.

It was starting to catch up to me. I knew that when the time was right, I would find the way. I had the desire, but for the time being, I just kept on reading these books. I couldn't get enough.

Reading was great therapy for me, because I could pursue the topics that helped me heal at my own pace. I was pretty private about my grief, and didn't want to burden others with it. Some people told me "You should be 'over it' by now." Well, they hadn't walked in my shoes! You don't get over stuff like this. I had to get through it in my own way, and in my own time. They were *my* issues that needed to be resolved, and only I could resolve them.

It was strange how my need for answers came and went. I would be doing fine for a few months, and then I'd need another fix. It was as if my spirit knew that I hadn't finished grieving and understanding yet, that I still needed more. It was weird how sometimes the very book I needed seemed to appear at that critical moment. I'm sure there are a lot more great books not listed here that have come out since my loss, but the following books have been especially helpful in my healing process.

WIDOW BOOKS
- *I'm Grieving As Fast As I Can: How Young Widows And Widowers Can Cope And Heal* by Linda Sones Feinberg
- *Being a Widow* by Lynn Caine
- *Loss and Found: How We Survived the Loss of a Young Spouse* by Kathy Young and Gary Young

BOOKS BY OR ABOUT SPIRITUAL MEDIUMS
- *Talking to Heaven, Reaching to Heaven* and *Healing Grief- Reclaiming Life After any Loss* by James Van Praagh
- *The Eagle and the Rose* and *Proud Spirit* by Rosemary Altea
- *One Last Time, What if God Were the Sun?, Crossing Over* and *After Life* by John Edward
- *Lessons from the Light* and *Walking in the Garden of Souls* by George Anderson and Andrew Barone
- *The Other Side and Back* and *Life on the Other Side* by Sylvia Browne
- *We Don't Die: George Anderson's Conversations with The Other Side, We Are Not Forgotten* and *Love Beyond Life* by Joel Martin and Patricia Romanowski

BOOKS ABOUT NEAR-DEATH EXPERIENCES
- *Embraced by the Light* by Betty Eadie
- *Saved by the Light* by Dannion Brinkley

BOOK ABOUT AFTER-DEATH COMMUNICATION (WITHOUT A MEDIUM)
- *Hello from Heaven* by Bill and Judy Guggenheim

AND ALSO...
- *Love Never Dies: A Mother's Journey from Loss to Love* by Sandy Goodman
- *The Wheel of Life: A Memoir of Living and Dying* by Elisabeth Kübler-Ross, M. D.
- *The Afterlife Experiments* by Gary E. Schwartz, Ph.D.
- *Some Go Haunting* by Brian Edward Hurst

<u>Humor</u>

"Laughter is the tonic, the relief, the surcease for pain"
—*Charlie Chaplin*

Before Darren's death, I had a wonderful sense of humor. It was the one characteristic that I looked for in friends, as well as in people I dated. If you could make me laugh, you were in. I had a very juvenile sense of humor- I still do, ask anyone who knows me. I loved making up funny names for bodily functions, or goofy nicknames for people; and my speech has always been peppered with colorful words. I enjoyed imitating voices and making obscure references at inopportune moments. Nothing was funnier to me than people falling down. I'd laugh first and then ask if they were okay. I've always loved to laugh and to make other people laugh too, so did Darren.

During the first week after Darren's death, I didn't laugh much. It just felt wrong to laugh. But after a while, I realized that laughter was probably what I needed most. I didn't feel like myself if I didn't laugh. I had some of my favorite funny movies on tape, so I thought I'd try watching one of them to make sure I was still alive. They had always made me laugh in the past, and I sure needed it now. *"Pee-Wee's Big Adventure"* was one of my favorite comedies. I knew every line of the movie, and could recite every word. I couldn't help but laugh as I watched it again, and when it was over, I actually felt alive again, not dead inside! I don't know what I would have done if I had lost my sense of humor, too.

Another favorite movie was *"So I Married an Axe Murderer"* starring Mike Meyers. (Yes, it's a comedy.) The best parts are whenever the lead character's father appears, also played by Mike Myers. Again, I knew all the lines, and frequently yelled out parts of the movie for no reason. "Head, paper, now!" (Those who have seen it are laughing.) I decided to watch it again and laughed hysterically. Laughter was good medicine.

In fact, technically speaking, laughter actually enhances the immune system and decreases the production of stress hormones, cortisol and epinephrine. It also increases the levels of beneficial hormones, beta-endorphins and human growth hormone. Laughter has a positive effect on the cardiovascular system: blood pressure is lowered, and resting heart rate decreases. These benefits are similar to exercise. Grieving people definitely could use more of all of that. I recently heard a radio interview in which a stand up comic who survived cancer requested that people donate funny movies to cancer centers because they aide in the healing process.

During the second week after Darren's death, my mom managed to get me out of the house and took me to see the movie *"Dumb and Dumber,"* starring Jim Carrey. (I loved his *"Ace Ventura"* movies, and was excited to see this new one.) I laughed so hard that I cried; happy tears this time. As soon as it came out on video, I bought it; and whenever I needed a good laugh, I watched it. My mom said that after she saw me laughing again, she knew she could go home. Watching funny movies was a little bit of escapism, but who wouldn't have wanted to escape my life at that time? Laughing was good for me. I noticed how much more alive I felt when I laughed. My whole body tingled. I knew that if I could laugh, I would somehow be okay. Laughing helped me get through this devastating time in my life.

I also had every episode of *"Beavis and Butthead"* on tape, which I thought was the greatest show ever. I would watch my tapes and laugh for hours at those two fools. I could not help but laugh at some of their stupid comments and antics, especially when critiquing music videos. I even began joking about myself and my situation. It made it a little easier to cope. When I was around friends and family members I found myself trying to crack jokes and be like the old me, so that they wouldn't worry. I tried to be my normal, happy self. When I was alone, I still cried a lot; but I needed laughter to bring some balance back into my life. It couldn't all be misery.

Another thing that was very helpful in my healing was listening to funny talk-radio shows in the morning or afternoon, whenever I woke up, as I got ready. I found that if I could start my day with a laugh, it made life more bearable, and it still seemed worthwhile. When I was still living in Chicago, I listened to Howard Stern, Mancow, and Kevin Matthews. I don't know how I would have made it through some days without my daily dose of these programs.

Also, when I met Matt, we shared the same juvenile sense of humor, and he made me laugh again and helped bring me back to life. He was so silly, and I loved that about him. I go more in depth about this in the "Falling in Love Again" chapter, but I could not have fallen in love with a humorless stick in the mud. He also did great impressions, especially Butthead. I knew I had found my match.

Before my loss I had a well-developed sense of humor. Now, I allowed myself to use that sense of humor while I went through the process of grieving. I gave myself permission to laugh, and crack a joke. That's who I was- and who I still am. Darren's death didn't change this essential part of my identity. Everyone's sense of humor is different, and yours may be very different from mine. The following movies helped me lighten my mood when I needed it. Maybe they will work for you too.

FUNNY MOVIES
- *"Pee-Wee's Big Adventure"*
- *"Ace Ventura- Pet Detective"*
- *"Ace Ventura- When Nature Calls"*
- *"Tommy Boy"*
- *"Dumb and Dumber"*
- *"So I Married an Axe Murderer"*
- *"Austin Powers- Man of Mystery"*
- *"Austin Powers- The Spy Who Shagged Me"*
- *"Austin Powers- Goldmember"*
- *"Beavis and Butthead Do America"*
- *"There's Something About Mary"*
- *"South Park: Bigger, Longer, and Uncut", or the TV show*
- *"Deuce Bigelow, Male Gigolo"*
- *"Jay and Silent Bob Strike Back"*
- *"Saturday Night Live Presents: The Best of Chris Farley"*
- *"Napoleon Dynamite"*
- *"The Family Guy"*

Having a Good Cry

"Life is like photography. You use the negatives to develop."

—*Swami Beyondananda*

After Darren died, I was amazed at how many tears my body could produce. It seemed as if I was crying more often than I wasn't crying. Then, if I didn't cry for a whole day, I felt like there was something wrong with me. As time went by, especially after I had moved on and buried some of my grief, the tears became less of a daily routine and more of an outlet for my pent-up emotions. Sometimes the tears came naturally and sometimes they needed a little encouragement. I always felt cleansed after a good cry, so I did certain things to bring them on when I needed it, because I discovered that crying is healing.

There were a few sure-fire ways I had to start the waterworks. First, there was music. I would listen to certain sad songs, like the ones I listed in the music chapter, and the tears would fall like rain. Then, I would let my mind wander through all my pain and sorrow, and the tears kept coming. Crying actually relaxed me and I often did it right before bed. Afterward, I slept like a log. Even when I was younger, I often used music to help me purge my emotions after disappointment or heartbreak. This was a tried and true method for me.

Another way to get the tears flowing was to look at old pictures of Darren and me, or to read old cards and letters from him. This trick *always* worked, although sometimes I couldn't bear to look at pictures of him because it brought on more depression. But, for the times when I felt I needed to cry, I just broke out the photo albums or our wedding video.

Just as I watched funny movies to make me laugh, I watched sad movies to make me cry. Although most people wouldn't consider it a sad movie, "*The Crow*" had special meaning for me. Darren had loved its action and cool music. After he died, the movie took on new meaning for me. In the movie, The Crow returns from the dead on Halloween night to avenge the wrongful death of his fiancée.

Brandon Lee, who played The Crow, actually died in a freak shooting accident during the filming of the movie. He was only 28-years-old, the same age Darren was when he died. A beautiful love story balances the violence in the movie. The message is that love never dies, even in death. The song played during the credits *"It Won't Rain All the Time"* by Jane Siberry is so beautiful and haunting, that I bought the soundtrack. I would listen to it over and over. It gave me hope and helped me heal every time I listened to it.

One day, my mother-in-law told me that my father-in-law mentioned that every time he saw a crow, he felt that it was Darren. She couldn't understand why a noisy, ugly crow would remind her husband of their son. It was following him and he sensed Darren in this crow. Now this is a man who is very cynical and doesn't believe in life after death, so for him to say this, it must have been a moving experience. I understood the connection and told Darren's mom about the movie. In the movie, Brandon Lee's character manifested as a crow when he returned from the dead.

Shortly after Darren's death, my cousin Julie loaned me her copy of *"Ghost"* with Patrick Swayze and Demi Moore. Although I had seen it before, it was now more personally meaningful. One night, I sat on my couch with a box of tissues and cried my eyes out, hoping that the movie's portrayal of death was accurate and not just a Hollywood fabrication: that those in spirit are actually right there with us, knowing everything that goes on in our lives, and are able to help us.

This movie was also my first introduction to the wonderful world of mediumship. Whoopi Goldberg plays a medium, and gave me hope that there actually were people in this world who could talk to dead people as she did in the movie. Although it came out years after Darren died, I loved the movie *"Dragonfly."* It stars Kevin Costner, a cynical doctor whose wife dies while pregnant. He starts getting unmistakable signs that his wife is trying to contact him from the other side, and leads him on a journey of discovery. It was amazing. I wished it had come out when I lost Darren.

Another movie I liked a lot was *"Bounce,"* starring Gwyneth Paltrow and Ben Affleck. She plays a young widow. It hit a little too close to home when she found out about her husband's death. I also found it interesting that when she started dating again, she told the man, played by Ben Affleck, that she was divorced. I guess she wanted him to think she was normal.

In the early stages of my grief, there were just a few movies that helped me heal through tears; now the list has grown. All of them have death or grief as a theme. They are…

SAD MOVIES

- *"Ghost"*
- *"The Crow"*
- *"Moonlight and Valentino"*
- *"What Dreams May Come"*
- *"City of Angels"*
- *"To Gillian on her 37th Birthday"*
- *"The Sixth Sense"*
- *"Bounce"*
- *"Dragonfly"*

<u>The Internet</u>

"Education is our passport to the future, for tomorrow belongs to the people who prepare for it today."

—Malcolm X

It was 1995 when Darren died, and I still didn't know how to use a computer. The computer age was here, and I was behind the times. I decided that I had better get up to speed and prepare for the future, since I had no idea what mine now held. New technology was very intimidating to me because I knew nothing about it. I did some research, shopped around, and finally bought a computer.

I felt so proud of myself as I learned how to use it. Not only was exploring the internet a lot of fun, but during this whole process, I found a sense of independence that I hadn't known before. Buying the computer made me feel empowered, because I found that I could make a decision on my own. I didn't have anyone to answer to or to get permission from to make this big purchase. It also made me feel like I was no longer out of the loop. I don't know why I had ever allowed a computer to intimidate me. They are so user-friendly, a monkey could operate one.

There were so many cool websites to look up. The whole world was at my fingertips. Learning to use the computer was challenging, but it felt great to use my brain, to make decisions, and to solve problems again. Anyone who has lost a loved one knows how your mind can just melt down. Making even the simplest decision can be mind-numbing.

The act of teaching myself a valuable new skill was very rewarding. I didn't know what kind of work I might eventually be doing, but I knew that I would now be financially responsible for myself. I still had a lot to learn about computers, but I now knew some of the lingo and had enough skills to get by.

There are so many great websites out there now for people who are grieving the loss of a loved one. A lot of them have links to related sites and bereavement support groups, chat rooms, as well as lists of recommended reading. Here are some of my favorites to get you started:

Laura Hirsch

GRIEF WEBSITES

- www.after-death.com- Bill and Judy Guggenheim's website, authors of *Hello from Heaven*, a book on direct after-death communication (ACD). This site has links to bereavement support groups, and lists many incidents of ACD's in books, movies, and the media.

- www.groww.com- Grief Recovery Online (founded by) Widows and Widowers. Tons of great information and support.

- www.widownet.com- An information and self-help resource by and for widows and widowers.

- www.youngwidow.com- The original and only interactive website and nonprofit organization exclusively dedicated to young widows and widowers.

- www.youngwidowsandwidowers.com- Practical advice for young widows and widowers, by a fellow young widow. Offers free newsletter, support group, online dating for widows and widowers.

- www.bestpsychicmediums.com- Education and resources for understanding spirit communication and a "genuine and legitimate psychic mediums" list.

- www.ofspirit.com- Holistic, spiritual, and self-improvement articles, interviews, links, and weekly online magazine.

- www.griefandbelief.com- Ofspirit.com's sister-site; devoted to people dealing with grief. Great links to other web resources.

- www.vanpraagh.com- Medium James Van Praagh's website, good grief related resources.

- www.griefnet.org – Directed by a clinical grief psychologist and grief educator. The site includes support groups, Kidsaid, memorials, a library, and other resources.

More Tragedies

"Earth has no sorrow that heaven cannot heal."

—*Thomas Moore*

Within 13 months of Darren's death, I had to cope with three more deaths in the family. First was my paternal grandfather, who still lived with my grandmother in northern Wisconsin. He died three months after Darren did. The day he died was both Mother's Day and my grandparent's wedding anniversary. Upon hearing the news, I instantly felt so much compassion for my grandma, because I had just lost my husband, too.

Driving with my sister, Kim, I received an unexpected gift on my way to my grandpa's funeral. Out of nowhere, a magnificent giant double rainbow appeared in the sky. My mom was driving in the car ahead of us, and must have seen it too. Knowing that I was waiting for a rainbow, she opened her window to point it out. This was my sign! I had been waiting to see a rainbow for three months, ever since the priest had said at Darren's funeral "I have put the rainbow in the sky as a sign of my everlasting love for you." Now, one rainbow for Darren and another for my grandpa told me they were together and safe. I felt a sense of peace wash over me as a stared at the rainbows, intuitively knowing that they were there for me.

Nevertheless, the funeral was an emotional ordeal for me. I tried not to think about why I was really there, and spent my time talking with relatives whom I hadn't seen in a long time. Grandpa's death was so close to Darren's that I was still in that desensitized mode where I didn't feel my emotions fully. I was numb. At the cemetery, my grandma let out a wail that just tore what was left of my heart out. I'll never forget that heart-wrenching cry.

The second death, six months later, was Darren's grandfather. His funeral was held at the same funeral home as Darren's. It was like re-living Darren's funeral. Darren's mom felt guilty because she couldn't grieve for her father, because all she could think about was her son. The only way I could get through it was by blocking a lot of it out and socializing. My sister, Kim, came with me for moral support. I told Darren's relatives about my upcoming move to California- only a month away-

and they all wished me well.

I had been living in California for a few months, when I got a phone call that my paternal grandmother passed on. I guess she just gave up after my grandpa died. This was the fourth death of someone I loved in just a little over a year. I decided I couldn't go to the funeral. I couldn't handle any more grief! Who was going to be next? My dad was very understanding and told me not to feel obligated to come. So instead, I talked to my grandma and told her I loved her. I hoped that she understood why I couldn't go and I grieved for her in private. She knew how much I loved her and that I was thinking of her. My relatives understood that I had been through a horrible year and didn't need another setback in my healing.

I was just starting to rebuild my life, yet I felt so vulnerable at this time. I felt that all the people I loved could die at any moment. I was just waiting for the rug to be pulled out from under me again. It seemed that just when the dust was starting to settle, someone else was gone. The only good thing was that it made me appreciate the people who were here that much more. In my anxiety, not knowing who might be next, I wanted everyone to know how much I cared for them. My family and friends must surely have been getting exasperated listening to me telling them that I loved them all the time. It's scary to realize that you have no control over what happens. After four deaths in a little over a year, I learned that losing someone you love does not make you immune to losing someone else you love.

After this string of deaths, I became extremely fearful and paranoid about everything Matt did or wanted to do. I could feel the tension in my stomach whenever he spoke of doing something that I considered even remotely dangerous; body boarding at night, mountain-biking alone, scuba diving, driving to work, breathing (just joking on the last one). I just couldn't handle losing him, too.

After a while, I will admit, I started to get a bit ridiculous. He was torn because he respected where I was coming from, but at the same time, he didn't find these things dangerous and felt that he was missing out because of my fears. Matt had been wanting to buy a dirt bike ever since I met him; but I was so afraid that he would be killed riding it, that he stopped bringing it up to avoid upsetting me. Although he was working as a sales rep in the dirt bike industry, Matt, bless his heart, went along with my wishes and was the only employee without one. Finally, after talking about it with my sister and convincing myself that I was being too much of a control freak, I surprised Matt and told him it was okay if he bought a dirt bike with the bonus money he had worked so hard to win at work. I decided to trust that God would keep him safe for me. I thought that I might lose him to a breakup, not death, if I couldn't come to grips with my fears. It was a big step for me. I had to stop trying to control everything, and have some faith. In the end, the ear-to-ear grin on Matt's face when he finally got his bike made it all worth it.

Going Back To Work

"The courageous man is the man who forces himself,
in spite of his fears, to carry on."
—General George S. Patton

I had just started working at my friend Laura's modeling agency a few months before Darren died. It was just the two of us, and I knew Laura needed my help. After Darren's death I just couldn't go back to work. My heart just wasn't in it anymore, I explained to her. I needed some time alone. Laura understood, and told me that if I felt up to doing any promotions or trade shows, I should just let her know and she would book me. This was such a relief. I could go back when I was ready. She was a great friend during this time.

I wasn't able to face the world yet. I couldn't make it through a whole day without crying. Feeling vulnerable and small, I was an emotional wreck, and would have been useless on the job. After about a month, one of the other modeling agencies I was registered with called me to go to an interview for a trade show job. I hadn't worked for them much, and didn't want to decline and have them not call me again. I explained my situation, but said that I felt up to it. The agent was very sympathetic, and gave me all the information for the interview.

Modeling is a fickle business; you never know when you'll get your next job. I realized that I had better take the opportunities that presented themselves to me. I went to the interview, and when the agency called to tell me I got the job, I was shocked. I couldn't hide from the world forever. It would be good for me to get out and begin some kind of routine again. It was only a three-day show, so it wasn't too much of a commitment.

On the day of the show, during the hour-long drive to the convention center in downtown Chicago, I felt so strange. The world was different now. I was different now. As I walked to our booth in this giant convention center, I felt transparent, as though the hundreds of strangers I passed knew exactly what had happened to me. I was one of the walking wounded, and wondered if there were other people walking past me who also had internal injuries. I was truly on my own for the first time. I felt

119

like I was walking on a tightrope without a safety net.

One thing I struggled with that day was whether or not to wear my wedding ring. I did, mainly so it would deter men from hitting on me or asking me about my personal life. Well, it didn't work. The first day of the show, one of the sales reps at the booth saw my ring and asked me if I was married or engaged. I paused, caught off guard at this line of questioning, and decided to be honest. I said "Neither, actually… my husband recently died in a car accident, and I still wear my ring out of habit, I guess." He was stunned. How do you respond to that? He asked some questions, and I was very straightforward, curbing any emotional reaction. I had to learn to talk about it without breaking down. By the end of the three days, everyone at our booth knew my story. They were respectful and considerate, which allowed me to be myself and do my job.

Working the trade show was a good experience, and I was encouraged to keep doing it. It felt good to rejoin the world. Even though I was going through my own personal hell, getting back to work took my mind off my private life and restored a bit of confidence. I met new people, I laughed, and I even had fun. For a short time, I could forget about my own pathetic life.

After working the trade show, I called Laura and told her I was ready to come back to work. She booked me for a few beer promotions, but I soon realized that I couldn't do this with a clear conscience. The money was great, but promoting alcohol, a contributing factor in Darren's death, made me feel like a hypocrite. What if I talked someone into buying the beer that was (as we used to jokingly call) "one for the ditch?" This was no longer a joke to me. I wouldn't be able to live with myself if I had any part in an alcohol-related car accident. I had already lived through that devastation personally.

I called Laura and the other promotions coordinators I worked for and they all understood my predicament. For the same reason, I couldn't go back to work at the restaurant, either. Alcohol was served there. What if I over-served someone? I didn't want that kind of responsibility. So, I stuck with working just the trade shows, and I felt very good about my decision. I had a clear conscience, I was doing something productive, and I was having fun again. It felt a little strange to realize that my old lifestyle didn't fit the new me anymore. I had become not only financially responsible for myself, but also ethically responsible for the consequences of my choices. Laura booked me for both the Food Marketing Institute Convention and the National Restaurant Association Convention in May. The two shows were a week apart. Since Laura and I would be working at the same booth, and lived near each other, we carpooled every day. It was at the second of these two shows, the National Restaurant Association Convention that a new chapter in my life began.

Falling In Love Again

"And the day came when the risk to remain tight in a bud was more painful than the risk it took to blossom."

—*Anais Nin*

The first day of the National Restaurant Association Convention, May 22nd, was also my mom's birthday. I was working for a large food company with a chef who was carving samples of a new turkey product, which I put on little buns and served to show attendees. The chef was really funny and we had been having fun all day, joking around with people, and I was in a great mood. The chef ran out of turkey, so I was left standing there with empty buns. Just then, a young man with a scruffy beard, who I guessed was around my age, 27, approached and asked me what I was sampling. I immediately noticed his beautiful blue eyes. Being the smart-ass that I was, I replied "It's a wish sandwich." "What's that?" he asked. "You wish there was meat in it," I answered. He laughed at my lame joke, and then we talked for a while as we waited for the chef to return with the turkey. Matt Hirsch, as his name badge read, ate his sandwich, said good-bye, and went on his way.

Laura and I took our lunch break at a juice drink booth. Matt happened to be there also, with the woman he was working for. We waved hello. Laura and Matt's colleague struck up a conversation, and Matt motioned for me to come over. We started talking on a more personal level. He was a sales rep for a start-up food company from California. He was in Chicago for the show and to drum up new business and would be leaving in about a month. I didn't say much about myself, but since I was no longer wearing my wedding ring, I'm sure he assumed I was single. He was very sweet. He even seemed nervous talking to me. When Laura and I were walking back to our booth she said "I think he likes you. Do you think he's cute?" I wasn't sure how I felt about this possibility. "No, he doesn't" I nervously responded. "It's hard to tell if he's cute with all that facial hair," I laughed, "But he has great eyes." "I think he likes you." Laura repeated. I blushed and felt like a schoolgirl.

Laura and I had found some plastic roaches at one of the other booths on our break, and, with mischief in mind, I garnished a few of the turkey sandwiches with them when we got back to our booth. The reactions they provoked gave me a good laugh. When Matt came over again, I served up my new specialty. "Oh, now I see what you really think of me," he laughed. He asked me what else I did for fun around here. I told him that I was a loser and that I just went home and played with my dog; (which was true) but I could make some recommendations on where to go while they were in town. Matt had a hard time looking me in the eye, which made me not look him in the eye. He asked if I ever went to the Riverboat Casino. I told him that I wasn't much of a gambler, but that I had brought good luck to everyone else the one time I had gone. "Would you want to go again?" he asked. "Yeah, I'd go again." I answered. *Did he just ask me out? Did I say yes?* Matt asked how he could get in touch with me. *Oh, crap, I think I did say yes.* Panicking, I told him to come back to the booth tomorrow, and we'd figure it out. This would give me time to decide if I wanted to go through with our "date."

Although he said he'd see me tomorrow, I wasn't really convinced that he'd show up. Laura was excited for me. She was sure he'd be back. The next day was a tough day emotionally for me. It would have been my third wedding anniversary, so it was nice to have a distraction. As promised, Matt returned. This time, he was all dressed up in a suit and tie. He was dressed more casually the day before. I was walking past him with an empty tray, and did a double take when I saw him. I thought "Wow, he cleans up nicely." He was definitely cute. We talked for a while, and it turned out that the place they were staying was only about 15 minutes from my house. How convenient. I gave him my phone number, and told him I was leaving town in a week and would be gone for 11 days. We'd have to go out before I left or put it off until I returned. I thought it would be nice to get out of the house and get to know him better. Matt seemed really nice- not pushy or aggressive. I thought he'd be safe to go out with because he lived across the country and would only be here for a month. I could maybe make a new friend and test the waters as to what it would be like to be on a date with another man. No strings attached.

He called me the next day and we talked for an hour and totally hit it off. I told him that he'd probably think I was a weirdo. "Why, what do you mean?" he asked. "Well," I said, "I like stupid humor, like Beavis and Butthead." With that, he did the best imitation of Butthead I had ever heard. I screamed with delight: "Oh my God, no way! Do it again, that was perfect!" He did more Butthead imitations and I, in return, did Beavis. This was great! He was as silly as I was. If nothing else, we could do Beavis and Butthead imitations on our date. Then he got serious. He started talking about his bad luck with women. He had only had one serious relationship that he ended because his girlfriend had cheated on him twice. He said that he was too nice, and that nice guys finished last. I let him finish his story and saw this as my chance to explain my situation to him up front. "You think *you* have bad luck," I laughed. "Wait till you hear *my* story." In a lighthearted way, I told him: "Until February 11th I was married, and then my husband was killed in a car accident, and the guy that I dated before my husband was stabbed to death." I finished, "Now that's bad luck". There was silence on Matt's end of the line for a moment, and then he said "Wow, I'm speechless." If I wasn't ready for this, he said, he would understand. I told him that I really need to get out and find some enjoyment in life again. We could take things at my pace, he assured me.

I was relieved that Matt was so understanding. As we talked, I discovered that he was five years younger than me. This came as a surprise to both of us; but we didn't care. We seemed to be so much alike that age didn't matter. We decided on dinner and a movie instead of the Riverboat Casino for our first date, and that we'd meet before my trip. We talked a while longer, and I hung up the phone with a smile on my face.

I immediately called my sister, Kim, to tell her the news. I had already called her the day I met Matt and told her "I think I said *yes* to a date." "What do you mean, you think?" she'd asked me. When I told Kim that "Matt" was his name, she said, "I like him already. His name means, 'a gift from God.'" I told Kim all about our plans and asked nervously, "What if he tries to hold my hand?" She chuckled. "If you think it's right, you'll know." "What if he tries to kiss me?" I persisted. "You know," she said, "I feel like the older sister here, giving you dating advice. You sound like a teenager, not a 27-yearold woman." I told her that I was scared because I hadn't been out on a date with anyone for years, this was new for me. Kim helped me laugh at myself. It was just dinner and a movie, after all. "Go, and enjoy yourself." she said.

I drove the night of our date because Matt shared a rental car with his business associates, and I felt bad stranding them without a car. Besides, I knew where I was going- and if things didn't work out, I could leave when I wanted to. We had dinner at a Mexican restaurant. At first, we were both kind of shy and nervous, but then our shared sense of humor helped to break the nervous tension. In no time, I felt like I had known him my whole life. He made me feel so comfortable and at ease in his presence. I could just be myself. It was a great feeling.

Next, we went to see a movie. I felt his arm next to mine on the armrest. It just felt natural to want to hold his hand, so I slid my fingers between his. He looked at me and smiled, and squeezed my hand. I knew he didn't want to rush me and was glad to see me make the first move. Things were going so smoothly that neither of us wanted the date to end. After the movie, we went to a near-by restaurant to talk. We played a game where we asked each other questions, a "getting-to-know-you" game. I'd say "My turn," and ask him a question. Then it would be his turn to ask me a question. This went on for hours.

We finally left the restaurant, but still didn't want our date to end; so I drove around and played tour guide, even driving by my house to show him where I lived before dropping him off. I got out of the car to say goodnight. I was nervous; but I said "It's my turn," continuing our game. "Do I get a goodnight kiss?" "Do you want one?" he asked. I answered "Would I have asked for one if I didn't?" "I guess not." With that, we simultaneously took out our gum and had our first kiss.

Wow! Talk about electricity! I knew I was in trouble. We said goodnight, and I drove home with an ear-to-ear grin. It was the best first date I had ever been on. We went out three more times before my trip. By the time I left, I was completely infatuated, and could tell that Matt felt the same way. I felt very guilty, because I would be in Florida on the second half of my trip with my mother-in-law and sister-in-law, and they didn't know about Matt. I hated the feeling of going behind their backs, or having a secret.

The first part of my trip was to Atlanta to visit Moe. A month earlier, I'd helped her move there from Milwaukee. She had to have my blessing, she'd insisted, before she'd accept the job offer in Atlanta, because she didn't want to leave me in my time of need. I remember telling her, "Moe, go for it. If I've learned one thing, it's that life's too short. Do what will make you happy." She reminded me of this five years later, at her wedding. But, I digress.

The trip would give me some breathing space, and a chance to decide if I was ready to pursue a new relationship with Matt. From Atlanta, I talked to him on the phone every night for at least an hour. Some breathing space! I owed Moe about $100.00 for the phone bill by the end of the trip. I felt even closer to Matt by the time I got to Florida. I was falling in love with him, and tried, to no avail, to talk myself out of it.

I didn't want to open my heart up again and end up getting hurt. I knew that Matt would be returning to California soon, but I couldn't stop thinking about him. He occupied my every thought. I was supposed to be a grieving widow, and here I was, falling head over heels for a new man. What was wrong with me? I really struggled with this one and then, finally, let myself off the hook. As I had told Moe, life was too short. If I could have some happiness in my life after all that I had been through, then I needed to let it happen. You can't control who you fall in love with, or when.

I figured that I had two choices. First, wait until I was done grieving, whenever that would be- then hunt Matt down across the country, and take a chance that he was still available and interested in me. Or second, seize the moment. I chose the latter because, as I knew all too well, there are no guarantees in life. Matt was a once-in-a-lifetime opportunity. Guys like him don't grow on trees. I had sacrificed enough recently, and wasn't about to sacrifice Matt too.

Many people are under the false impression that when a widow starts seeing another man, she is done grieving. Wrong! It doesn't mean that she has forgotten about her deceased husband. Dating again is part of a widow's grieving process. It's part of her inner healing. There's no shame in living and loving again. I was not some vulnerable, little thing that people thought I was. I was not being taken advantage of either. I was making a conscious choice. It takes a lot of courage to take a risk and open up to being hurt again.

Dating again doesn't mean that you are in denial either. I knew the reality of my situation. I had started dating again because I wanted to fill the void in my life, and end some of my loneliness. How long was I expected to be miserable? I shouldn't have to feel guilty too, I didn't do anything wrong. Matt was the best thing that could have happened to me. He didn't think of me as "the poor young widow." He liked me for who I was.

Before I met Matt, I had been working through my grief. I let out my feelings. I talked about them. I cried until I couldn't cry anymore. I stayed home for months confronting my grief. I was in a good place emotionally by the time I met Matt. I wasn't pretending that nothing had happened to me. I knew I'd be harshly judged whenever I started dating; so in that sense, I'd be damned if I did, and damned if I didn't.

In Florida, I came to grips with my guilt, and decided to tell my sister-in-law about Matt. If I hadn't been certain that Matt and I were going to have a relationship together, I wouldn't have said anything. It was difficult, but I felt that she deserved to hear it from me. I considered her a friend, and I guess in a way, I was trying to feel her out to see if her mom was ready to hear my news. She assured me that the family knew that I would eventually find someone else, but she felt that it was too soon to tell them. They were still in so much pain from losing Darren that they didn't need to feel as if they were losing me too. My sister-in-law was very supportive, but protective as well. She cautioned me that Matt and I had just met, and not to rush things. I was glad I told her. It relieved some of my guilt, but mostly, it made me more confident that it was okay for me to move forward with my life, while I was working through my grief.

On my last day in Florida, I woke up early, and took my walkman out on the balcony. I was watching the boats pass by on the ocean and I noticed that I was actually thinking about Matt instead of Darren as I listened to love songs playing on the radio. I felt good, not sad. This would be a new beginning for me, and I couldn't wait to get home and pursue this budding romance. I had something- and someone- to look forward to again.

I called Matt as soon as I returned, and told him that I'd be over soon. A romantic surprise was waiting for me when I arrived. Matt wasn't there, but his roommate said he'd be right back. I was instructed to wait in his room. A trail of rose petals led me to a gorgeous bouquet of red roses, where another trail of rose petals led to a card. I sat on the bed reading the card, and heard Matt's voice coming from the bathroom, telling me to close my eyes. He was there after all. What was he up to? I heard the door open, and then I felt his face rubbing up against mine, minus the beard. I had told Matt that I would like to see him clean shaven. As expected, when I opened my eyes, there was a handsome face under all that fuzz. We hugged and kissed and it felt like it was the first time. We'd missed each other so much.

We went to my house and I remember asking him how long he thought it took to fall in love with someone, thinking that it was just me moving too fast because of my loss. He asked, "How many dates have we been on?" I answered, "Four." "Four dates is how long it takes." he responded. Then he added, "Actually, for me, it was love at first sight. I walked around the corner at the convention, and knew I'd marry you the moment I saw you." It wasn't just me.

From that moment on, we saw each other almost every day. I dreaded the time when he'd have to go back home, and so did Matt. We made the most of our time together. We spent our days having a blast. Even when we did nothing at all, we'd have a great time together. We were like two little kids. We rode mountain bikes (where I kicked his butt), played laser tag, and of course, watched Beavis and Butthead. Also, among our fun: while impersonating Butthead's voice, Matt made crank calls to strangers with funny names out of the phone book (like Harry Bush), as I recorded the conversation on the other line so we could play it back and laugh some more. "Uh, huh, huh… Is Harry Bush there?" "Speaking" "Uh, huh, huh, I said Harry Bush." Click. This was big fun.

One day, we went to the grocery store and put embarrassing items in other people's carts when they weren't looking, and waited to see their reactions. We put a box of condoms in one man's cart, and inconspicuously followed him around the store giggling, as he looked for a place to stash them. We did the same with an enema kit, Preparation H, and adult diapers. I know we were being immature, but it was so funny, and we had the best time! It felt so good to laugh again, and to have fun with another man.

Matt also gave me my space for bad days when they came up. Sometimes, usually after drinking a few glasses of wine, my grief would take over and I would start crying, and Matt would just hold me, hand me tissues, and listen. He was so good to me, and so gracious to accommodate my grief. I felt bad that I was crying about Darren in front of him, but he understood that I was still going to need time to get past this grief. He was also confident enough to know that my grief didn't lessen my feelings toward him. They were two separate issues. Matt knew that I loved him, and that Darren wasn't a threat to out relationship. Grief and love can co-exist. I didn't stop loving other people when Darren died, why couldn't I find room in my heart to love someone else too? Matt was my angel- he allowed me to do what I needed to do to heal, and he never felt slighted.

This is the part I almost didn't include, but then decided that it is far too important to omit. (Dad, if you're reading this, you might want to skip the next four paragraphs, thanks.) I've always been a very private person regarding sexual matters. I didn't even talk much about sex around my best friends. I was always pretty vague when asked about my sex life because this was a private matter between my partner and me. As a young married woman with a healthy sex life, it was very difficult to suddenly become celibate. I had been out of the dating pool for eight years; the eight years in which AIDS climbed to epidemic levels in this country. I was so terrified of contracting AIDS or some other sexually transmitted disease that I felt like I'd never be able to trust someone enough to want to have sex again. I used to tell Darren all the time how grateful I was to be married, and not have to be in the dating cesspool. I didn't want to dive in headfirst now.

It was a big step for me to become intimate with another man; so when I was ready, I first had to make sure that Matt had a clean bill of health. I asked him to get tested. He wasn't hurt or angry, and thought it was a good idea. He had only been with a few other women, but it only takes one. I knew I was fine, because even though I was married and monogamous, I got tested routinely every year at my annual exam. We were both relieved when his tests came back negative.

Maybe I was being a bit paranoid; but I had heard too many horror stories and wasn't about to become another statistic. I'm a little old-fashioned, I guess, when it comes to talking about sex. Nevertheless, it's important to mention it because it's a big issue with widows. Sex is a big part of marriage and when your partner is gone, you wonder who will fulfill that missing part. We are all sexual beings, and we all have needs. My advice is not to let others dictate what is right for you. If you are not ready, don't rush it. If you are ready, don't be foolish. It's not worth it. I understand how your self-esteem all but disappears after the loss of a husband, and you become very vulnerable to a man's affections. Sex can and should be a mutually enjoyable experience, and can really help fulfill your physical and emotional needs, and make you feel alive again. Just use caution, protection, and your head, and you won't have to live with regret or worse.

And yes, it was weird to think that Darren could "see me" having sex with someone else in what used to be *our* bed. In a strange way, I blamed him for putting me in the position to have to make that choice in the first place, so anger was at play here too. I almost felt like I was getting back at him for leaving me. I just had to keep telling myself that now it was *my* bed, and that it was just a piece of furniture. I had to take the emotional attachment away from it. I didn't dwell on thoughts like these because if you think about it too much you realize that your grandparents and anyone else on the other side can also see you in the act. Talk about creepy.

As things turned out, Matt's business in Illinois for didn't turn out as planned. Things weren't happening as quickly as expected, and he had a choice to make. He could stay in Illinois and find another sales job, or he could move back home. He told me that he didn't want to go back to California without me. I told him that I didn't want him to leave and that he could stay with me until we figured things out. I'd always wanted to see California, so we planned a trip on my birthday at the end of August.

We went there for a week. I loved it at once and could easily see myself living there. Matt's family picked us up at the airport, and they were great. His younger brother, Tim, was our chauffeur for the week, showing me all of the beautiful places and tourist attractions. As I've already mentioned, I went snorkeling for the first time, and Matt caught a lobster which we cooked for dinner. We also went jet-skiing, which was a blast. One night, we made a bonfire on a private beach in Malibu where some of his friends lived. At that moment, I decided that California was where I needed to be.

As soon as we returned to Chicago, I put my house on the market and it sold within a month. It was a non-contingent sale, closing in 45 days. Perfect! We'd be in California before Christmas. In the meantime, I either sold or gave away everything I didn't need or want. I sold a lot of furniture with the house, keeping only my bedroom set (so that Dakota would feel at home when we got there). I was truly starting over.

With the move to California, I could leave the old "me" behind. I could shed my skin and find that new identity I was looking for. The move was symbolic: when I looked back, I saw darkness, when I looked forward, there was light. I felt a parallel between leaving the cold darkness of Illinois winter behind me, along with my grief, and heading toward sunny California and a new life.

Even before I met Matt, I'd thought about leaving Illinois anyway. I was considering either moving by Moe in Atlanta, or to the condo in Florida, or back to Wisconsin. The house Darren and I had built was now just a shell of my life. It was no longer a home; it was just a house. I just wanted to get rid of this burden I felt I was stuck with. It had taken every ounce of strength in my being not to just run away and abandon the house and my responsibilities; but I stuck it out, and now the time was right for me to move on.

I loved living in Southern California, it was a completely different lifestyle than I was accustomed to, but it fit. I certainly didn't miss the weather back home. I didn't regret moving so far away, though I did feel homesick for my old life and the people in it. Not only had I lost Darren, but I also lost a lot of his family and friends. I still keep in touch with some of them, but our relationship has changed. I also missed being only two hours away from my old friends and family in Wisconsin. It didn't seem fair. If someone had told me that I was going to be widowed at age 27, meet a new love and move to California six months later, I would have thought they were completely insane. But that is what happened to me in a very short time. It took some getting used to.

Being with Matt helped me rebuild my self-confidence, slowly but surely. When your whole world comes crashing down around you, you become very fragile, and expect to find tragedy around every corner. With Matt by my side, I had the strength to get out and face the world again. It wasn't such a scary place with him holding my hand. I stopped feeling like a victim.

When I was first widowed, I felt very frightened and lost. Then, as my self-confidence started to resurface, I became more determined to make it through this tragedy, and come out on top. I found courage and strength I didn't know I had. Yes,

I took baby steps; but baby steps lead to big steps. Each step I took gave me more confidence, and I began craving more. I took chances. I would even say that I became self-centered, and did what pleased *me*, instead of everyone else for once in my life- and it felt great! I said what was on my mind. I lived my life with integrity. I knew that I could never be the same person I was before Darren died; but I liked this new me even more. I had lost my husband; but I had re-created myself.

It was important for me to realize that there wasn't just one perfect person out there for me to love. That's a myth perpetuated through fairy tales, greeting cards, and the movies. You don't just fall in love, get married, and live happily ever after. When we met, I thought that Darren was my Prince Charming, my soul mate, my one true love. After the unthinkable happened and he died, I thought that my one chance for happiness was gone, and that I was doomed to live the rest of my life alone. That idea faded when I fell in love with Matt. I found that I had room in my heart for more love. But I had to force myself not to compare the two of them.

If you idolize the dead, no one else will ever measure up. No one is perfect. Darren wasn't perfect, Matt wasn't perfect, and I wasn't perfect. Comparing people is an easy trap to fall into; but if you expect someone to live up to certain unrealistic expectations, you will always be disappointed and unhappy. You love every person in your life differently. You love them for who they are, and you learn to appreciate the unique qualities they possess. Matt was not Darren, and I could not expect him to be. He was a wonderful, loving man with his own personality and quirks. It was different than what I had been used to for so long, but it was also exciting, fun, and romantic. I felt like I was getting a second chance.

Getting Remarried

*"If we listened to our intellect, we'd never have a love affair.
We'd never have a friendship. We'd never go into business,
because we'd be cynical. Well, that's nonsense. You've got to
jump off cliffs all the time and build your wings on the way down."*

—Ray Bradbury

Although Matt and I knew from the beginning of our relationship that we wanted to get married, this was a big step for me. I had this illogical fear that if I got married again, Matt would die too. Marriage meant being widowed at some point, I reasoned. Matt proposed to me shortly after we moved to California, twice actually. First, while Moe was visiting, so that she could see the ring, then he officially proposed to me a second time when we were by ourselves on the beach. I thought I should wait two years before marrying again; it seemed like a reasonable amount of time. When that time was drawing near, it was next to impossible to get all of my friends and family members to California at the same time to try to organize a wedding. So, we decided that if everyone couldn't be there, it would just be the two of us, so no one's feelings would get hurt. I had already had the big stressful wedding, and Matt didn't care either way.

Matt and I were married on March 29, 1997, on a beach overlooking the Pacific Ocean in Carmel, California. I thought it was the most breathtakingly beautiful place I had ever seen. I wasn't nervous about the wedding until I actually started walking down to where Matt was waiting for me to begin the ceremony. I just hoped that I had Darren's blessing to get married again. I also prayed to God that lightning wouldn't strike twice in the same place, and I wouldn't lose Matt too. I don't think I could live through that again. I had to let go of my fear because I kept going back to a big lesson I learned in losing Darren: to appreciate what I had, when I had it, because there are no guarantees in life.

We wore the traditional wedding gown and tuxedo, and rented a limousine to drive us from the hotel to the ceremony, around the scenic 17-mile drive in Pebble Beach for pictures, and back to the hotel for dinner at an elegant restaurant. Two other couples having dinner each sent us a bottle of champagne. There were bats darting around outside the window of the restaurant. It was so cool. Now, most people don't find bats romantic, but I had an affinity for them after a semester long project in a college class. I was a member of the fictitious Bat Preservation Society, and learned more about bats than I cared to; for instance the beneficial uses of bat guano. Anyway, seeing bats on my wedding day was a good sign.

Our hotel suite had an awesome ocean view, and we saw a comet from our balcony on our wedding night, another good sign. After dinner, we slow-danced in our room. We each had a song for the other. My song for Matt was "*Because You Loved Me*" by Celine Dion, and his song for me was "*I'll Stand by You*" by The Pretenders. Matt had bought that song for me when we first started dating. It was an incredibly romantic, stress-free weekend. We had only ourselves to think about.

I sometimes regret that the people we loved weren't there to share our day, but we really enjoyed ourselves. We videotaped the entire ceremony, so everyone was able to see our wedding on tape. It felt good to be married again, and not be considered "a widow" anymore. I had a wonderful husband who loved me, and I realized that I could be happy again. I'd always believed that I'd only get married once. However, because my first husband died, I didn't like to think of myself as being *re*-married because my first marriage didn't fail; if that makes any sense. Yes, it was my second marriage, but I felt that there was a big difference between being widowed and being divorced. I didn't choose to become widowed, and didn't like the stigma attached to having this be my second marriage. Maybe they will come up with new terminology someday to show that there is a distinction.

A week after the wedding, we moved into our new house. Now that I was married again, had a new house and new in-laws, I felt as if I were truly starting a new chapter of my life. My sister, Kim, got married in Illinois a month after we did, so Matt and I were congratulated by all of my relatives there. Most of them had already met Matt at my cousin's wedding a year earlier, but it felt good to reintroduce him as "my husband." Kim actually wore the dress I had worn when I married Darren, and though she had altered it so much that it didn't look the same, it was something special that I was able to share with her. I felt honored that she wanted to wear it.

Having a Baby

"A baby is God's opinion that the world should go on."

—Carl Sandburg

After Matt and I got married, we "stopped preventing" my getting pregnant right away. I'm sure that on some level, part of the reason that I didn't want to wait was the guilt I felt for putting off having a baby when I was married to Darren. I knew that life could be so fleeting, and saw no reason to wait. I no longer believed in "forever" and "happily ever after." I believed in making the most of every moment I had left, and in appreciating what I had while I had it. I certainly didn't want to die without experiencing motherhood. If there is one thing I've learned about myself, it's that I was put on this planet to be a mother. I absolutely adored children, and couldn't wait to have at least one of my own. After losing Darren, I felt this sense of urgency to do everything right away, or I might miss out on life.

I became pregnant six months after we married. During my pregnancy, I asked Matt's mom what her secret was for giving birth to three kids naturally, with no drugs. Her third child was even delivered at home, yikes. Talk about pressure. She had to know something I did not. She said that she simply prayed to God for assistance. I didn't think my faith was that strong, but I was still determined to give birth without drugs. If she could do it, I could do it too. You hear all these horror stories from friends and family, it was nice to hear a good childbirth story. I never did well with medication, and was terrified of taking the drugs they give for childbirth. Plus, the thought of a needle in my spine for an epidural, or the major surgery of a cesarean section was more frightening to me than the imagined pain of giving birth.

Matt and I went to classes that taught the Bradley Method, which focuses on natural, partner-coached childbirth. We learned a lot about relaxation and helpful positions during labor. Our Bradley instructor was also a Prenatal Yoga Instructor, and taught us safe yoga moves to practice at home. Although we were still nervous about what was going to happen, we felt prepared for the big day. We found out during the pregnancy that we were going to be having a boy. I was too much of a planner to not want to know when given the option. Matt was so elated to be having

135

a son. We went through the baby books separately and each circled the names we liked. The only name we both circled was Trevor. His due date was on July 4th, Independence Day.

I had false labor and was sent home from the hospital twice. When it was actually the real thing, ten days past my due date, my actual labor lasted a total of only six hours- short by first birth standards- and I delivered Trevor with no drugs! Don't hate me. With a combination of prayer, and the things I learned in childbirth class, along with Matt rubbing and pushing on my back for hours, we did it! The television was on in the delivery room, and the Tom Cruise movie *"Born on the Fourth of July"* was showing. I thought that was funny, since Trevor was supposed to be born on the fourth of July.

I had an amazing spiritual experience during the hardest part of my labor. While I was in the delivery room, with Matt helping and encouraging me, I had an overwhelming sense of Darren's presence in the room as well, just above me. Sensing him there as I grew tired from pushing, I remember opening my eyes and looking up. I just knew he was there, cheering us on. It gave me an additional rush of energy to keep going. I had tears of joy in my eyes, because I knew Darren was with me, supporting me as Matt was. I didn't see his spirit or anything, I just felt him there, strongly enough to break my concentration during hard labor. It was as if he burst through the door to get my attention. During my pregnancy I had wondered if he would be there, and he was.

A child is a true miracle, making you a part of something bigger than yourself. I helped in God's miracle, and I felt blessed to be trusted to care for this beautiful child sent from heaven. If you ever doubt the existence of God, have a baby. With Trevor's birth, I was re-born. I now had another new identity. I was someone's mom now. I never knew I could love anyone so much. This was a different kind of love from anything I had ever experienced before. It was as though my heart now existed outside my body, and within Trevor's.

As soon as Trevor was born, I knew I would be ready to give my own life for his. With that protective motherly instinct kicking in, I knew I would do anything to protect my son from harm. I was just mesmerized by every little thing he did. I couldn't believe that I had grown this child inside my body, much less given birth to him. I remember thinking how amazing it was that the day before he was born, he was living in fluid and after he was born, he was breathing air.

I knew then that the loss of a child has to be the greatest loss of all. I remember feeling so much empathy for Darren's mom after I had Trevor. He was only an infant, but I couldn't imagine how I would be able to cope if I ever lost my own child. I couldn't fathom the idea of him dying before me; it was unthinkable. I don't like to compare grief, but originally, I thought my loss had been the greatest. Now I felt differently. I had been closer to Darren than anyone else in my life, but he wasn't my child. Now that I had a child of my own, I understood my mother-in-law's pain a little more. When you lose a child, you lose part of your past, present, and future. I had another husband, but she would never have another son. Even if she could, you just can't replace people. None of us would ever have another Darren.

Now, just because I am mentioning it in this section, I am not suggesting that having a baby is a tool to heal grief and that people should rush right out and have a baby. However, in hindsight, the experience itself and the love and joy my son brought to me helped to heal my broken heart after the loss of my husband.

<u>Forgiveness</u>

"Forgiveness is the fragrance the violet sheds on the heel that has crushed it."
—*Mark Twain*

When I first learned that Dave was driving the car that killed Darren, I was furious! A few days later I began to feel sorry for Dave, and even asked him to be a pallbearer. That initial feeling of forgiveness was short-lived and was replaced by rage, blame, and even thoughts of revenge. I've discussed this in the chapter on anger; but I bring it up again to show that as angry as I was at one point, I was eventually able to find true forgiveness in my heart for Dave. It took me five years and a lot of inner healing first, but it did happen.

After Matt and I moved to California, I stayed in touch with Rico and his sister, Kathy. They would tell me about what was happening in Dave's life, whether I wanted to hear it or not. I remember that my stomach would flip over and knot up any time Dave's name was mentioned, and I would feel like I was having an anxiety attack. Finally, I had to ask Rico not to bring up his name anymore unless I asked about him, because it was so upsetting to me. It was a slap in the face that Dave was still living his life as though nothing had happened.

Over the next few years, I felt my anger softening up a bit, and I even began asking Rico about Dave and Kristine occasionally. I no longer felt a knot in my stomach when Dave's name was mentioned. One day, I told my sister, Kim, that I was thinking about calling Dave, to tell him that I forgave him. She thought it was a good idea. We agreed that hating someone hurts the angry person more than the person they hate. Holding on to anger was causing me to experience the pain of Darren's death over and over again. I needed to let it go.

For a long time, I tried to convince myself that I didn't have to forgive Dave. I felt that what he did was unforgivable. There was no way I could forgive him for being so reckless with my husband's life. He didn't deserve my forgiveness. I would punish him by not forgiving him, I reasoned. I wasn't going to forgive him just because it was the right thing to do or because I was "supposed to" forgive people. It needed to come from a place of wholehearted pardoning. This required me to resolve what happened in my own mind and heart to be at peace with it first.

Every so often, I would be reading a story about forgiveness or watching a program on TV in which a murder victim's relative forgave the person responsible for the death, and I felt my anger for Dave softening. Such things always brought tears to my eyes and inspired me to want to forgive Dave. I thought, if this person can forgive a stranger who deliberately intended to murder their loved one, than maybe I can find a way to forgive Dave for what he had done.

I didn't really know what to say to Dave, but I didn't want to call him on whim, only to realize later that the forgiveness I was feeling was only temporary. So I waited another year after my initial conversation with my sister to decide if my feelings were true. After enough time had passed, and my feelings hadn't changed about forgiving Dave, I talked to my sister about it again. I told her that I felt I was ready to call Dave, and believed that in order to have closure on Darren's death, and truly recover, I not only had to forgive Dave in my heart- which I did but I had to let him know that I forgave him. I realized that the bottom line for my healing was to focus on Dave's *intention*. It was not premeditated murder, which made a big difference. Kim agreed, and suggested that I write down everything I wanted to say, in case I got too emotional. Now I had to work up the nerve.

A short time later, Rico told me that Dave was having a lot of problems in his marriage and also with his health. Rico thought that the root of it all was Dave's failure to deal with Darren's death. I was glad to hear that Dave was finally being affected by it, as he had been so stoic up until now, and never showed any emotion. I said that I had been thinking of calling him. I asked Rico for Dave's phone number, but asked him not to tell Dave, because I wasn't sure if I was ready to make contact. Kristine asked about me all the time, Rico said, and she missed me a lot. Although I felt bad about our friendship falling out, as long as she was with Dave, I hadn't wanted to talk to her. It was too painful. I missed her too, and thought that I might call her first, and ask how Dave would feel about talking to me.

One day, I wrote out all of the things that I wanted to say to Dave; and while Trevor was taking his nap, I gathered my strength, sat down on my bed with my list and a box of Kleenex, and called to talk to Kristine. But when Dave himself picked up the phone and said, "Hello," in that old familiar voice, I chickened out and hung up. I was sure Dave would be at work. My heart was pounding, and my breathing sped up as I contemplated calling back. I took a few deep breaths, and told myself that Dave was the person I really needed to talk to. So I picked up the phone with my hands trembling, and hit redial.

"Hello." It was Dave again. "Dave?" I asked, even though I knew who it was. "Yes," he replied. "Do you know who this is?" I asked. He said, "No." "It's Laura," I replied. His voice got excited, and he said, "Oh my God, Laura, I knew it was you, but I had to hear you say it." We both started crying uncontrollably. I got out my notes, and through my teary vision, I could barely see what I had written. I told him that Rico had given me his number, that I had learned he was having some problems, and so I decided it might be a good time for me to call. Between sobs, I managed to tell him that not only did I forgive him for killing Darren, but that I needed to tell him this, in order to have closure. And that while I still believed he needed to be accountable for the accident, I knew in my heart that he had never intended to kill Darren. He had loved Darren like a brother. He really needed to hear that. I asked if time had given him any more clarity about what exactly happened the night of the accident.

He went over his story again for me; and although there was nothing new, he now took responsibility for what he had done and apologized to me. I really needed to hear that. We cried and talked for almost two hours. Kristine had recently moved out. Dave, who had been home unexpectedly, was having a really bad day. He couldn't believe that I had picked this moment to call. My phone call, he said, made his day-no, his life! I ended up trying to help *him* deal with what *he* was going through. I explained how his grief was the source of his problems and that he needed to talk about it, and somehow learn to forgive himself. I knew he was in pain, and that I could give him some of the help he desperately needed.

We talked about Darren a lot, and reminisced about some great times we'd all shared together. We talked about our children, and congratulated each other on being parents. Our sons are only four months apart in age. Dave said that Kristine missed me, and needed me in her life, and that she would love to talk to me too. I promised I would call her soon. I let him know that if he needed to talk to me, he should feel free to call. Healing the pain of old, unresolved wounds was what we both needed. I felt so good when I put the receiver down. This was the best phone call I had ever made in my entire life!

I was so elated; I was walking on a cloud. My mom (who now lived with us), my brother Joey and I took Trevor down to Zuma Beach in Malibu about an hour after my conversation with Dave. It was a cloudy, gloomy day, but there was one ray of sunlight beaming down through the clouds and lighting up the ocean, and there were dolphins playing in the sunlit water. Darren's mother always associated dolphin sightings at their condo in Florida as a sign from Darren. On that day, so did

I. It was amazing how that ray of light cut through all the gloom. I thought of it as a direct parallel to my phone call. My call to Dave cut through years of darkness and grief, and left light in its place. I felt so at peace, and so proud of myself. I was overflowing with joy. I felt an inner warmth and love which I can only describe as God, filling up my entire being, and I knew that Darren was right there with me, smiling.

The next day, my mom and I took Trevor to the park near our house. As I pushed him on the swing, I looked up in the sky, and saw a giant rainbow encircling the sun, taking up half of the sky. I pointed it out to my mom. She had seen it too. There were tears in my eyes, it was so spectacular. I'd never seen anything like it before. It was a sign for me from Darren saying, 'Way to go, Kiddo.' I reminded my mom of what the priest had said at the funeral: "I have put the rainbow in the sky as a sign of my everlasting love for you." She started crying too. The strange thing was, it was a clear, sunny day, with not a cloud in the sky; and it hadn't rained in a long time. I knew that the rainbow was meant for me.

A few days later, I called Kristine. We picked up right where we left off. She thanked me for calling Dave, and said I'd never know what that phone call had meant to him. We talked for over an hour, catching up and reminiscing. It was wonderful. I never expected the act of forgiveness to change my life as much as it did. My intent was self-healing and closure, but the result was greater than I ever dreamed! My willingness to open my heart and forgive had a ripple effect. It touched many other hearts. Kristine and I promised to keep in touch… and have we ever! We exchange pictures of our children, send each other letters, and talk on the phone. She even came to visit us in California with her son. It felt so good to have my friend back in my life.

The day after my phone call to Kristine, I was driving alone in my car when for some reason I looked up at the sky. I saw another identical rainbow circling the sun, just like the one mom and I had seen after my phone call to Dave. Again, sunny day… no clouds… no rain. This was no coincidence. I felt certain that Darren had put the rainbow there.

Dave and Kristine eventually divorced and I have kept in touch with them both as friends. I told Kristine that I had written this book, and she wanted to read it. I sent her a copy, and she loved it and thought that Dave should also read it. I wasn't sure if I was ready for him to do so, but the next time I spoke with him, he said that he was ready to read it, and I mailed him a copy. A few months later, I received an unexpected letter in the mail from Dave's mom, thanking me for the book. She had asked Dave if she could read it. Her letter made me cry and brought the forgiveness part of this experience full circle for me. In the letter she said that she wanted me to know that they have never forgotten Darren or how his loss has affected me and Darren's family, and that they also have daily reminders of what has happened that they live with. She also thanked me for forgiving her son, and told me how much it has helped him heal from the torment that he has endured. I was blown away by her letter, and her courage to send it.

Dealing with my own pain, I had lost sight of their loss. It was a comfort to hear that they also grieve deeply for his death, and that they haven't forgotten. I've learned that just because people don't tell you how much they are hurting, it can't be assumed that they are not. I had no idea how deeply Darren's death had effected so many other people, for so long. I also asked Dave what he thought of the book. He said that when I sent it, it was too hard for him to read the whole thing, but he read all of the parts pertaining to him, and they were all true. He had no problem with anything I wrote, and thinks it will help a lot of people. It meant a lot to me to have his blessing, after some of the things I had said about him. Now, when we talk on the phone, he still calls me a Carnie, and we joke around like we used to, and have a unique bond that many people wouldn't understand. Just staying in touch is healing for us both.

It's ironic, but forgiving Dave was really more of a gift to me than it was to him. I thought I was doing him a favor by forgiving him; but this simple act has had so many positive effects on my life. I feel as though a weight has been lifted off of me. I no longer carry around the harsh burden of anger. Letting go of my pain did not mean letting go of the love that Darren and I shared. It has also helped me forgive other people in my life who might have slighted me in some way. "If I can forgive Dave for killing my husband," I tell myself, "I can surely forgive this, too."

Forgiving Dave has brought me peace. It has allowed me to let go of the past and truly move on with my life. I read somewhere that "to forgive is to set the prisoner free and discover that the prisoner was you." That gave me chills, and it really stuck with me. I also received the added bonus of helping another human being heal old wounds, and to top it off, I restored and strengthened my bonds with a great friend, Kristine. I couldn't feel more proud of myself.

There is a little more to this part of the story. If you are reading this sentence, then you are reading the second edition of the book. The original *Widowed Too Soon* came out in August of 2004, and I updated a few things for the second edition in 2006. The following things happened after the original story was published.

In October, 2005, I was going on a trip back to Wisconsin for my 20-year high school reunion, and was going to be staying with my sister in Illinois. I thought that it would also be a good opportunity to see Dave again. Although we had been talking on the phone occasionally for the past five years, we hadn't seen each other in over 10 years, since shortly after the accident. We were both excited and were looking forward to our healing reunion.

The week before my trip, Kristine called me to tell me that Dave had been in a life-threatening motorcycle accident, and was in a coma in the Intensive Care Unit. They didn't know if he was going to survive. He underwent surgery, including removing six feet of intestines. Things did not look good.

Before my trip, in a conversation with Dave, I had told him about a new energy healing technique I had been doing called Reiki, and he mentioned that he wanted me to try it on him when I came to visit. I had no idea at the time what was going to transpire before I got there.

When I got to Illinois, Kristine told me that although a week had passed since the accident, Dave was still in Intensive Care, and had to be put into an induced coma following another surgery. She told me that Dave had mentioned to her before the accident that I was now a Reiki Master, and that he wanted me to do some healing on him when I came to visit. If ever he needed a healing, it was now.

I decided to go see him in the hospital, even if he didn't get to see me. I had been expecting just to go out to lunch with him somewhere to have this part of the story come full circle, but what was about to happen was nothing short of a miracle.

I went to the hospital, and was greeted with hugs and thanks by Kristine in the ICU, along with Dave's mom, and Dave's girlfriend, Kristina, who had been on the back of the motorcycle during the accident. She was in a wheelchair with a badly broken leg and cuts on her face. Apparently, a woman in a minivan pulled out from a driveway and plowed right into them, and kept on driving. The accident happened less than a mile from the house that Darren and I were living in when he died.

Anyway, Dave's mom told me that Dave was sedated and was in and out of consciousness, but that earlier that day, he was awake and looking up at the ceiling. She asked him if he saw Darren, and he nodded "yes" before going under again. I knew Darren was going to be there for this monumental "reunion."

I was escorted by my "sister" Kristine into Dave's hospital room. I barely recognized him with all the tubes in his nose and throat. He was in bad shape. I looked around his room, and saw pictures of his two kids. I knew what I was about to do was for them. Dave couldn't go yet. The TV was on above the bed, and the monitor next to his bed listed all his vital information.

I decided to get started on the healing right away before the nurses came back and asked what I was doing. Kristine stood on one side of him, holding his hand, and I began. I called in Darren to assist me in healing his friend. I used a few different methods of energy work; a combination of Reiki, Quantum Touch, and of course, prayer. I began the breath work and started running the energy, with one had on Dave's stomach, and the other on his forehead.

Suddenly, the TV began to change channels on its own (which had been stuck on the same channel for two days), the lights in the room flickered, and the monitor flashed and changed numbers. Kristine and I looked at each other and smiled, and said together "Darren's here." (You will understand this reference more after reading the chapter called "The Touch Lamp.") I felt my hands heat up as I worked on Dave's wounds and broken foot for the next 30 minutes or so.

During the healing, I felt so much energy running through me, and I felt Darren's energy working with me. I remember thinking, ten years ago, I wanted to kill you with my bare hands, now I'm using those very hands to heal you, and I'm praying for you to live instead of die. Talk about full circle. This act for me was more healing and powerful than any reunion could have possibly been. Dave twitched a lot during the healing, but never regained consciousness while I was there. I hoped that on some level, he knew I was there. Kristine said that it was the most beautiful thing she'd ever seen.

After I returned home, Dave made a miraculous recovery. When he could speak again (he had a tracheotomy), he called Kristine, and in tears, said that he had to talk to me right away. When I got home from work later that night, which was actually Dave's birthday, he said, "I don't know what you did to me with those magic hands of yours, but you and Darren brought me back." He explained that they had only given him two hours to live when he got to the hospital. After I was there and did the healing on him, he made the fastest recovery they had ever seen, and he went from the ICU to a rehabilitation facility; and went from a wheelchair, to a walker, to a cane, to walking on his own in a month. The hospital staff was amazed. Dave credits this to me. I may have helped him heal, but he also healed me.

So, I got to see Dave on that trip, but he didn't get to see me. Ironically, (or not) I had to go back to Chicago four months later for a fitness certification on the golden anniversary of Darren's death. It was 11 years on February 11, 2006. I called Dave to tell him I was coming, and we planned our reunion- again. As my plane was touching down in Chicago, my cell phone rang. It was Kristine. She didn't know I was coming because it was very last minute. I was only there for two days, and didn't have any time to socialize, but we made a date to go to breakfast, the day I was to see Dave for lunch.

I had Kim drive me over to Dave's house, partly because I didn't have a car, but also, she was there for support and as a "safety net." I was unsure if I was going to possibly have some repressed anger or animosity toward Dave, being back in the town we used to live in. But, I didn't. We got to Dave's house, and hugged hello. He had the biggest grin on his face. He showed us his scars from the accident and surgeries, and we talked to his younger son for a while. Dave's girlfriend, Kristina was also there, and obviously happy for Dave to be experiencing this. Dave guided us around town to show me how everything has grown since I lived there. We even drove past our old house, which was now painted an ugly color. It was all very surreal. Then we went to lunch at a local greasy spoon, which had been one of Darren's favorites.

Dave's older son came to see me at the restaurant. I couldn't believe he was in high school. I remember the day he was born. We also called Rico from the restaurant, and he was so happy to hear from me. I think he was in shock to hear who I was dining with, and where. I had to catch my flight home, so we drove Dave back to his house. I got out of the car to give him a hug goodbye. I knew that my energy toward Dave had completely shifted. As I was standing there, hugging the man who was driving the car that killed my husband, a voice in my head clearly said, "Now this is the true meaning of forgiveness." I felt my eyes tearing up. What a beautiful lesson to learn. I thank Dave for allowing me to learn this lesson with him.

I received this new definition of forgiveness from a friend shortly after my meeting with Dave: "Forgiveness isn't a verb, but a noun. It isn't something to "do" but a place to get to with the grace of God. It's the light at the end of the tunnel, the feeling of peace, the breath of fresh air that you come to when the healing process is complete and you are ready to let go of that which was binding you." I couldn't agree more.

Part Five

<u>Spiritual Transformation</u>

About My Spiritual Transformation

"We are not human beings having a spiritual experience.
We are spiritual beings having a human experience."

—Teilhard de Chardin

This section includes all the "after-death stuff." Some people will want to skip right to this section, which is understandable, but the rest of the story will make more sense if you know the background information from the beginning of the book. Trust me. I'm the type of person who likes to read ahead to the good stuff too, but it will be more enjoyable if you start at the beginning and read the whole story. So, all you peekers, go back!

Our beliefs about life, death, and the afterlife are shaped throughout our lifetime and are closely linked to our prior experiences with death, our religious beliefs, and the beliefs of people who are close to us. The depth of our grief depends to some degree on these beliefs. Questioning my prior beliefs and finding my own truth were my keys to finally being at peace with Darren's death. The questions that arose from losing Darren were not answered to my satisfaction by the belief system that my church taught, so I decided to look elsewhere for answers.

Because none of the grief books that I read following Darren's death acknowledged the spiritual aspects of the grief process, discussed the afterlife, or the possibility of any type of after-death communication, I turned to other types of books for the answers I needed. The comfort that these books gave me by assuring me that Darren was okay, and that he still existed in another form, was immeasurable. But reading these books were only the beginning of my spiritual evolution.

I want to incorporate the spiritual aspects of loss in this book because understanding what happens after death has been so vital to my healing. This section of the book was the hardest for me to write because I know that I still have a lot to learn. Nevertheless, I want to share what helped me heal, in the hope that my story may help others with their struggles. I have had many extraordinary experiences which have led me to a deeper understanding of the afterlife, and of how we are still connected to our loved ones, even in "death."

A major part of my final healing was the result of being able to connect with Darren in the spirit world, through the assistance of spiritual mediums and through direct after-death communication. My hope in sharing such personal information is that someone without the means to have this type of experience may benefit vicariously through my experience, and know that the truths that I discovered are universal, and not exclusive to my loss. In fact, over 60% of the population reports that they have felt some connection or communication with someone that has passed on.

It is not my intention to shove my spiritual beliefs down your throat, or suggest that I have all of the answers; I certainly do not. My own spiritual transformation didn't happen overnight. It has been over a decade now since Darren passed on, and I finally feel like I am beginning to understand things. Connecting to people in the spirit world may not be for everyone, but it changed my life and everything I had previously believed in.

I want to share with you what helped me through my grief, and what I believe to be the truth. If my experience helps someone, I am gratified. You don't need to be an expert on a topic to know the truth. I didn't study metaphysics for years; rather, I had experiences that helped me connect to Darren in his existence on the other side. I knew he was there, and I was comforted.

My intention in this section is to open people up to a possibility that may help them get through their grief. I'm not trying to prove something. It would be futile to try to prove the existence of something you can't scientifically prove. How can you "prove" that you love someone? You can't, you just know it in your heart. Sometimes, seeing is believing; but other times, you have to believe first, in order to see.

Religious Beliefs

"Change your thinking; change your life."

—*Ernest Holmes*

(Warning: This chapter may offend devout Catholics.)

I don't intend to bash anyone else's religious beliefs- people can believe whatever they want to believe. I'm simply sharing what happened to me, and how my beliefs were challenged by my husband's death. Nothing brings your beliefs more into focus than the death of a loved one. It makes you examine life itself. Our religious upbringing helps shape how we grieve. One has everything to do with the other. A belief in God and the afterlife are at the heart of most religions, it's all of the manmade parts of organized religion that are damaging. Looking back, I find it no wonder that my grief was so painful and lengthy.

I was raised in the Catholic religion, but I wasn't a regular churchgoer. I was baptized, had my first communion, and was confirmed Catholic, however I never fully embraced the religion. I often wondered why there were so many different religious denominations, and why everyone believed that their religion was "right" and the others were "wrong," and that only believers in their religion made it to heaven when they died. When I asked about this in religious classes I attended at our church, I never got a straight answer. At least, I never got one that made any sense.

As a kid, going to church was a hassle. I had to wake up early and wear a dress, which I hated. Then, during the entire service we had to kneel, and then sit, and then stand; and then sit, and then kneel, and then stand. I thought, I'm tired, can't I just sit here? I could never find what page we were on in the book, and I didn't want to say the wrong thing out loud, or talk out of turn, so I usually just mouthed everything, so I looked like I knew what I was doing. Receiving communion grossed me out. I didn't want to put the wafer in my mouth after the priest had touched it, or had his fingers in someone else's mouth, and I didn't want to eat Christ's body. Gross! I mainly just enjoyed the music and singing along.

I didn't feel connected to God in church because I was too worried about doing and saying everything right. Only in the comfort of my own bedroom, as I prayed before I went to sleep every night did I feel a spiritual connection to God. Then, along came the introduction of the creation vs. evolution debate in school to add even more confusion. I had always excelled in science, and was pretty analytically-minded. So, when Darwin's Theory of Evolution was taught, I thought that it sounded far more logical than what the church had taught me. In college, I had an anthropology class which further explained the evolution of man, and I saw "evidence" in the form of prehistoric remains that had been discovered. I always wondered, "Why couldn't both theories be partially true?" Couldn't God have created the universe, and then everything in it naturally evolves? Why did it have to be one or the other? It was yet another thing that made me question my religious upbringing.

As an adult, before Darren's death, I felt that the Catholic Church's beliefs were rigid, outdated, hypocritical, chauvinistic, and elitist. Don't even get me started on the whole sexual molestation scandal involving Catholic priests. Talk about hypocrisy! The message I got from my church was: if you follow our rules, you'll go to heaven when you die. That's what church was all about, earning your place in heaven. But who in their right mind would debate the church? No one knows for sure what happens when you die, so people just go along with what the church tells them. They're supposedly the experts. If you disobeyed the rules when you were living, when you died, off you would go to the fiery pit of hell with the 99.999% of the other people on the planet who were too ignorant to share and slavishly follow these beliefs. Unless, of course, you went to confession, then you would be forgiven and receive a free pass to heaven no matter how many sins you committed. That sounds about right! (Sarcasm.)

I considered myself to be a disgruntled Catholic, and I didn't go to church often. The church's rules contradicted many of my personal beliefs. Still, Catholicism was the only religion I knew, and I didn't want to rock the boat. I believed in God and prayed every night, but I always felt more spiritual than religious. Spirituality, to me, was more about my personal relationship with God, and my personal search to find greater meaning and purpose for my existence.

Organized religion seemed to be full of man-made rules designed to control people by using guilt and fear as a means to that end. Organized religion is a business which depends on money to keep it going. Who do you think pays for all of those beautiful churches?

After Darren's death, I was forced to examine my beliefs about the afterlife. I realized that it was my religious upbringing, particularly the church's views on heaven and hell that were causing my hang-ups about processing my loss, preventing me from healing. It is hard to erase 27 years of believing that if you did certain things while you were living, your soul would go to heaven when you died; and if you did or didn't do certain other things, you'd go to hell. I couldn't believe that God, who I was supposed to love and honor, could be so harsh and judgmental. That was not my idea of unconditional love.

When my parents got married, they were of different religions. My mom converted from Lutheran to Catholic so they could raise their children in one religion. She told me that when she was going to religious classes to convert, a Catholic priest told her that in order to go to heaven when she died, she had to be baptized in a Catholic Church, and that her baptism in the Lutheran Church meant nothing. He also told her that if she got into argument with someone and then died before going to confession, her soul would go to hell. She didn't agree with these things, but had to go along with it. This always bothered her, but she felt she had no choice but to pretend that she believed it.

The whole idea of confession always intimidated me. I was never sure what exactly were considered sins, and why a priest in a little booth had a more direct line to God than I did. Whenever I had to go to confession, I never felt that I committed any sins, but had to confess to other things that weren't sins in order to be in there. I wasn't breaking any of the Ten Commandments, but like any other kid, I occasionally swore or lied to my parents, but apparently, those things are equivalent to killing someone.

If I believed what my church taught, Darren's soul was now in hell. He didn't go to church every Sunday, had premarital sex, used birth control, took God's name in vain on occasion, and didn't confess these "sins" to a priest before he died. Why would I want to belong to a church that would like me to believe this? I didn't want to believe that my husband's soul was in hell. These are not very comforting thoughts for a grieving young widow. I was confused. Which was it? Was Darren's soul now in heaven because he was baptized as a baby in a Catholic church as the priest at the funeral suggested? Or was he in hell because he did or didn't do all of these other things while he was living? Talk about mixed messages! My religion seemed to fail me when I needed it most.

My religious beliefs were also challenged after Trevor was born. Matt and I didn't belong to a particular church, since we had different religious backgrounds, and I thought "How can I teach a child about God, religion, and spirituality if I don't have all the answers myself?" There are more reasons than I've already mentioned as to why I felt so detached from the Catholic Church, but I think I've said enough. It was this detachment that led me on a quest for answers, and eventually to a place where I felt I belonged. I wanted my son to love God, not fear him. I didn't want him to live most of his life, as I had, believing he would go to hell when he died if he didn't follow all the church's rules. The God I loved was not vengeful. I felt I had to recover from the distorted images of God that I had learned in my Catholic upbringing.

Matt was raised as a Christian Scientist. Although he was no longer practicing, he was also more spiritual than religious, and didn't believe in all of his church's man-made rules, particularly the church's belief in shunning medicine. Neither of us was interested in converting to the other's religion. The major dilemma for me after the birth of our son was regarding baptism. Christian Scientists along with many other religions don't baptize infants. Matt wanted me to explain why it was necessary to baptize Trevor, and I honestly couldn't find an answer. It no longer made sense to me. Why would I want to raise a child in a religion to which I no longer felt a connection? The Catholic religion would have you believe that if you don't baptize an infant in a Catholic Church, and the child dies, their soul will go to hell. Matt's religion didn't teach that, and I honestly didn't believe it myself. Although I felt a bit guilty about it, I did not have Trevor baptized, since I would only be doing it to ease the fears and hang-ups of others.

Trevor was too young to know the difference, so I decided to do some research about other religions and beliefs. I felt that there had to be something else out there for us. Freedom of religion is one of the greatest things about living in America. You are not stuck believing what your parents believed. You have the freedom to choose for yourself, and believe what resonates within you. I read books about other major religions, and even went to some churches I thought I might like; but none of them seemed to fit right.

Then I found a book that made sense to me. It was called, *Finding Your Religion- When the Faith You Grew up with Has Lost Its Meaning*, by Reverend Scotty Mclennan. Reverend Mclennan related stories about people who were on the same path I was on. He spoke of spiritual development as a process- as a journey, not a destination. I liked the metaphor he used of religion being like climbing a mountain. There are a lot of paths up the mountain, but the view from the top is the same, no matter how you get there. I could relate to that. I began to feel like I had choices about my spiritual and religious beliefs. I didn't need all of the answers today.

I did find a lot of answers in other places as well that made me feel justified in changing religions. Just to be sure, my mom and I went to an Easter service at a Catholic Church near our home in California in 1999, the year after Trevor was born. I remember sitting there listening in disbelief to some of the things the priest was saying and wondering if all these people actually believed this stuff, or if they were just going along with it. I purposely didn't go up for communion and knew that this would be the last time I would attend a Catholic service.

I felt a bit blasphemous turning away from the church I had known my whole life, but I wasn't rejecting the idea of God, just the organized religion I had grown up with. I was free to choose that, right? I only needed to look at my son to know that God existed. Then, it dawned on me: I was looking for a church to give me what I already had inside of me. Once I stopped looking outside and started looking inside, I found what I was really looking for: a connection to God and to Darren in the spirit world. I had only to look inside my own heart to find God. I had been searching for the meaning of life and why I was here, and I wasn't finding those answers in any church. Don't misunderstand me, please. I know that others have a profound connection to God while they are in church, which is great. It just wasn't my experience with the religion I was raised in. I needed to find a different path to God.

When you are a child, you don't question your religion. You believe that what you are told is truth. As an adult, I found that I had choices. I didn't have to blindly believe things that didn't make sense to me. When we question something, one of two things happens: we end up either changing our minds about it, or embracing it more fully. When it is our religious beliefs that are in question; if they are true, they will stand up to the scrutiny; if they are faulty, they will be easily thrown out to make room for new ideas. In my case, the more new-thought, spiritual ideas that I was opening up to were contradicting the religious beliefs with which I had grown up. For me, it was the spiritual beliefs that made sense and resonated within me. It was time for a change. I almost felt as if I needed to be deprogrammed.

I don't believe that any one religion is right. There is truth in all religions. Most major world religions have two things in common. First, is a belief in God, or whatever you want to call our creator. Second, is a belief that the spirit transcends death. My difficulties concerned certain church's man-made rules, trying to be passed off as God's rules. I was able to see the difference.

I was eventually able to make peace with my religious dilemma. I just listened to my heart, and believed what resonated as truth within me. I no longer felt guilty about not wanting to follow the Catholic religion. You don't need to belong to a particular religion to have faith and a connection to God. I know people who go to church every Sunday, and who are not even sure if they believe in God. They are just going through the motions. They believe they will earn a place in heaven by going to church every week, regardless of their beliefs. I equate that philosophy with the saying: "Going into a church doesn't make you religious; any more than going into a garage makes you a mechanic." I believe that it is how you live, not how you worship that matters the most. God is everywhere, and in all things. He hears what is in your heart, from wherever you are. You don't need to be in a church for God to hear your prayers.

My connection to God, to those in spirit, and to the universe is stronger now than it has ever been, and I found that connection within me, where it has always been. Ironically, once I accepted the idea that I didn't need a church to find a connection to God, I was introduced to a church whose teachings both Matt and I could agree with. We decided we could raise our children according to ideas and values taught there. Matt would never convert, but the new religion was a lot closer to his background than Catholicism was. However, my mom and I became members of the church, as she had never embraced Catholicism either. We feel good going to our church and we truly enjoy it. We don't feel that we are "bad" if we don't go. That is the way it should be. We feel that we are a part of a spiritual community. There is no dogma or doctrine.

A supportive spiritual environment is important for children, which is why finding a church of like-minded individuals was important to me. I just needed to find one that resonated with my lives and beliefs. If my children decide when they are adults that our church is not their choice, I'll encourage them to search for their own answers.

I was hesitant to divulge the name of the church we now belong to, because the answer for me may not be the answer for you. We are all on our own spiritual paths. However, I'm sure there are a lot of people out there who are in the same boat I was in, and would appreciate being pointed in another direction, as I was. So, for anyone interested in checking it out, it is called Religious Science, founded by Ernest Holmes (author of the cryptic quote at the beginning of the chapter.) The religion is founded on his book, *"The Science of Mind."* To learn more, do a Google search or go to the website www.religiousscience.org.

The Paranormal

"Sit down before fact like a little child, and be prepared to give up every preconceived notion, follow humbly wherever and to whatever abysses nature leads, or else you shall learn nothing."

—*T.H. Huxley*

My religious beliefs were not the only factors responsible for shaping my ideas about life, death, and the afterlife. The experiences of people close to me and the stories I had heard about the "paranormal," or things that couldn't be explained rationally, were also strong influences.

We've all heard our share of ghost stories. There was always something scary or evil behind them. The ghosts were never friendly like Casper. Certain houses in town were said to be haunted, and you didn't want to go inside, especially at night. Also, I watched plenty of scary movies that supported these concerns, such as *"Poltergeist"* and *"The Amityville Horror."* So, I grew up thinking that spirits were something to be feared. As I got older, I began hearing some intriguing stories that I couldn't explain within the context of my belief system.

After Darren died, I recalled stories from friends and family members who claimed to have had paranormal experiences. I asked them to repeat their stories. I needed to know there was more to this existence than just life on earth. I needed to be sure that Darren still existed; otherwise, what was the point of our being here? I had started reading books on near-death experiences and was opening up my mind to new possibilities, but as a natural skeptic, I wanted "proof" from people I knew personally.

One of my most memorable experiences with the paranormal occurred during college. My senior year, I lived in a big house with eight roommates. One of them had a brother who was killed in a car accident that year. It was a horrible time for her, and we were all very concerned about her mental state. At one point, she awoke in the middle of the night screaming, saying that her brother had appeared at the foot of her bed and then ran and disappeared under the door. Some of my roommates thought she was losing her mind, but I believed her.

She also had a very vivid dream about her brother in which he related details of the accident which no one knew. She insisted that it was more than a dream. She had such a peaceful look about her when she related it to me. She also said she saw a partial apparition of her brother from the chest up appear on the wall while she was talking to her boyfriend. She was so startled that she couldn't speak. She could only point for her boyfriend to look at what she saw. He saw nothing. I called her after Darren died and asked her to review these incidents for me. I knew that she was very sane and hoped that maybe someday I would have a similar experience with Darren. Hearing her story gave me hope and comfort.

Another story I remembered was one that my friend Brenda told me. We had been friends since high school and just like my college roommate, Brenda was completely sane, so I trusted that what she told me was true. When Brenda was 16, her grandfather died in the hospital. He had been on morphine and was totally incoherent, so the family went home because there was nothing they could do at that point. The hospital called the family at 2:00 a.m., saying that Brenda's grandfather had died. Her mother came in her room to tell her the news. Brenda went back to sleep, and when she woke up, she saw her grandfather standing at the foot of her bed. She also clearly saw his reflection in the closet mirror behind him. She glanced away for a second to look at the clock to make sure she wasn't dreaming, and when she looked back, he was gone. She said that she was not scared at all, but comforted by his appearance. She found out later that her grandmother saw him in her bedroom as well, but it scared her so much that she never slept in that room again.

Another story that stuck with me came from my sister. Kim's sanity is questionable. (Just kidding.) One of her good friends in high school died in a freak car accident. She fell off the hood of a moving car that another friend was driving in the high school parking lot and was accidentally run over and killed. Kim visited her friend's grave one evening and while she was kneeling down and crying, she felt a hand on her shoulder. She turned around to see who it was, but there was no one there. Kim got so spooked, that she ran to her car and swore she would never return at night again. I was comforted by the idea that a spirit is able to touch us, and that we can feel its touch.

I also remembered my grandma telling me many years earlier that she had a near-death experience during surgery. She mentioned something about floating above her body as she looked down on herself on the operating table, and about traveling through a tunnel toward a bright light, and seeing bright colors all around. She said that she heard the doctors calling her back. They later told her that she had been clinically dead for a brief period. At the time, I thought she must have been having some drug induced hallucinations, but now I was intrigued to hear her story again.

I remembered something else: after my old boyfriend Rick died, I visited his grave on his birthday the year after he died. It was the first time I had been there, and I wasn't sure where his grave was. As I searched for his headstone, I saw a child's pinwheel sticking up out of the ground, near where it was supposed to be. Suddenly, although the day was calm, the pinwheel started spinning out of control. Startled, I looked around to see if the leaves on the trees were moving and I even licked my finger and held it up to see if I felt a breeze, but there was no wind. I walked toward the spinning pinwheel, and found that it was right next to Rick's headstone. I thought that was a little odd. I crouched down, shed a few tears, and talked to him for a while. I remember saying, "I'll see you when I get there." The pinwheel had slowed down and even stopped while I was there, but as I got up and started to walk away, it started spinning really fast again. I kept looking back at it as I got closer to my car, and it was still going strong. I took this as Rick's way of getting my attention, acknowledging me and saying, "Hi," even if no one else would believe my story if I told them.

My overwhelming desire to connect with Darren on the other side (if there was another side) kept me searching for answers. I couldn't rest until I found them. Every night, I prayed to God for a sign that Darren was okay. I don't know what I was expecting, maybe a full-bodied apparition of Darren appearing to me and telling me exactly what I needed to hear. That would be too easy. I wanted a sign, but I feared it at the same time, because I didn't know what would happen. I probably got plenty of signs, but I wasn't aware of them, or else I dismissed them as something else because I wasn't fully convinced that after-death communication was possible. Whenever some weird thing would happen to make me wonder if it might be some sort of sign or spiritual connection, I would write it off as something else.

For example, shortly after Darren died, I would be fixing my hair in my bathroom mirror and one of the vanity lights above mirror would blow out in front of me. Mind you, the house was only a few months old; lights shouldn't blow out that soon. The first time, I thought it was a fluke; but then it happened again, and again. This scared me, so I chalked it up to faulty wiring or bad light bulbs. It couldn't possibly be Darren giving me a sign, could it? No, I preferred to think it was just my imagination, or a bad electrician.

Also, shortly after Darren's death, I'd be lying in bed reading or watching TV with Dakota at my feet. Suddenly, Dakota would stand up and sniff the air, and look around the room, then look at me; or suddenly jump down on the floor and start sniffing around, and then jump back up and cuddle up next to me. I'd say to her, "Did you see something, girl?" She sure acted as though she had. It was kind of spooky to think that Darren might have been in the room, and that Dakota had sensed or seen him. The first time this happened, I got spooked, and I hid under my covers and told him to go away. Later, the thought of him being around comforted me greatly. I wondered why I couldn't see him. It reminded me of the movie "*Ghost*," where Demi Moore can't see Patrick Swayze's spirit, even though he is always with her.

The most dramatic example of something paranormal happened a few months after Darren died. I was getting a massage in my bedroom from Rico's sister, Kathy, who was also friends with Darren in high school. I was lying face down on the massage table at the foot of my bed talking to Kathy about Darren. Suddenly, her hands tensed up and she asked me "Which side of the bed was Darren's?" Thinking it was a strange question, I said, "Why do you ask that?" She said that she could see Darren sitting on the edge of the left side of the bed. (The left side was his side.) I said, "What do you mean you can see him? What is he doing?" She said he was just sitting there listening with his chin resting on his hand. She could see his spirit, she said, just as she had seen her grandmother's spirit after she died. I was pretty freaked out by the possibility that Darren had actually been in the room. Why could Kathy see him and I couldn't? Kathy was very calm about the whole thing, as though it were an everyday occurrence. A few moments later, she said that couldn't see him anymore, but we continued to talk about her other experiences like this.

In the months that followed, she helped me open up to new spiritual ideas. She always comforted me by assuring me that Darren was looking after me, and that he wanted me to be happy. She even met Matt and was very supportive of our relationship and gave him a few massages too. Her support was a wonderful gift! I wasn't sure at the time if I believed that she actually saw Darren, because I didn't see him; but it gave me hope that there really was more to this life. I was open to the possibility that other people had these types of gifts; it was just shocking to hear things like that in the beginning.

Finally, another incident occurred that made me wonder about spirit influence in our lives. I was out of town helping Moe move to Atlanta, and I had left Dakota with my in-laws. Being a Siberian Husky, born to run; Dakota somehow escaped and ran away. She was never let off her leash because she just bolted. My mother-in-law got in her car and tried to find her. She saw Dakota in a field near some railroad tracks, and knew that if Dakota crossed them she'd never catch her. She kept calling Dakota's name, but Dakota kept on running. My mother-in-law was crying and thinking, "How can I ever tell Laura that now her dog is gone, too?" Out of desperation she cried out "Darren, if you ever loved me, send your dog back to me!" Suddenly, the mischievous Dakota, who does what she wants, when she wants to, turned around and ran right to my mother-in-law! She knew in her heart that Darren had returned Dakota to her. She told me the story when I got home and I knew it was true. I don't know how I would have gotten through some days without Dakota, and it comforted me to think that Darren had made her come back home for me.

A lot of other strange things happened to me in the years after Darren's death, when I actually "got it," and I will discuss them later on; but even early on, things were happening that made me question everything I had previously believed or not believed. New possibilities were presenting themselves to me. I still had many unanswered questions and insecurities, but I believed that the answers were out there if only I chose to follow that path and discover them.

<u>Questioning</u>

"The first key to wisdom is this- constant and frequent questioning...
For by doubting, we are led to question, and by questioning,
we arrive at the truth."

—Peter Abelard

Soon after Darren's death, I started questioning my own existence and mortality. Death forces you to be introspective, to think about the bigger picture. When someone you love dies, it forces you to analyze your own life. The death of a loved one is a test of faith; and if your faith is weak to begin with, as mine was, you are in for a long journey.

Darren's death changed everything for me. It forced me to think about things that I wouldn't have put any energy into before, things that I had always believed I thought I was too young to ponder. In addition to the constant "Why me?" and "What if...?" I was now having philosophical dilemmas, as new questions kept surfacing:

- Why did Darren die?
- Was it really his time to go?
- What is my purpose for still being here?
- Does God have a plan for me?
- Was this part of the plan?
- Was I supposed to learn a lesson from this?
- Was I being punished?
- Was this some type of balancing of karma from a past life?
- Is there reincarnation?
- Will Darren reincarnate before I get there?
- If everything happens for a reason, what possible reason could there be for a 27-year old to lose her husband?
- If there are guardian angels, where was Darren's?
- When is it going to be my time to go?

- Are there really accidents or was this part of a grand plan?
- Where is Darren right now? Above me, next to me?
- Can he see me? Even when I'm going to the bathroom or having sex?
- Did he want me to get remarried? Is there jealousy in heaven?
- What does he do all day in heaven?
- Can he communicate with me somehow to let me know he is okay?
- Has he been trying to contact me, and I just don't get it?
- Can he be with me and his mom at the same time?
- If life is a circle, and the soul eternal, did I choose this life before entering it?
- Did I choose these circumstances for my own growth?
- Was I insane? (Just kidding.)

These were just some of the questions I asked myself after Darren's death. Some of them may sound silly or trite, but I actually thought about this stuff. My internal dialogue was totally chaotic. I needed to know the answers to all of these questions so I could replace this anxious, longing, aching feeling with some kind of peace. I didn't know if I would ever have all of the answers, but something was driving me to find out more.

After Darren died, people would say things like, "It was his time to go," or "On a soul level, a person knows it is their time to go and they start making preparations ahead of time." These ideas made me question some things that happened before Darren died, making me wonder if maybe he did know on some level that it was his time.

For example, there was that conversation we had about life insurance. Was that just a coincidence? It took place just before the accident. Also, before we moved into our new house, Darren insisted that we buy all of the furniture before we moved in. He wanted everything to be perfect, no empty rooms, and no loose ends. I couldn't understand why we couldn't move in first and then look for furniture. Was Darren making sure I was going to be settled and secure before he had to go?

Shortly before Darren's death, we were in bed one night, and he initiated a conversation about confessing all the things that either of us had ever done and either never admitted, or else lied about during our eight-year relationship. He said, "It's all water under the bridge now, we're married and have never been closer, so why not? I promise I won't get mad if you won't." I was glad that he felt so close to me, so secure with our love that he was willing to be completely honest. I'd always felt that he wasn't completely truthful about some things, and it turned out that I was right. It was as though we were wiping the slate clean, free of all secrets. After Darren died, I thought long and hard about this conversation. Was this part of his preparing to go?

I also recalled Darren's last comment to me on the night he died: "Don't forget to say good-bye to Dakota for me." What was that "for me" all about? Why couldn't he do it himself? Also on the night of the accident, Darren had said that his shower was the best he'd ever had, and that his spaghetti was the best he'd ever eaten. (It was from a jar.) Why had these things been so special that night? Did he somehow know that they'd be his last?

As I've mentioned, Darren had been so determined to go out that night. Earlier in the week he had said, "I don't care what you say, I'm going out on Friday night," as if I had ever told him he couldn't. The comment was out of character. Was he *supposed* to be riding with Dave? Even Rico and Dave thought that certain things that happened were uncharacteristic of Darren that night. Darren had driven on the way to the bar and had gotten lost, even though he had been there many times and knew his way around. Darren didn't smoke- but he smoked cigarettes that night. He'd also tried to pick a fight with some guy, which wasn't like him at all, and Rico had to step in to prevent things from going too far. Darren had told him, "You got my back, right man?" Also, just before Rico got in the other car with his friend, Darren poked Rico in the chest, and said, "I'll see you there, man."

This has haunted Rico ever since. Did he mean the other bar... or heaven? What tormented me for the longest time was that if Darren's blood alcohol level was zero, then why had he allowed Dave to drive his SUV, especially knowing- as he must have- that Dave had been drinking and smoking pot? Was it *supposed* to happen that way? Darren often tried to get me and other people to drive home when we went out to dinner, just because he was being lazy. But he had promised me he was going to drive that night. Why did he break his promise? Was there something bigger happening here?

Another oddity: four months before Darren died; the two of us were at a Halloween party, hosted by a girl I worked with. Her mom was a palm reader and told me during my reading that I wouldn't be with Darren forever, and that it had to do with him, not me. I was upset by this, and thought that Darren should have his palm read to see what she would tell him. He refused, saying "She'll probably tell me I'm going to die or something." A prophecy? My friend who hosted the party came to Darren's funeral and I remember saying to her, "I wish your mom could have predicted this." I'm sure she didn't have a clue what I was talking about.

I couldn't stop thinking about things like this. It's funny how the mind works under the stress of tragedy. My mind was debating the logical and the supernatural. I struggled with an inner conflict: was I reading too much into these things, or was something bigger involved? I didn't know, but I thought about it constantly. I kept trying to find a way to make sense out of what had happened, to make the pieces fit somehow, even if it meant stepping outside the lines of conventional thinking.

The Quest Continues

"The church says that the earth is flat, but I know that it is round,
for I have seen the shadow on the moon, and I have more faith
in a shadow than in the church."

—Ferdinand Magellan

I never stopped thinking about Darren; but after I met Matt, my quest for answers was put on hold for a while. My energies were concentrated on my relationship with Matt. For the time being, my grief would have to take a backseat. Oh, it reared its ugly head quite often, believe me, but I tried not to let it interfere with the new life I had begun with Matt. I thought I could leave my grief behind in Illinois when we moved to California. Guess again.

At that point in my life- four years after Darren's death- I was happily married to Matt, and we had Trevor, our beautiful first son. My life was good. At the same time, I knew I still had a lot of unresolved grief, and that I needed to find peace with it in order to be the best wife and mother I could be. It wasn't fair to Matt or Trevor for me to become upset or lost in my own world at times, for reasons they couldn't understand. I needed to work through many unresolved and complicated emotions. My religious and spiritual beliefs were still pretty sketchy; and I had not yet forgiven Dave.

My true spiritual transformation began when I read the book *Talking to Heaven*, by spiritual medium James Van Praagh, which I referred to earlier. Reading this book was an epiphany for me, an awakening to the truth. It was a real eye-opener to new possibilities for me. I felt such a sense of peace after reading it. From that point on, I was fascinated with and drawn to the spirit world. I was desperate to have my own reading by a medium, but I didn't want to be taken for a ride by some fraud who takes advantage of innocent grieving people. I wanted the real thing. I had to try this if it really was possible to communicate with Darren. I had so many unanswered questions, and no chance to say good-bye.

I also wanted proof that the spirit lives on. I needed to know for certain that heaven was not just another fairy tale; but unlike Santa Claus, the Easter Bunny,

167

and the Tooth Fairy, you have to wait until you are dead to find out that it is not real. That would just be way too cruel. Although my grief left me emotionally vulnerable, I didn't just fall off the turnip truck. I was an intelligent, educated person. I used to think that only weirdoes were into this type of thing. Now, I realized that people who seek assistance from mediums are those who have lost someone they loved. Who else would have the desire to talk to dead people? Love is the driving force here. Unfortunately, the unscrupulous charlatans out there spoil it for the truly gifted mediums. I needed to be cautious.

I went to James Van Praagh's website only to discover that he had a three-year waiting list and no longer did private readings. Disappointed, I kept reading books by other mediums. Each one strengthened my conviction that it really was possible to contact deceased loved ones on the other side. Although I believed the stories I read about other people's experiences, I wanted to have my own reading to completely erase my skepticism that communicating with the dead was real, and to give me the comfort in knowing that Darren was indeed safe on the other side.

I shared my new ideas, as well as the medium's books with Darren's mom. We have developed a very special bond since Darren's death. She had always said that we were each other's link to Darren. I still call her "Mom," and always will, for she has been like a mother to me since I was 19 years old. She is to me, as I am to her, the one person who understands the need to piece together the bigger picture behind Darren's death. We talk about all aspects of our loss and we have been there for each other listening like no one else can. We can discuss all the spiritual aspects that accompany a death, with no judgment from one another. Together we explore the spiritual side of life, sharing our thoughts and experiences, our tears, and our healing.

I began researching websites that relate to spirituality and grief. One day, while I was looking up James Van Praagh's website to see what was new, I noticed that he had a section called "referrals." I trusted him, and I figured that his referrals would be legitimate. One of the referrals he listed was a man named Brian E. Hurst, who lived not too far from me. I wrote down his name and phone number for future reference, thinking that when I was ready for my own reading, I'd call him.

In 1999 and early 2000, James Van Praagh published two more books. In both of them, he refers to Brian E. Hurst as one of his spiritual teachers. Now I really became excited about getting a reading from this exceptional medium. I didn't care if people would think I was crazy for wanting to do this, I had to do it to find closure…and peace. I decided I was finally ready to give Brian a call. The message on Brian's answering machine indicated that he only took appointments on the first day of each month, and that the appointment would be two months later. I made a mental note to call on the first of the next month.

Part Six

<u>After-Death Communication</u>

My First Reading with a Spiritual Medium- Brian E. Hurst

"The most beautiful thing we can experience is the mysterious.
It is the source of all true art and all science.
He to whom this emotion is a stranger, who can no longer pause
to wonder and stand rapt in awe is as good as dead:
his eyes are closed."

—Albert Einstein

It was March 1, 2000. I had been calling on the first of the month for six months trying to get an appointment with Brian Hurst. The phone line was always busy; and by the time I'd get through, all appointments were already booked. He took appointments only from people who had lost loved ones in the past five years, and it was now just under five years for me at this point. I told myself that if I didn't get through this time, I would start looking elsewhere. The line had been busy for about thirty minutes, and it didn't look promising. Suddenly, I heard dialing instead of a busy signal, and Brian himself answered the phone. I told him I couldn't believe I had finally gotten through, after trying for six months! He apologized, and said that his earliest appointment was for May 16th, two-and-a-half months away. Eagerly, I grabbed the opportunity. The delay would give me more time to prepare.

Brian took my name and address so he could send me instructions and a map to his house, where my reading, or "sitting," as he called it, would be held. I never told him who I was trying to contact, but the skeptic in me thought "Now that he has my name, he can investigate me." Erasing that thought from my mind, I tried not to pre-judge him. Wait and see what he comes up with during the reading, I told myself.

I was so excited when I hung up the phone. I had to try not to think about it too much until the day got closer because the anticipation was overwhelming. In the meantime, I began to prepare myself as much as possible by studying books about readings with mediums, so I knew what to expect. I also looked up a few websites that Brian had mentioned in his letter. They featured him and explained what he does. A detailed description of Brian's reading with James Van Praagh's mother appears in *Healing Grief,* which conveniently came out at this time. The timing couldn't have been more perfect. I felt confident that I was going to a reputable person.

I realized that going to see a medium was a bit of an unconventional approach to help heal grief, but the main issues that I was struggling with required this type of assistance. I briefly debated whether or not to tell anyone that I was going to see a medium. But I couldn't keep it a secret for very long. First, I told my sister, and although Kim was skeptical and didn't believe in this sort of thing, she said, "If that is what will bring you peace, then do it." Next, I told my mom, because she would have to watch Trevor while I was gone. She didn't know much about mediums either, but she was encouraging as well.

Finally, I told Matt. I explained why I needed to go, what I was looking to get out of it, and that it had nothing to do with my love for him. I was reaching out to find the peace for which I had been yearning. Matt was very supportive and told me that he hoped I would find what I was looking for. I wasn't living in the past, I told Matt. I expected that the reading would improve our future because I would, hopefully, finally be okay with the darkness I had been carrying around in my heart for five years. That was a pretty tall order, I hoped Brian could deliver.

In his letter, Brian requested that I write to the person in the spirit world who I wanted to contact, explaining that I will be seeing a medium, noting the day, the time, and the location. I should also ask that the person in spirit to please "come through" and give the medium a message for me. I was told to leave the letter out in my home for several weeks to attract the attention of any spirit visitors. I might have tried this if I had lived alone, but I wouldn't have wanted to explain it to anyone I lived with or any visiting family members. I believed that Darren could hear my thoughts just as easily as read the letter. So instead, I just talked to him, asking for him to come through and give me messages that let me know without a doubt that it was him.

May 16th finally arrived. As Brian suggested, I brought an audio cassette to record the session. He had a recording device that could start and stop the recording by using a foot pedal. I was feeling a mixture of excitement and nervousness. I had also put a pack of Kleenex in my purse, because I knew I'd cry if we connected with Darren. Brian had stated in the letter that there was no guarantee that the person I wanted to come through would, so I tried not to get my hopes up too high. It was hard to keep from having high expectations or preconceived notions of what I wanted to hear. I found myself putting conditions on what would make the experience real or not real. "Okay," I told myself, "If Brian tells me that I put a picture of Darren in my purse just this morning, then I'll believe this is real." Brian had even said in his letter that spirits will usually not say what you are expecting them to say because they are anxious to demonstrate that the medium is not simply reading your mind, since that is what most people think they are doing.

So I went to the reading with an open mind and love in my heart, as the letter had suggested. I arrived a few minutes early, and before I got out of the car, I sat there for a few minutes looking at Darren's picture that I had brought along and said a silent prayer that he please come through for me. This was the moment I had been waiting five years for, I didn't want to leave disappointed. After a few deep breaths, I went to the door and knocked.

Brian was an older gentleman, with a British accent, and the most beautiful, light eyes. He invited me in, and asked me to have a seat in the front room while he finished his preparations. Before he left the room, he asked me if I was here to contact a parent. I said no. I'm sure that by looking at me, the loss of a parent would be a likely guess. I was 32-years-old, but most people thought I was in my twenties. Brian asked if it was a child that I wanted to contact. Again, I said no, without offering any more information. He said that yesterday he'd had a reading with a woman whose son had come through, and shared a few validations from her reading. He said that he hoped we were successful today as well, then excused himself and left the room.

This line of questioning made me feel a little skeptical again. Was Brian trying to eliminate people before we had even begun? I knew I didn't look like someone who had been widowed. I decided to remain open-minded and give him and the reading a chance. Brian finally called me in from the next room and we began. My heart was pounding and my palms were sweating. "Please, Darren, please come through," I silently begged, "I need to hear from you, and know that you're okay."

My Reading with Brian

When Brian does readings, any spirit who is on the other side is free to come through, so I got a lot of names of people I didn't know at the time, who were later validated by family members. I've left them out of the following account. My own responses to what Brian said are in italics. My thoughts, or why the message was significant are in parenthesis.

Brian started by telling me about himself: that he's been doing this for 42 years, and has worked with many bereavement support groups, including Mothers

Against Drunk Drivers, Victims Against Violent Crimes, Bereaved Parents USA, and Compassionate Friends. I told him that I have read a lot of books, including those by his student James Van Praagh, so I understood how this process worked. Brian began by saying a prayer and opening up his sensitivities, so that hopefully, somebody in the spirit world would make an appearance and give him some information that made sense to me. He added that if I understood something, I should speak up, because my voice might encourage them to give further meaning to the message. Brian also explained that he sometimes receives symbols or images. He might understand the basic idea, but his interpretation might not be quite right. Hopefully, what he was seeing, hearing or feeling would make sense to me.

Brian addressed his spirit guide, Dr. Grant, who assists him on the other side with his connections and asked him if there was anyone that I knew, or who knew my family who would be able to give names, messages, information, or evidence from the other side that would be helpful or uplifting to me. Brian began:

- "Somebody's got a Polish background there."
  I responded "Yes." (Darren's dad's family is Polish.)
- "Dr. Grant comments that often you're in a hurry to get things done; but it seems that what has happened a little while back has kind of frozen you up a bit, you're feeling a little shocked by it. You wanted to get everything done quick, quick, quick; very zippy and quick. That's why communications appealed to you when you wanted to study; journalism, the media, and that sort of thing."
  "That's true," I replied. (My major in college was communications, with a public relations emphasis, and yes, my life had definitely slowed down since Darren's death. Brian was off to a good start.)
- "I'll describe what I see: next to you, there appears to be a fairly tall, slender, youngish man. Is that who you are trying to contact?"
  "It could be," I squeaked out. (Tears started streaming down my face.)
- "Is it your brother?"
  "No."
- "It could almost be your brother."
  "Why do you say that?"
- "I don't know... I feel like there's kind of a bond or connection there between you. Were you married to him?"
  "Yes," I answered. (Bingo! This was what I was waiting to hear.)

- "It's your husband, okay. But it was like you were just very good friends, good buddies. There was a tremendously strong friendship here. This man is a very good-looking man. He's not overweight, kind of tall."

  "Correct on everything," I said.

- "He was standing right there beside you for a moment, but he's faded from my vision. I saw him with my third eye quite clearly for a moment, and then he was gone."

  (Why couldn't I see him? I wondered.)

- "Dr. Grant, Laura's lost her husband apparently. Is this her husband trying to get through to us, and is he able to give us any messages that Laura would understand, please?" "I don't think he knows much about the subject of spiritualism. This is not something he would have investigated."

  I said, "No, he wouldn't."

- "You've gone into this since he's gone over, haven't you?"

  "Yes."

- "My condolences, I'm sorry that you've had this shocking experience because you're very young to be left on your own. It's not nice for you. I'm very sorry for that. I hope I can succeed in getting something from him that will make sense to you. This is what we are trying to do."

  "Thank you."

- "The deceased person is talking about a David. He's telling my guide about someone named David."

  "Yes, there's a David." (I wish I had asked for more about Dave, but that was all he said. But it was very impressive that out of the thousands of names out there that he came up with David right away.)

- "There is a great deal of love to you. There were a great deal of feelings of annoyance and rage about being dead. He wasn't happy about it at all, initially. It looks like he's coming around. He's getting a little more resigned to the fact that he is in another dimension, but he didn't like it at all when it first happened. He was very annoyed to be dead."

  (I could believe that!)

- "I see an image of a boy on a skateboard, flying up and down. I don't know who this was, whether it was him when he was younger, or a friend who skateboarded and took risks. I can see an image of somebody trying to fly up over a plank, up on a cylinder, like they're trying to go over it, like a seesaw."

177

> *(I didn't know this at the time, but Darren's mom confirmed later that*
> *he loved skateboarding as a young boy.)*

- "I feel like he should have a brother, shouldn't he?"

  "No."

- "Do you know if there was a brother who was born and lost, or miscarried?"

  "He was adopted, so I don't know about his biological family."

- "I see. Dr. Grant, I think he needs some help. He doesn't know what to do. Could someone help him, please? They (those in spirit) tell me that you are the most enlightened one in your family, that none of the others are into this subject at all. You're the only one. You feel a bit isolated because nobody else believes in this. They're all kind of cynical and skeptical. They're into this world, and the material, and not as much concerned with anything beyond this world. So, you are the exception in the family. That's what I'm told. I'm sure the family are nice people; they're just not spiritually minded. They're not into this."

  I said, "Some have potential, maybe after they hear about this."

- "I hope so. At one time, I feel that there's a connection here with the Great Lakes area. Is this Chicago? Were your parents from Chicago?"

  "His parents are."

- "Okay, because they're definitely telling me that there's a connection here with Laura, with the Great Lakes area, with Chicago, and with a parent."

  "I grew up in Milwaukee, Wisconsin which is a Great Lakes state, and I lived in Chicago for five years with him. My parents are from Milwaukee, and his are from Chicago." (How did Brian know this? We were in California.)

- "It looks like someone playing in a band. It looks like musical instruments, like brass instruments and percussion, and there are drums and cymbals. Somebody's got drums, and they're beating them, and they're linking up with nightclubs and musical events. Does that make sense to you?"

  "We went to a lot of concerts together, and to clubs to see bands." (This reference could have also been to my maternal grandfather who was a drummer in a band that played in nightclubs.)

- "I see. Did you know whether your husband had gone skiing at one time?"

  "Yes, he used to ski."

- "Because I see an image of this tall man going down a snowy slope on skis. Does that make sense to you?"

"Yes."

- "Were there times when he would raise his voice, and speak loudly in a room, so people would hear him? He was very sociable and wanted people to hear what he had to say. I feel like he wanted to be the center of attention; he was very attention-seeking. He wanted people to hear him, to see him, and to know he was there. This was a very extroverted, a very get up and go, very active, very dynamic sort of person. Do you understand?"

    I smiled and said "Oh, yeah, that was him."

- "One of his parents had a serious problem, was it an alcohol problem?"

    "His birth parents?" I asked.

- "Yes."

    "I don't know anything about them."

- "He's met some of his biological family over there, who would not have approved of what happened about the time he was born. Was he out of wedlock or something?"

    "I don't know."

- "Okay. You can see how very difficult this work is to do."

    "It amazes me."

- "Looks crazy, but I'll say it. Something about Easter eggs. Has it ever been a tradition to do something with Easter eggs?"

    "We do an Easter egg hunt every year, and we just took our son on his first egg hunt."

- "That's what they're indicating symbolically to me. Somebody's been aware of the fact that you've been doing something with Easter eggs."

    (Here comes the big one.)

- "Did your husband die in an accident? They're saying, 'to do with the road,' 'on the road,' is that it?"

    "Yes" I answered with tears in my eyes again.

- "Was your husband in his late 20's, early 30's?"

    "Late 20's"

- "28, that's what I feel, around age 28. I feel like this was an automobile accident; it was on the road that he died, and I feel like it was fairly quick. I don't see long lingering, or being on life support and all of that stuff. I feel like it was very quick. There was really very little pain and suffering because it happened so fast. You know, he didn't have time to think about it before it happened, and suddenly he was out of his body and on the other side. They seem to think your husband was driving very fast."

I nodded to everything as he said it, and added "He wasn't driving."

- "Or the person who was with him was driving very fast. The person beside him was driving very fast... okay. The car was going very fast... yes. It was unsafe driving for the conditions of the road. I see that he was the innocent victim of someone else's craziness."

    "Yes" I validated. (Oh, my God! Brian had just described exactly what had happened. Darren's age, that he was killed instantly, someone else's craziness had caused the accident, unsafe driving for the conditions... I couldn't believe that Brian knew all of that.)

- "Yeah, I'm sorry. That's always hard to take when he didn't do it himself, but somebody else caused his death, you know. I don't know why I keep thinking he's your brother, because it looks to me as if you've had a tremendous spiritual rapport with this man from the moment you met him, didn't you? I don't want to shock you- I may shock you, but they say to me that you were brother and sister in a past life on earth. It was a family connection."

    "Really?" I questioned.

- "Yes, you had been brother and sister, but this was in a past life on earth, in a past incarnation. This time, you came back as husband and wife. It may sound weird, but I have to tell you that. That's why I thought he was your brother, you see. You really understood each other and had a terrific rapport, a terrific friendship and were very close. You had a natural understanding, like twin souls. I feel like that."

    "Absolutely."

- "You took life very lightly, and very easily; and it didn't bother you most of the time. You were kind of very... 'Let's try this, let's do that'... you wanted to have a different finger in all kinds of pies, didn't you? Experiment with different kinds of things. Life was like a candy box... 'Let's try this candy, let's try that one.' It was a very easy, pleasant life you had until this happened to you."

    "Yes, it was."

- "It may be that sometimes tragedy comes to people because it's a spiritual lesson that we're learning from it. In other words, maybe it was to deepen your thought, or deepen your understanding, or deepen your urge to seek truth. It may be that if you hadn't had something like this happen, you might have gone through life a bit like a butterfly, you know, flitting from one thing to another, without perhaps going into anything very deeply or very seriously, or asking questions. And it may feel like God is a bit harsh sometimes. It may seem like that sometimes, when people you love get taken away from you. I would understand how you would feel about that, definitely, that you feel it isn't fair. Why did it happen to me? I can understand that. At the same time, looking at it from the overall point of view, it has led you into a deeper path of thought, philosophy, and understanding. So, there is good coming out of what appears to be a tragedy. Good will come out of this. Although at the moment, it seems hard for you to understand how that could ever be possible. But it will. Good will come out of it."

   "I hope so." (Very well put.)

- "Somebody else wanted to marry you, didn't they, at one time? You turned him down, did you?"

   I said, "He talked about it." (He was talking about Rick, of course, my ex-boyfriend who died after Darren and I got married.)

- "Someone else talked to you about getting married, and you turned him down. You said, 'No, I don't think so.' You made the right decision. It wouldn't have been right to marry him. I'm not talking about your husband; I'm talking about this other man."

   (I wish I would have asked if Rick was there!)

- "Your mother might know who Helen might be."

   "I know a Helen. She's my mother-in-law's mother." (Darren's grandmother.)

- "I see. They're talking about a Helen. I think she is a spirit lady, and it looks like she may be helping your husband in his new environment. She may be trying to help him. I think there's a great love and affection from Helen to him. He was the little boy she made a fuss of when he was small, did she?"

   (Darren's mom confirmed this later; I hadn't known at the time that Helen was alive when Darren was a child.)

- "Do you know if he would ever complain about his knee joint, or his leg? I think he hurt himself a bit while skiing once, didn't he?"

   "I don't remember." (Darren's mom confirmed later that he had hurt his leg once in a skiing accident.)

- "Dr. Grant told me to tell you that your husband is not in the room with us. He was here briefly; but for some reason, he found it difficult to stay materialized, so that I could see and hear him. He has gone back to the other dimension. So they're trying to pick up some signals from him if they can. Something that would make sense. This is the trouble. They're not always in the room with us."

(After a moment, Brian continued.)

- "February... anniversary... Is that a birthday, or an anniversary of a death?"
  "The anniversary of his death... February 11th."
- "I see, so you've been re-married for what... two years?"
  "It was just three years."
- "I see, so your first husband's death took place, when?"
  "Five years ago."
- "Yes, I see, I understand. Well, in a sense, you did the right thing, you got on with your life... and your present marriage is all right, is it?"
  "Yes!"
- "It's working. It's always hard when you've lost someone in a tragic situation like this; it's very hard. Hopefully, he's kind and understanding; and hopefully he realizes that you've gone through a bit of a trauma. He tries to do his best."
  "Better than I could ever imagine."
- "Did you have Italian ancestry?"
  "My first husband did."
- "There's something there about Italian background."
  (Darren's mom's family; and also Darren's biological family were Italian.)
- "Oh, you have Native American Indian background. They said: 'Oh no, she's Native American Indian.' Okay, that's your secret, you're Native American Indian."
  (It was interesting that Brian used the word "secret." Some of my relatives believe that one or both of my dad's parents were part Native American Indian, but other relatives disagree.)
- "Dr. Grant seems to be explaining to me that it seems your first husband is reluctant to become too close because he doesn't want to interfere with your progress, and your life, and what you're doing now. He doesn't want to interfere. He respects your right to go on, to be married again, and be happy with someone else because he was no longer around. What can you do? And you wanted to be married, and there was nothing wrong with that. From

what I'm getting here, he's sending a great deal of love, and he seems to be satisfied that you are all right, and that you're married to a good man who loves you, and that things are working out."

(But I wanted him to "interfere." That's why I was there!)

- "Are you trying to get a little girl?"

  "We're talking about having another baby."

- "I think you will have another baby. So, by your current husband, you have a little boy?"

  "Yes."

- "Right, and the children are going to be wonderful. I see two children for you. It may be next year or the year after, but I think you're going to have another baby. How old is your boy- one?"

  "Yes, going on two." (I had Damon, my second child a year and five months after the reading.)

- "Ok, I'm sorry I couldn't get you your first husband's name, he didn't give it to me."

  "It's Darren," I answered.

- "Oh, Darren. I didn't get it at all. He wasn't able to get his name through to me. But I got through pictures, memories… you know, the skiing memories and such. It's definitely not a strong connection, because he's moved on… he's moved away from the Earth. He came down briefly but couldn't hold the vibration. He was pulled back to his own dimension. He tried to get through a few bits and pieces, but I couldn't make sense of some of it. I did the best I could. I don't think we'll get much more from him."

  (I didn't want him to go yet!)

- Dr. Grant, is it possible to pick up any signals from Darren? Maybe he can still say something interesting. I know he doesn't want to pull you emotionally because he wants you to be happy with your present husband and doesn't want you to get too nostalgic or too involved with memories of the past. He wants you to kind of let it go. It's hard, because it's part of your experience, you know, and you've shared times together- good times- and it still comes back into your thoughts. Of course it does. But I think Darren feels like he's been advised by people over there not to intrude. So, I feel we make a brief contact with him and he wants you to get on with your life, here and now, with your present husband and little boy."

- "Is your present husband connected to Chicago?"

"We met in Chicago."

- "Oh, because there's also a link with Chicago with your second husband. You met in Chicago, there's the link."

  (There's no way Brian could have researched that one.)

- "It looks like they want you to concentrate on being happy in your present situation. Your late husband is doing fine on the other side, he's okay now. He's met up with family, and with his biological family and with other people around him, friends, and he's doing all right. He knows that he has to let you go. So, this is the feeling I'm getting strongly, you see; so don't linger on those things too much. Enjoy the present."

  (That's great, but I still wanted more from Darren.)

- "May...May, are there birthdays this month?"

  "My mom's birthday and my wedding anniversary with Darren are in May."

- "Because I know May is a very significant month for you, to do with a birthday or anniversary."

  "Also, my current husband and I met on my mom's birthday, in May." I added.

- "I see. Is there anything else to tell her please? Any other information? Helen is dead; we said that, didn't we?"

  "Yes."

- "She seems to be the only one who's really taking a strong interest in this and is trying to help. Was she connected to your first husband?"

  "She's his grandmother. Is there's anything I can tell her daughter? Darren's mother and I are still very close."

- "Does Helen have any messages?" "She says she has great feet and legs, and has no more problems with them. So, I don't know if she had a problem with them at one time."

  "I wouldn't know about that."

- "Swelling or pain, maybe the other lady would know about that. She gives her love to everyone who remembers her."

  (My mother-in-law later confirmed that Helen had had cancer that affected her feet and legs so badly, that she couldn't drive or get around. Because of this, my mother-in-law said, Helen had given up her will to live.)

- "There seems to be a link here with Toughy Avenue in Chicago, or the

North Chicago area, near Toughy, is it?"

"There is a Toughy Avenue in Chicago, I know."

- "Toughy, T-O-U-G-H-Y, and Devon Street. Someone may have lived there at one time."

"I'm not sure." (This turned out to be one of the biggest validations. Darren's mom confirmed that the adoption agency that they adopted him from was located in this area. We speculated that maybe Darren's birth mother lived around there too.)

- "I see magazines around you, you see… but have you not done any more with your writing?"

"I used to write a lot, but I've been doing more reading these days."
(Maybe Brian was on to something?)

- "You will find out things when you get home, that's what I'm told.

"Okay."

- "Did a member of your current husband's family say he shouldn't marry outside his religion?"

"Not that I know of."

- "I think it may be an older woman. I'm not sure about this, but ask your husband if he understands what this is all about. Of course, he totally disregarded it because he loves you, and he married you."

"The only older female is his mother, and she's fine with it" (Later, when I asked Matt, he told me that she was concerned about our being different religions. Who knew?)

- "That's good; she should be… because really, you know, whatever your religious beliefs are, we all survive death anyway. We don't need to be saved, or a member of any stupid religious sect that says you've got to be this, that, or the other. People are going to survive death anyway. But where you go depends on who we are, and what we are thinking, and what we are all about as people. That's how it works. When you die, you go to people who share your attitudes, values, and belief systems, who think the kinds of thoughts you think, and like what you like. There are all those different levels of consciousness, as we know."

"I'm glad to hear you say that."

- "We have to bring it to a close. Dr. Grant says there's not much more he can tell you. Your life seems to be going along very smoothly, very nicely. You seem to have a very nice family, and a nice, cute boy. I think this is a good life. I don't see any other major disasters or tragedies. I think you are going to handle things quite well; and you know, later on, when the children get a bit older, I can see you getting into some kind of social work. You'll be involved with some kind of social work later on. I don't know what, but I think the way will be shown to you. You will be directed when the time comes."

*****

Brian and I talked for a while longer. I thanked him, and paid him for his services. I showed him my picture of Darren that I had brought along, and he confirmed that he was indeed the person who he had seen standing next to me, although at first glance he thought the person in the picture was a woman because of Darren's longer hair. Brian also told me that he was going to mention it to me earlier, that the person standing next to me during the reading resembled a young John Travolta. The John Travolta comment was the ticket for me. We used to tease Darren all the time saying that he looked like John Travolta. (An interesting side note, as I am transcribing this, there is a talk show on TV in the background and the guest is John Travolta. Just thought I'd throw that in.

My Feelings about Brian's Reading

I left Brian's house with my cassette tape of our session, and I tried to digest everything that had just happened. At first, a lot of it didn't make sense to me, and I thought he was mistaken about some things. He had given me the names of about 15 people whose identity I didn't know. Later, most of them were confirmed for me by Darren's mom and by Matt's dad. It had to be hard for Brian, because so many families were connected to me. There were my relatives, Darren's relatives (from both his biological and adopted families), and Matt's relatives- most of whom I didn't know. Some of the biggest pieces of evidence that Brian's reading was the real thing were the facts that I hadn't known at the time of the reading, but which were later confirmed by Darren's mom.

I played the tape again on my 45-minute drive home. This was a lot of information to process. I couldn't believe that I just made contact with Darren in the afterlife! This was really possible! As I drove past the street where I worked, I thought to myself, "If the people I work with knew where I had just been, they'd freak out!"

I must admit that I was initially a little disappointed with my reading because even though I was warned not to, I expected Darren to come through with specific things that only I would have known and I had certain things in my mind that I wanted him to say to prove that it was real. It is human nature to focus on what's wrong, instead of what's right; and my reading was no exception. Because there were a few things and people mentioned that I couldn't validate, I questioned the authenticity of the entire experience. If I had instead focused on the things that he said that *were* true, and the things that I *did* understand, I would have realized how truly extraordinary my reading had been.

I'm glad that I researched how this process works before I had my reading; otherwise, my initial skepticism may have stayed intact. Basically, I had to understand that the way this process of communication works is not the way we communicate on Earth. It is more like telepathy. The spirit world is a world of thought. They don't have mouths and voices to communicate verbally, so they communicate with the medium through their senses, usually through a series of images and messages transmitted through thought. The spirit usually tries to show survival evidence by communicating messages that the person having the reading would understand, for instance memories from the past, and knowledge of things happening in your life since they've passed on.

Also, I had to look at the process from Brian's perspective. Basically, a total stranger is judging his authenticity on what he says or doesn't say, and his ability to describe the symbolism of what he is seeing, hearing, and feeling. What a difficult undertaking! For Brian, it is like a game of psychic charades, trying to figure out what the messages mean to the other person. Just because he didn't describe exactly what the symbolism of a message meant to me, didn't take away from the fact that the symbols were accurate and meaningful to me. He did his part, I had to make sense of it all.

I also had to look at it from Darren's perspective. No one had ever tried to contact him in spirit before, so he didn't know what to do in order to communicate. The medium has to raise his vibration and those in spirit have to lower theirs in order to communicate on the same level. That is why Brian's guide on the other side, Dr. Grant was assisting him with this process. Darren was not into this type of thing on Earth, I would imagine the first time was difficult for him. After confirming some of the messages I received after the reading with others and having future predictions prove to be accurate, I knew this was the real deal.

Why I Began to Believe

- First of all, Brian said that Darren materialized next to me, and he accurately described what Darren looked like.
- He told me the nationalities of Darren's family, my family, and Matt's family.
- He knew that I went to college and studied communications.
- He described what Darren's and my relationship was like, and his personality.
- He knew that no one in my family was spiritually minded.
- He mentioned David, by name.
- He knew that Darren liked to ski.
- He knew about our connections to the Great Lakes area, specifically mentioning Chicago, as well as Matt's link to Chicago.
- He mentioned a link to clubs and musical events, which we did together.
- He described how the accident happened, Darren's age when he died, and the circumstances surrounding his death. This validation alone should have been enough proof for me, but I was too stubborn and skeptical.
- He accurately described what my life was like before and after Darren's death.
- He knew about Rick's wanting to marry me, and that it wouldn't have been a good idea.
- He mentioned that his grandmother, Helen, who he also named, was helping him out on the other side.
- He knew that February was the anniversary of his death, and that May was a significant month for me.
- He knew that I enjoyed writing.
- Finally, Brian had almost told me, he said, that when he saw Darren materialize, that he looked like a young John Travolta. My mother-in-law and I teased Darren constantly about his resemblance to John Travolta.

But, the most astonishing pieces of evidence were the things I didn't know at the time of the reading that were confirmed later:

Validations after the Reading

- Darren's mom confirmed his love of skateboarding.
- Darren's mom confirmed that he injured his leg while skiing.
- Darren's mom also confirmed that Helen, his grandma, was indeed living and fussed over Darren when he was young, and that she had cancer which

so devastatingly affected her feet and legs that it undermined her will to live.

- She also confirmed the uncanny significance of the North Chicago area, near Toughy and Devon Street; it was the location of the adoption agency that Darren's parents adopted him from.
- Brian knew that Matt and I had different religious backgrounds, but I found out from Matt after the reading that his mom was concerned about his marrying outside their religion. How could Brian have known that? I certainly hadn't.
- Brian said that I'd have a second baby in a year or two, and I gave birth to Damon one year and five months after the reading.

Hello!!! Just because Brian didn't tell me *exactly* what I wanted to hear does not change the validity of the messages that did come through. What are the odds of him hitting on all of those personal items, including things I wasn't even aware of? In my heart, I knew that it was Darren that came through, and that the information that Brian shared could have only come from the other side, not by any amount of thorough detective work. It wasn't so much that the messages themselves had so much meaning, but that a total stranger could give me such personal details, and reveal so many facts that I was not aware of at the time of the reading.

This was my proof that there is truly something beyond this life. I feel that my first reading had to be very factual in order for my skeptical mind to believe that this was real. I needed tangible proof. I needed facts; names, places, events, and I got it. I now knew for certain that Darren was on the other side, with other loved ones, and that he was fine. This knowledge gave me peace and closure, and helped me grasp the bigger picture of what life and death are all about. Years of therapy couldn't have done what this reading had done for me! It gave me an immeasurable amount of tranquility.

Some of my own religious conflicts were resolved as well; mainly when Brian assured me that we all survive death, no matter what our religious beliefs are. Also, just from having this connection, I knew that what my church had been saying about heaven and hell my whole life was wrong. Darren had broken many of the church's rules that were supposed to send him to hell; but he wasn't in hell, was he? He was with other loved ones, he was okay, and he knew what was taking place in my life. No wonder the church frowns on this type of activity; they don't want you to find out the truth!

My reading with Brian gave me a new perspective on life and made me eager to pursue my spiritual explorations. There had to be others like Brian out there, and I was curious to see what other messages there might be for me from the spirit world. For the time being, I was comforted to know that the bond Darren and I had shared on Earth continued, and that he was aware of what was happening in my life and was happy for me. This helped ease my guilty conscience that he would be mad if I moved on with my life and remarried. Also, the fact that so many spirits came through in my reading, (15 friends and relatives of people close to me, whom I didn't name to avoid confusion) gave me the comfort in knowing that I am never alone.

There were even little things that Brian said would happen that seemed insignificant at the time, but when they actually happened, I had to go listen to the tape again to make sure I was right. For instance, he mentioned that I was going to be around someone who is having trouble with their pager. A few weeks later, I was doing a freelance makeup event, and the makeup artist next to me was having a problem with her pager not working, and it wouldn't stay clipped on. To her it was a nuisance, to me, another validation.

The first person I called to tell about my experience was Darren's mom. We were both crying as I read her the parts of the reading about Darren. I also sent her a copy of the tape. She confirmed some things that I hadn't understood, and this made the reading more meaningful for me. It was a very bonding experience for the two of us. I thought long and hard about telling my close friends and family members about my experience. I feared being disbelieved or ridiculed. Worse yet, I worried that they would think that I had gone off the deep end and needed to be committed!

When I finally did start talking about the reading, I would start off the conversation by saying something like "You are going to think that I've completely lost my mind, but I have had the most amazing experience and I'd like to share it with you." I was so relieved by everyone's willingness to be open-minded. Skepticism is natural, I believe; and I had been one of the biggest skeptics out there. But I had to know for sure if communicating with the dead was real or not. I had even been prepared to expose the reading as a sham. Instead, I became a believer.

My Readings with a Second Medium- Sherry Lynn

"The mark of your ignorance is the depth of your belief in injustice and tragedy. What the caterpillar calls the end of the world, the master calls a butterfly."

—Richard Bach

I expected that a personal reading with a medium would give me the closure I needed to finally be at peace with Darren's death. Instead, it left me wanting to find out more. I knew there had to be other gifted mediums out there. I was a little bit nervous the first time, because I didn't know what, if anything, was going to happen. I figured that if I did it again I'd be more relaxed. Also, I wanted more details specifically from Darren himself. It seemed that he didn't know what to do either, so maybe it would be better for him a second time around. My spiritual journey was just beginning.

One day, about four months after my reading with Brian, our local newspaper ran a small ad with an angel on it that said, "Sherry Lynn- Spiritual Medium, Healing one Heart at a Time," and it gave her website. I tore out the ad from the paper, and decided to check out her website, and see what she was all about. Maybe Sherry Lynn was the person I was looking for.

After checking out her website, I decided to call her to book an appointment. Sherry (I'll refer to her as Sherry from here on) could do readings over the phone, and even on line, but I wanted a human contact, and an in-person reading. In fact, many mediums prefer phone readings because they are not influenced by the person and their non-verbal communication. I left a message on Sherry's answering machine, and she called me back the same day. We hit it off right away. I asked her a lot of questions, and she answered all of them to my satisfaction. She was just what I was looking for. Sherry did her readings differently than Brian. With the help of her spirit guides, she was able to ask for a specific spirit, rather than hope that the person I wanted to come through actually would. Then, by the specific information that comes through, and the way it comes through, you know it is actually them. This style worked for her.

A lot of people have preconceived ideas about what a psychic or a medium can and cannot do. I certainly used to feel this way. I remember thinking that if a person really was psychic, then they'd know why I was there. It doesn't quite work that way. I decided to keep an open mind when I went to see Sherry. If she could just get Darren to come through (and not have other spirits take up my time) I would be happy. I wanted a full hour with just Darren, not just ten minutes with him and then have other spirits hog the spotlight. I now knew that he was safe on the other side, and that this type of communication was possible and real, I didn't need that anymore. I needed more personal messages from him.

Sherry said that she could feel a spirit's emotions that their personalities really came through, so there would be no doubt that it's them. Sometimes, she said, it's not the message itself that is most significant; but rather the way it comes across, that lets you know who is coming through. The content of the message confirms the spirit's awareness of what is going on in your life. I asked her how she received the messages. She said that she is shown a series of images- like a movie- and the words of the message come across like tickertape. I found all of this fascinating.

I had my reading the following week. (I was glad I didn't have to wait two months this time.) The day of the reading, I was more excited than nervous. I couldn't wait to hear from Darren. On the drive over I talked to him in my mind and asked him to be there, and to please come through for me. Sherry and I greeted each other with a hug. There were some candles lit around the room. I made myself comfortable on the couch to the side of her. She wasn't what I expected, either. I'd imagined she would look like the stereotypical gypsy or fortune teller depicted on TV, with a crystal ball, dressed in some elaborate layered gown. Instead, she was a casually dressed, ordinary mother of two teenage boys, whose pictures were prominently displayed in the room. She was so warm and had such empathy for me. I knew she truly wanted to help me. I had my pen, paper, and Kleenex ready. Unfortunately, Sherry didn't record it as Brian had, so I had to take notes as fast as I could.

Sherry asked me Darren's full name, and when he passed. She closed her eyes and was quiet for a few minutes. I could feel my heart racing as I anticipated her every word. Soon, everything came so fast that I could barely keep up, trying to write it all down. (Again, my responses to Sherry's messages are in italics; my thoughts or why the message was significant are in parenthesis.) Sherry began:

- "The first thing I am getting is that Darren is very sincere and very calm. He says it is a humbling experience to talk with you again. The first time was for them, this one is for us."

(I'm already crying.)

- "He says it's time to discuss facts and the ultimate meaning of why these things happen, to put the pieces together, and to resolve open-ended questions. He wants to help you with your spirituality and help you move forward. This will be a boost in your spirituality."

(Finally, some answers.)

- "He has a matter-of-factness about him, structured, like a business meeting. He has things to accomplish here, an agenda, and he's rubbing his hands together, like 'here we go.' About your healing and grieving, he says he's very proud of you. You've been going up, up, up... and now you're stuck. He wants to help you bring it up again."

(I was stuck, that's why I was there)

- "He wants to talk about your future. The area of concern is with your future endeavors, and how to personally apply yourself, and give meaning to what you do."

(I had been questioning my purpose in life.)

- "He says not to belittle what you do. Your work with makeup is part of a grand plan. You are working on your connections with people. In the future, you'll be helping people who have lost someone by being a shining star. From you, they'll learn that joy can be recognized through pain; that every day isn't great, it is a struggle. Not that you'll be a martyr, but people will relate to the truth within you. A sort of, I did it- so can you."

  I asked, "How can I help others, when I don't feel totally healed myself?" (Sherry didn't know that I was a makeup artist or that I was thinking that there was more I was supposed to be doing. It was a talent, not a passion).

- "You will heal yourself as you heal others, he says. You don't need to be completely healed before you can help. You can benefit others right now; this is a wonderful time, because you are not too much past your loss."

  (I'd always wanted to have my experience help someone else, but I didn't know how.)

- "Darren is talking about the strong parallel between what you do now and what you will be doing. Now, by putting makeup on people, you make them feel beautiful, inside and out. You make them feel good about themselves. Most women feel naked and incomplete without makeup. In the future, you'll help make people ready to face the world again."

(What the heck am I going to be doing?)

- "He's also showing me a parallel between covering up scars with makeup and covering up emotional wounds. Wounds can heal, but the scar remains and they are never forgotten. But, there are ways to cover the pain without denying it exists, and to put on a fresh face and start anew. He also says that makeup is symbolic of bringing color to people's faces, and bringing people back to life. He says this is honorable work, it's God's work."

  I finally asked, "What does he mean by saying I will help others. How exactly am I going to do that?"

- "Darren asks if you've ever thought of writing a book about grief for young widows."

  I laughed and asked, "Who would read it? And what do I have to say?"

- "You'd be blown away by how you'll touch people and how your story will help them heal. He asks 'Wouldn't you have bought a book like that after this happened to you?'"

  "Yes!" I answered. (There was nothing around that I could relate to written by another young widow.)

- "He says that millions of women are waiting for your book, but that there's no pressure. 'Just kidding.' He says."

  "Sure, no pressure at all." (I laughed, that was just like him. This is when the seed was planted for me to write this book.)

- "He says that the reason you will be drawn to this work is to make sure he didn't die in vain, and that you didn't go through all of this for nothing."

  (This really made me cry. Then Sherry asked if I had any questions for him.) I asked, "Why did this happen to us at such a young age?"

- "He says that the answers will come along the journey to share your story. It will become clear that there is a reason for everything. But there is a need for you to help people who have experienced a similar loss."

  Then I asked the question I've wrestled with since day one, "Why was Dave driving the night of the accident?"

- "He gives an abrupt answer. He says, Dave was supposed to drive because I was supposed to be the passenger and die. It was my time; I understand that now. It was a chosen plan. Our souls agreed. We had made a contract together before we were born." Sherry added that she felt that Darren and

Dave had been together in a past life. "They were brothers," she said. "I feel this strongly."

(Wow! Not the answer I was expecting, but one that gave me a lot to think about. I wondered if this was the same past life in which Darren and I were brother and sister that Brian had mentioned in my reading with him. Would that have made Dave and I brother and sister as well?) "Is Darren mad at Dave?" I asked.

- "No, nothing could be further from the truth. Darren does not have an ounce of anger toward Dave; he did his job and fulfilled his contract."

  (Dave would be glad to know that, I thought.)

- "There were other reasons for the accident. It was an 'agreed' experience. Dave's own experience is yet to unfold. It is just beginning. Darren knew that his time here was short. Dave was meant to experience driving and killing a friend. Now he has a need for inner healing. The accident was a catalyst to heal old wounds and Dave can now take an instrumental step in healing and remembering who he is."

  "What about Darren's parents? What are they supposed to learn from this?"

- "Appreciating life, not taking anyone for granted. This is not a punishment for them. It is hard because they lost a child, but this is an opportunity for them to grasp the bigger picture as a result of their tragedy. Through their pain, to know how blessed they were to love him for 28 years, and be grateful for their time together."

  "Does he have any messages for them?"

- "Yes, for his mom. It's all for mom. He says he is so proud of how she's connected with her spirituality. She's on the right track. He wants to encourage her to keep going, mom. He's really choked up talking about his mom." Sherry started to cry herself as she added, "He wants to tell her that the spiritual journey is the purest way for her to find meaning in losing her son, and that she will. 'Don't stop until you do, mom,' he says, 'please don't stop until you get the peace you seek for losing me.' That's what he wants for her, to be at peace with what happened. He's very emotional about the pain she is in. He has so much to say to her. This is the most emotion I've felt coming from him. I can feel how close they were."

  (Sherry is crying as hard as I am at this point.)

- "He wants to relay the love he has for her for the pain that she's in. He's so sorry for the pain he's caused her. They did this, contracted with one another, their souls agreeing that in their lifetime, he would leave her in some form, the physical form. It was for her personal growth and the strengthening of her soul. He agreed to leave her, for her to find her inner strength, but he has never truly left her side. He has just changed form. As his mother connects to her spirituality, they will reconnect, and be closer than ever. They are bonded forever, not just in this lifetime. The sooner she gets a handle on her spiritual understanding, her true inner strength, specifically to know that spirit is everywhere and behind all things, the sooner she'll have him back in her heart and in her life. He's trying to get her attention, and he'll continue to do this until she gets it, no doubt."

> *After we both regained our composure, and stopped sobbing, I asked, "What was my role? Did I have a contract with him too?"*

- "Your role in his passing is to help his mom, Dave, and the women who will read your book heal, and to heal yourself in the process. You are to help people grieve losing him. You've done a beautiful job so far, and he's so proud of you. Also, you were supposed to experience each other in a marriage that ended tragically, so that you would connect with your spirituality, and learn the truth about how spirit works, and be able to express it simply to others." Then she paused, and said, "I don't mean to take away from your relationship in any way, but I feel you two had more of a brother-sister kind of love, and were not overly romantic."

> *"You could say that."*

- "It was planned that way, so you would be able to move on."

> *"Okay."*

- "He wants you to know that he sent you Matt."

> *"He did?" (I knew it! I knew this comment was coming from Darren because Sherry didn't know my current husband's name was Matt.)*

- "He says that Matt could give you the things that I couldn't. He planned the way you met, and he's very proud of himself for hand-picking Matt for you. It was his way of providing for you after he left. Darren knew what you needed, and he knew that Matt had what you needed. He is very happy for you."

> *(I knew I had help, and now it was confirmed. It was a relief to hear the message again that he was happy that I was with Matt.)*

- "Your challenge will be to merge your two worlds. Part of who you are is your past. You need to merge being a widow and helping others; with being a wife and mother and being happy. You've lived through it, now you need to tell your story to help others."

"What should my book be about?"

- "He says, 'Laura's journey.' But I'm told that you have a specific spirit guide who will help you with this. We can talk about this another time, okay?"

*****

Then Darren gave me a few ideas about the book he said I should write, but he added that this is just to get the ball rolling, it is my choice. You have free will to do it or not do it, he said. It was good to know that I had a choice in something. Sherry and I continued to talk after my reading. I was there for two hours, and when I left I felt like I was walking on air. As I drove home, I felt so free and peaceful. I just had a conversation with my late husband. How weird is that? I didn't care. I felt great!

Over the next few weeks, I couldn't get the idea of writing a book out of my head. I called some friends and family to tell them about the reading, and they all thought the book was a great idea. I really wanted something good to come out of this tragedy. Maybe this was it. I didn't really want to re-hash the most horrible time in my life; besides, I was happily married with a beautiful son. But something about it resonated with me. It's not like Sherry told me I would find the cure for cancer; but writing a book to help others make it through a tragic loss was something I could see myself doing.

I was pushed further in that direction when a male friend I went to grade school, high school, and college with died in a vehicle accident, leaving behind a wife and two children. His wife was the younger sister of a girl on my gymnastics team. When I heard the news, I felt so awful because I knew too well what his widow was going through, and I felt I needed to do something. I decided to share my story with her in a letter mentioning some of the things that helped me through my grief. At first I thought my letter had fallen on deaf ears, but a year later, she wrote back, thanking me for my letter that she had kept and re-read. I cried as I read her letter because I knew that sharing my story helped another grieving person. Knowing that I had been able to help her get through a horrible ordeal warmed my heart. Even if she had never written back, I realized as I wrote to her that this was part of my calling, and that I had to write this book. (Also, when your late husband suggests that you should write a book, it's definitely worth consideration!)

My Spirit Guides

After a month or so, I decided to call Sherry and seek out my spirit guide who was supposed to help me with my book. Perhaps, I thought, I'd be able to decide if I wanted to undertake this after all. I'd given the idea a great deal of thought by now, and was leaning toward doing it. I didn't know where to begin or what to focus on. There were so many issues involved with grief. Should I write it as fiction, or should I tell my story in a straightforward way? I was hoping for some clarity; and besides, if nothing else, at least I'd know who my spirit guides were.

My next reading with Sherry called upon one of my spirit guides and added another dimension to my spiritual awareness. My spirit guide, who was to help me with the book, is a Native American Elder, a wise one. He is of Lakota descent and is named "Late Deer." "Deer" represents grace and "Late" because grace came later in life. He was my editor-in-"chief" as he humorously put it. He said that he knows spirit, because he is spirit. Although I felt personally motivated to write, I was beginning to feel as though I was destined to do so. I asked Sherry how he could help me, not really understanding how that would work. She said that he could help me metaphysically, by helping me with my memory and by making sure that things were quiet so that I could sit down and write. I didn't know that this was possible. Late Deer said that by writing the book, I would be serving the world and that it was a great purpose.

Most importantly, he made me realize that writing would be a healing experience for me personally. Late Deer said that my drive would be strong to deliver my message before I delivered my second baby. (Again with the second baby.) My due date would be my deadline. After having baby number two, I would have my hands full. I needed to put a part of my healing behind me in order to more fully embrace a family of four, he said. He said that writing the book and having a baby is a parallel journey. I will be creating in both experiences. I will be creating a new life with the new baby, and creating another form of a baby, my book, which will be coming of me and from my heart. Both are precious and both will grow and flourish after they are born and have their own journeys and their own lives. The book will have a life of its own once you give it to the world and take its own course.

My questions about how to write the book, and what to include in the book were also answered, and I was amazed at the specifics. It had to be my personal story, told in a simple, straightforward way. He also told me that I had no idea how courageous I was. Rico had given me the nickname "Couragio," meaning courage in Italian, after Darren died. Late Deer said that courage means that it is okay to be sad and it is okay to be afraid, but you still keep moving forward. That's the courage. Courage doesn't mean denying the pain and the loss. It means feeling it and working through it and having the determination that in the long run, this tragedy isn't going to kill you too. That part made me cry.

I had other spirit guides who also made a brief appearance, but the main purpose of this reading was to connect with my guide for this book. I was also told that I have another guide who will be coming into my life later; something to look forward to. It was good to know that we all have spirit guides who can assist us in various ways, at various points in our lives.

Once I returned home and gave it some more thought, I figured that healing myself wouldn't be a bad idea, so I started writing down everything that I could remember, in no particular order. Whenever Trevor was napping, I was writing. I was amazed at how the memories just flooded back. Four months later, I had a rough draft pretty much completed, and I simultaneously discovered I was pregnant with my second child.

Group Readings

Sherry and I were becoming good friends. She was becoming my spiritual mentor, helping me answer the questions that I had been struggling with since Darren's death. I had the pleasure of attending small group gatherings at her home where she did readings for everyone in attendance. It was very interesting to witness other people get a reading, and to see how much it touched their lives. There were always many beautiful messages and tears of joy. In settings like this, Sherry was able to receive messages from someone in the spirit world, who directed her to the person for whom the message was intended. On one occasion, I was the recipient of such a connection.

My paternal grandfather (the one who died three months after Darren) came to Sherry with a personal message for my brother Ricky. She asked me if I knew "Eric's" grandfather. (Eric is my brother's real name.) I asked which grandfather, since they had both passed on. Sherry described his appearance accurately, so I knew immediately which grandfather had come through. Besides the message for my brother, basically telling him to quit being a pain in the neck, my grandpa gave me information about the circumstances surrounding his death, and cleared up the question of his heritage (which our family has always been uncertain about).

Regarding his death, my grandfather had been very ill, and was on lots of pain medication and had taken his own life, and he told me the reasons why. It was very comforting for me to know that you still go to heaven if you commit suicide. I had read different theories on this, and hearing from him let me know that spirits who cross themselves over don't spend eternity in-between worlds, or in hell, as I had heard in the past. The fact that *he* came to *me*, through Sherry, made it even more authentic. There was also a young girl at the gathering whose brother had committed suicide who also came through with loving messages for her. So that was a double validation that this was true.

My grandpa said that he *was* part Native American, and even named the tribe (Ojibwa), and said that when he and my grandmother went to get married, they wanted to shuffle them off to a reservation, so they put that they were white on their marriage certificate so they could get married the way they wanted to. (This was true; I later ordered a copy of it from the county.) This added to the family controversy. Ojibwa was the tribe that my dad always told me was part of our heritage. This is not a commonly known tribe, so I was pretty stunned.

Later, wanting to validate this message, I called my aunt to ask her what she knew, and she said that my grandpa's mother was 100% Ojibwa, and that she even had a picture of her. She didn't know her name, she only knew her as grandma. So I guess this validated what Brian had said in my reading with him when he said that my secret was that I was part Native American Indian. It wasn't a secret anymore, thanks to my grandpa.

The most amazing information that came out of my attending these small gatherings was my ability to connect to Rick, my ex-boyfriend who died soon after Darren and I were married. I hadn't expected such great information to come through, but it helped this part of the story come full circle. This time, I told her who I wanted to connect with. Sherry got quiet, and then she connected with his energy. Sherry began:

- "He had a bit of an attitude, is that fair to say? There was a tone to it that was part playful, and part sarcastic. It came off a little hard; but if you knew him, he was just kidding around. It really worked for him."
  "Yes, that's him all right."
- "If you got to know him, you'd know there was nothing to it. This was natural for him to give off that air. It served a purpose. It kept people at a distance. Rick had a tendency to push people out of his life- and then a few

chosen ones, like you, he let in. He distanced himself from so many people because he knew he wasn't going to be around long, and he did it for their sake. So... now he comes up with "honesty." He says that he didn't share himself with many people for their sake; but the truth is the more people who loved and cared about him, the harder it would be for him to go. Not consciously.

- "Now he's figured out that it's you who is here and he doesn't have to hide who he is. He's saying 'I'm sorry that I did that to you.' Sherry asks me, 'Did he hurt you when he broke up with you?'"

    "Yes, he did", I tearfully replied.

- "He's saying he's sorry he hurt you. I think he said some harsh things."

    "Yes, he did, to push me away."

- When this happened, when you lost him, for your experience it was just the beginning of a spiritual journey to help you understand that when you lose someone you love, they're not gone forever. They just come back in another form. You were meant to be out of that relationship when it happened. In other words, Rick's passing laid the groundwork for you to experience the loss of someone who you had known and cared for, before you ultimately lost your husband. It didn't happen so that you would get used to it. It wasn't intended to be cruel, or to make you feel like you were cursed and everyone you love dies, it was to help you experience it and have it under your belt, so when you lost Darren, you could at least fall back on knowing a little bit of what it's like. It was to prepare you for what was coming, to help you."

    "I thought of that after Darren died."

- "I want to touch on it from Rick's perspective. Why did he die at such a young age? His whole life was like a flash, like a shooting star. It was like a big flash, he came, he saw, he left. He was kind of wild. He lived on the edge, pretty much. His life was like a wild ride for him, and he never settled down, from what I'm getting. He was pretty crazy, because he felt there was no point to getting focused and settling down in a boring job in order to make a living to make ends meet. He knew his life would be just a flash. He'd be here and gone, might as well make the most of it, kind of go for it. He was not Mr. Reliable or Mr. Responsible at all; he knew there was no point in it."

    "Absolutely!" He always used to say he'd be dead by the time he was

thirty. I never understood why he thought that." "Can you describe what he looks like to me?" I asked. She laughed and said "You had to ask me, didn't you?"

- "There's a harsh energy about him. His skin is darkened, like it's tanned. His hair has that greased-back look, and it's shiny and dark. Maybe the goop in it made it look darker than it was. There's a dramatic look to him; he was noticeable, striking. He drew a lot of attention to himself on purpose. This had to do with his aura, with making the most of his life, and getting the most out of it."

    "Yes, he was beautiful. He looked like a young Brad Pitt. He was tan, and often slicked back his hair and wore a ponytail."

- "Did he work out? I see muscles in his arms."

    "Yes."

- "He took a lot of care to look good. He was a little self-centered about his appearance. It's really important to him to look good and be noticed. He did a good job at it."

    "He sure did."

- "He can get very sensitive if he wants to, and now he's saying to tell you that he's grateful. This is the 'Jell-O' side of him, his soft side. He says that he's grateful for what the two of you had, and he looks on it as a very special time. You were the only one who really understood him, who took the care and the time to get to know him. Many people didn't bother to see through his good looks. They never learned that there was someone deep inside there. But you did; you got it, and he's so grateful for that. You slowed him down a little, made him be true to himself when he was with you. He's appreciative of that, because if it hadn't been for you, he would never have done that. He's really grateful and sends his love. I don't feel that he's going to come into your life too often- that's just not his role. You've got Darren coming in when you need him."

    "Are Rick and Darren hanging out together? They never met, but I always thought they'd get along."

- "I get this good feeling about it, like they're buddies. You know what I keep seeing? Do you remember the part in the movie "Grease," where the guys kept their cigarette pack rolled up inside their short sleeves? Did Rick actually do that? Or is it just his personality that I'm getting?"

    "He smoked cigarettes, and he had a bad boy image. That's how he

> *liked to portray himself."*

- "So, when you asked about hanging out with Darren; yes, they're together and Rick's being a really bad influence on Darren, sort of like, 'Hey, let's get into some trouble.' Darren is like, 'Okay, here we go again.' Rick is the instigator, and Darren is like, well...what the heck? He knows better, Darren does, he understands the consequences. Although Rick is aware, he doesn't care."

> *"Some things never change."*

- "But yeah, they're pals. They get into mischief, but it doesn't matter now. Anything else?"

> *"Does Rick have anything to tell his family?"*

- "I don't think he's in the mood right now, because there's an audience. For him, he's still got to be 'that guy.' But he will talk to you privately. We can do this another time. But he's got to keep up his image. Right now, he's being a hot-shot, and he doesn't want to say how much he loves his parents because that wouldn't be cool."

*****

It was great to hear that Rick and Darren were hanging out together, getting into mischief. They were both like that. They never met each other while they were alive, but I'd always thought they would be good friends if they had met. I guess there isn't jealousy on the other side. I was amazed at Sherry's accurate description of Rick, both visually and personally. There was no doubt in my mind that he had come through. It was also nice to hear him apologize for hurting me. It was also funny that she got the image of the movie *"Grease"* when I asked if they were hanging out together, because who was the star of *"Grease?"* John Travolta.

My Feelings about Sherry's Readings

Sherry's readings had a more personal feel than Brian's. I felt as though I had been reunited with Darren. I realized that death had not robbed me of the love we'd shared. I know that Darren is still with me and always will be. I no longer believe in "death," and I can no longer look at life the same as before. It made me more consciously aware of my connections with others, both here on Earth, and in the afterlife. I know that love matters, it counts for something.

My reading with Brian just scratched the surface of my understanding; my readings with Sherry went much deeper, giving me a new purpose. These readings confirmed that life and love continue after we leave this existence, and I wanted to shout my truth to the world. A sense of closure, healing, and peace that I'd never dreamed possible now filled my whole being.

The things that Darren talked about in my first reading with Sherry especially his message for his mom- convinced me he had come through. He knew all of my worries and concerns, and could guide me because he knew what I needed to feel happy and fulfilled. Darren confirmed a lot of things that I already believed, for instance, that he sent Matt to me. He also talked about things that Sherry was unaware of, like my occupation as a makeup artist, my discontent with what I did, and my desire to do something more meaningful. His personality and sense of humor also came through in the way he phrased things. Even though Sherry hadn't described his appearance, which would have been nice, I had no doubts that it was Darren. Since that time, Sherry has done many more readings for me, and whenever Darren came through, she instantly recognized his energy.

Meeting my spirit guides was another eye-opener for me. It's comforting to know that I am never alone, that there are spirits who have unconditional love for me, and who are always there to help me. Some guides have specific purposes in my life, like my editor-in-"chief." Others have always been and will always be with me. I was amazed at the information that came out of this reading. It humbled me to know how little I knew about spiritual matters.

In later readings with Sherry, where I've received many messages from Darren, he has shown me how his spirit continues to be a presence in my life, how we are still connected, and how he works behind the scenes to help me accomplish things. A lot of things that I used to think were pure luck (or an unbelievable coincidence) I now understand that Darren has been helping me out, protecting me, and providing for me, after all.

Unfortunately for those seeking a good medium, Sherry no longer does mediumship readings, and instead now focuses on intuitive counseling and energy healing. It was very draining on her to be surrounded by grief on a daily basis. I would imagine so. She is still using her gifts, but in other ways. Even though someone couldn't go to her now for a reading to connect to their departed loved ones, she was very helpful to me in my connection to Darren, and in my spiritual growth, so I've included our readings in this book.

My Readings with Ruth Kramer

"The best and most beautiful things in the world
cannot be seen or even touched.
They must be felt with the heart."

—Helen Keller

Now, I wouldn't say that I was becoming a psychic junkie just yet, but this whole world of psychics and mediums was so fascinating to me. I felt like I was privy to some secret society. The fact that I could have a reading with Sherry Lynn anytime I wanted to, and possibly connect with Darren was *so* cool. It was pretty much all I had at that point. Sometimes I just needed some reassurance that he was still there.

Sherry Lynn was beginning to lose her objectivity with me because she and I were becoming good friends. It was hard for her to tell if the source of the information she was getting was coming from her own wishes for me or from the other side. She was biased, and she didn't want it to compromise the integrity of my experience. I had some questions that I wanted some guidance with, regarding the possibility of moving out of state. Although I was disappointed, I respected Sherry Lynn's professionalism when she suggested that I should probably see someone else, because she didn't want me to move. She referred me to Ruth Kramer, who also lived in our town, and Sherry Lynn went to her for personal readings, and just raved about her. I decided to give Ruth a try. Besides, now that I was writing a book that included these kinds of things, I could now call this *research*.

Ruth Kramer calls herself a Holistic Therapist and Teacher for Personal Growth. She does body work (massage) in conjunction with spiritual guidance. She is not technically a medium, but often does connect with those in spirit during her work. She connected to Darren as the others did, even though that is not her specialty. I went to see Ruth two different times; once for just spiritual guidance, and once for the bodywork with guidance combination. Both were amazing. The first time I met her was when I went in to her place of business to make my appointment. I was carrying Damon in a front carrier, who was six-months-old at the time.

We went inside, and I told the person behind the desk that I wanted to make an appointment with Ruth, and that I was referred by Sherry Lynn. She replied, "I'm Ruth," in the most charming British accent. She was young and bubbly, with the sweetest smile and dimples. We chatted for a few minutes and I made my appointment for later in the week. Our first reading covered a variety of topics.

During our reading, she began by saying that there was a little blond boy about this tall, (holding up her hand) who was jumping out at her. She asked if I had an older son, besides the baby that she had seen me with. I said yes. She went on to accurately describe some issues that we had been having with him. He wasn't talking as much as he should have been at his age, and it was very frustrating for him and for us. He couldn't tell us what he needed, and we didn't know how to help him. She was right on target when she described it as a sorrow that I haven't let out for a long time. I eventually told her the issues, and she comforted me by telling me not to feel guilty, and that my frustration was so normal, and gave me some more advice. This was pretty amazing in itself. Then, she continued with the following:

- "There's this other sorrow over here, this sorrow is yours, and it is pre-kids sorrow. Did your father die or something? Because there is this death here- I'm feeling a guy…your husband?"

    "Yes, my husband."

- "Ok… and there's a lot of unresolved stuff here- all these unspoken words, and stuff that wasn't said and done. I can definitely feel a man, but it's funny, because I want to say father. I almost feel as though he was more of a father to you than a husband, more of a friend than a lover."

    "The friend part, yes. We were very close friends. Another medium got him as my brother."

- "It's different, I am just seeing him in a fatherly role- maybe that's where he is now. And he has died, and that's why you've moved on and remarried. But you are missing some things about him. The parts that you are missing are that you have all of this stuff going on over here with your son, and he would have been a great place to turn. He would have been the one to calm you and soften your spirit, so that you could have coped with this a lot better. That's the part you're missing in him. You put on this great tough exterior, I can handle this, I can do anything, I am Mighty Mouse; but it's not actually who you are. You're someone who feels everything very deeply, on a very conscious level, more conscious than you care to admit to, including

206

to yourself sometimes, and he got that. He was one of the few people in the world who got who you really were. The tough exterior, the I can cope, perfect looking, perfect outer shell; he got all that, that there's so much more to you. I feel that he even got that more than your own parents would have gotten that. I feel like there were certain standards that everyone else expected you to live up to, even now, around you. And the only reason they expect it is because you expect it of yourself. But he didn't. There was something very comfortable about this…you could really be *you* here. And if you miss anything, that is what you miss right now."

"You're right."

- "He still walks with you… I know you know that. He's very fatherly, he's definitely there. He still walks with you."

"I know he does." This one really choked me up.

- "If he was like the brother, he would have been the older brother, that's what I mean by fatherly. You didn't have to take care of him. But you do over here, with your current husband. He's younger, his whole spirit is younger, and it's like having another kid."

I laughed and said, "You're right it is, and yes, he is five years younger."

- "It's like having another child sometimes, he's like a big overgrown boy which will be lovely for your boys- and it will come into great service for your older boy, because he'll really be able to get down to that level and help him. But that's what you miss. This was yours. You only had him for a few years, didn't you?"

"We were married for a few years, but were together for eight years."

- "Ok, that's what I'm seeing then. I've got that bit. So you dated for a while first, right, because you were young when you met him. He was supposed to leave. He was always supposed to leave, and not be here that long. He was here for a window of time to show you that you were loved, that you were nurtured, and he still walks with you. I want you to know that this is not gone, it's just…different; it's changed form. It's not the same, and I know sometimes it's like… So what? Who cares? He's not here. I haven't got someone to go to and say, 'What do you think about this?' Actually, you do."

"I know, I talk to him all of the time."

- "Yeah, and sometimes answers will come back when you're really still and quiet- you will hear answers. You hear answers in that belly of yours, because you have this gut that turns over a lot, you're a worrier. *(Very true)* You present this very put together, fabulous, I can do anything sort of appearance to the world, but inside you're turning over, you're churning over with real concerns. So voice them, find places to voice these concerns. There should be a girlfriend over here. He's showing me someone, because he's standing in this room, right here on your side here."

"He is, really?"

- "Did he have dark hair?"

"Yes."

- "Ok, good, it's definitely him then. Because this one, your current husband, doesn't look the same as him. I've got a totally different look here. Is this one blonder, lighter haired, sandy colored?"

"It was blond when he was young, now it's sandier."

- "And this one, your first husband, is dark. They're sort of like night and day looking."

"You could say that."

- "Over here is a girlfriend, and she's fabulous. He's pointing to her. She's wearing a dress which is strange, because she feels very active. I don't know if she's in your life, or she's coming in, but she's got dark hair too. Not a relative, or sister or anything. This is definitely a girlfriend. I almost feel like you could walk to her place. She feels really close, and she could give you that similar nurturing that he did. He's showing me her in this flowery dress. Her hair sits more shoulder length, sort of neat as a pin. But she worries too, and it feels like the two of you could get together and discuss how you really feel, and I don't feel like you've got that at the moment going on. I feel like she's not here yet, almost like a neighbor. She's a wonderful spirit, and very loving, with so much to give, and she also looks after herself. She also takes care of herself- which would be very important to you, hanging out with someone who also knows how to take care of themselves like you do. You do a very good job, and take time with your appearance. There's a certain routine, something that you do that you take care of you. And you're doing a pretty good job there and can always expand upon it, but there's something happening there that's okay with how you look after yourself. So there's this person coming in, so wait for her, she's coming."

"Okay." (I figured that she must be referring to me being a makeup

artist, and taking time to do my makeup every day. Also, I met my girlfriend/neighbor, Jenny, over a year after I had this reading, who has become a wonderful friend. I knew Jenny was the one that Darren was referring to the first time we met. The description was perfect. She lives down the street, is also a makeup artist and takes care of herself, she's a worrier, has dark hair, is active like me; we even belong to the same fitness center, we both have two young sons, our older boys struggling with the same things, and we can talk about anything. It was wonderful to know that Darren knew about her before I even met her. Jenny thought it was amazing when I told her about it, and we agree that she is my mystery friend, which makes our friendship even more special. After I read the description of her, the only thing that didn't fit was the flowery dress, until she mentioned that her favorite outfit was a flowery dress that she used to wear all the time until she had two kids and it didn't fit anymore. I couldn't believe that one!)

- "But you've got this three-and-a-half-year-old, and there are these organizations and places where you can be involved with other people who are struggling with the same issues. Because this is difficult. And you've been given this incredible challenge because you can do this. You wouldn't have been given it if it wasn't something that you could do; and it is you doing it, more than your husband.

  "Yes, that's true."

- I feel like he's this big, burly guy."

  "He's six feet tall, and has an athletic build."

- "Yeah, and it feels like he's supposed to be doing something different with his career too. It doesn't feel like he's real happy with what he's doing. There's something else he's supposed to do, and he might want to do something related with fitness. He's quite knowledgeable, and he's got a passion for it somehow, and he's quite good with people. And he's very immature and fun-loving. Not in a bad way."

  "Yeah, I'm kind of like that too; although it is hard to tell that now." (She was referring to the fact that Matt had recently received a job offer in Reno, NV, in the same industry he was working in at the time, the motocross industry, but the offer was to go to work for a competitor. He took the job and we ended up moving a month later.)

- "Well, that's why this (Darren) had to leave- because this was fatherly, and he's nodding at me, so I know I'm not saying anything that's going to insult him. He was very fatherly, and still is, and he watches over you all the time like a guardian angel. He was more like a guardian angel. I feel like your current husband has got this big sandy hair and he should be on a surfboard."

"He does body board, and used to surf too. And he has big curly hair."

- "Yeah, I feel like he's that kind of guy. And it's going to be fun to be with him, even though sometimes you want to go, 'Oh, brother, I can't believe he just said or did that.' But it's still good, and there's good humor, and your heart still feels good over here. I feel like you have a career question that you are supposed to ask me, and I'm just supposed to flow."

(I told her about writing this book, and asked her if I should pursue getting it published, or scrap the whole thing. She talked a little bit about it, and then said...)

- "For some reason, there's a city somewhere- it could be Chicago. Something about Chicago. Have you got any connections in Chicago?"

"That's where my first husband and I used to live."

- "Oh, okay, it could be that's why. Is there a lot of description in the book about Chicago?"

"That's where most of the story took place."

- "Oh, I just got chills. I just feel like there's someone in Chicago who's really going to be touched because it is their hometown. It would mean you going back there to sign, so it's going to be a bittersweet pill with this book, because it is going to bring up memories and things of all of that. And that's okay; it is going to have such a human value to it. There's no question, I've got you really big back there for just a short period of time for that whole purpose. It has to go back to its roots, to its original birth place. I'm definitely getting that from him- he's sending me back there, it's really big, the word Chicago, it's in lights. And it is right in the city; I want to walk you through the streets where all of the stores are. Were you actually in the city of Chicago?"

"We lived in the suburbs, but I worked in the heart of the city, on Michigan Avenue."

- "Because I've got you retracing steps. It's part of your healing. You see, things don't just happen for one reason, they happen for several reasons, as you know. What happens is when you're retracing your steps, and having your book published to serve the world, you still sort of serve your own healing too, your own process. So this is a huge part of that. This is the part where you never lay this to rest. He walks with you...maybe not for the rest of your life. He died suddenly, right?"

"Yes, in a car accident."

- "I feel that he's not done. He's going to want to come back and re-do some things. So he's not going to walk with you forever, because he's going to want to come back and re-live life, or finish something; complete something for himself, for his own spiritual journey. He'll stop walking with you on a daily basis. At that point, you'll be ready for that separation. It's not now, but at some point, that will need to occur for him so that he can continue with his own awakening journey. It feels like he is quite wise though, and that there isn't so much for him to learn, but more for him to experience-there is an experiential part of coming back that he'd want to do. And he'd want to come back as a man, not a woman. He's definitely a guy, and likes it, likes that male energy...and loves women, just loves women."

"He was definitely a guy's guy." (He loved to tease me about female celebrities he thought were pretty, and said things to get a rise out of me like, 'Just because I'm on a diet, doesn't mean I can't look at the menu.' So she was definitely describing him accurately there.)

*****

Ruth went on to talk about other things that she saw in my future, along with giving me great advice on certain personal issues. I thought that this reading was excellent. From the moment she saw me, she knew all about the concerns in my life, which is kind of unsettling, but it proved that she was legitimate. The way that she described both Darren and Matt was all of the proof I needed. I was much more relaxed and more myself than in my first reading with Brian. This spiritual stuff was becoming normal, and made so much sense to me.

I made another appointment with Ruth about a month later, just a few days before we moved to Reno. I wanted to see what this body work was all about and after packing up the entire household practically single-handedly, I was in desperate need of a massage. (Matt had to go to Reno two weeks before the rest of us to start his new job.) As soon as I walked in to see Ruth, she said that she was supposed to give me a warning to be careful with my right foot. She said that she wouldn't want to see me break it or anything, and that it can be avoided. I told her that I was packing up to move to Reno and that I was carrying big boxes and furniture by myself. She told me to ask my brother for help, and that he lived nearby and would be glad to lend a hand. She was right, he did live nearby. When I got home, I took her advice, and called Joey, and he was glad to help out. (Joey had moved to California a few years earlier.)

Anyway, we started off our session with a short reading before we got into the body work. She talked about my upcoming move, and accurately described what our new neighborhood looked like. She asked if we were moving into a brand new home because she said that she smelled paint and saw carpet going down. Our rental home was brand new and had never been lived in. I couldn't believe it. She said that the move was going to be good for me and for our family for so many reasons, and went on to describe them all.

Then, we moved on to the body work, and before I even got on the massage table, and told her what hurt, she intuitively knew that it was my lower back and shoulder blades that needed the most work. She also mentioned that I needed a new bed because mine was too soft. She was right; it was like lying on a hammock. It was nice while I was pregnant both times, but now it was time to get rid of it. Our session began and she talked throughout it, continuing our reading and adding affirmative statements. I felt as though I was healing my body, mind, and spirit. It was the most amazing massage I'd ever had. She used the perfect amount of pressure and knew just what needed the most work. She explained how it wasn't just her hands doing the work, but that she had lots of spirits guiding her.

Most people know this type of energy healing as Reiki. I knew about Reiki from Sherry Lynn, who tried it on me once. (Reiki is the gentle laying of hands for healing by consciously channeling Universal Life Force Energy to the recipient, through the hands of the practitioner. It is a non-religious healing art which began in Japan and is used throughout the world.) I could feel the heat radiating from Ruth's hands. I left there feeling totally relaxed and energized at the same time.

I don't want to start sounding redundant about how I felt about these readings so I'll keep it short and sweet. Basically, they were amazing and incredibly healing. To have yet another person who could connect with Darren on the other side and give me such accurate information was even more proof that all of these people weren't in cahoots to fool me and take my money. She was incredibly accurate and knew so much about my life, it was kind of scary. At the same time, it reassured me that there really are many people out there who have wonderful intuitive gifts that can help others in need; the challenge is to find them. I took Ruth's business card with me, in case I needed it after our move to Reno. She, like Sherry Lynn, could do this work over the phone as well as in person. It was like having a life line.

My Readings with a Third Medium-Vickie Gay

*"We are, each of us, angels with only one wing;
and we can only fly by embracing one another."*

—*Luciano De Crescenzo*

It was the end of October, 2002, five months after we had moved to Reno, NV. My mom and I decided to go to the newly renovated Reno-Sparks convention center for the Home Show, since we were in the process of buying a new home. It just happened to be the same weekend that the convention center was holding the Psychic and Creative Arts Fair. How convenient!

Once I saw that there was a psychic fair, we had to take a detour from the Home Show and check it out first. I was curious to see what kind of psychics, or more specifically, mediums, were in Reno. I was a bit apprehensive because I didn't know anything about any of these people. I didn't want to waste my time and money on a vulture that preyed on grieving people or some buffoon telling me I had a curse, and that if I gave them enough money they could remove it. Darren's mom actually had an unfortunate incident with one of these types in Florida. The woman is now being brought up on charges. Luckily, Darren's mom was smart enough to see the con, but a lot of others were not.

We walked around for a little bit and checked out the scene. I was a little uncomfortable imagining that all of the psychics knew my life story just by looking at me. Then I noticed one of the booths had a woman doing readings whose sign said that she was a medium. She looked to be a little older than me with a fair complexion and a long, thick mane of blonde hair. I expected her to be the one sitting on the other side of the table. She looked kind and really into what she was doing. I put my name on the short waiting list for my fifteen minute reading. The lady standing next to me was wiping away tears with a tissue as she waited for her friend who was being read and told me that she just had a reading with Vickie, and that she was very good. That was a positive sign that she was legitimate.

My mom took Trevor over to the stage area where they were playing some

215

cool New-Age music, as I sat down for my reading with Vickie Gay. I wish I would have had my tape recorder with me, but since it was unplanned, I wasn't prepared to record it. The following are the most important messages I received from our first reading. I wrote them down when I got to the car.

After a brief introduction to the process, Vickie said a prayer of protection, took both of my hands in hers, closed her eyes for a moment, and then began:

- "I'm seeing boxes, are you going to be moving?"
  "Yes, we are having a house built right now."
- "Ok, good. I'm being told that you should go check on it every day. Don't think you are being a pest, but you need to be on top of things."
  "We have been walking there every day to check on the progress. It is only a mile away, in the same complex we live in."
- "It is going to be fine, I'm told, but just keep checking on it."
  "I will do that." (We ended up having a major water leak that they wouldn't have told us about had we not seen it for ourselves.)
- "I have an older woman here, sitting in a rocking chair with a lap shawl placed across her lap. It is like an afghan, but smaller. She has gray hair, which she let go gray naturally. She says that she has been watching you at home with your family playing with some kind of train."
  "Oh my God, we just bought an electric train, and it is set up around a table in our living room, and my children and I sit in there a lot watching the train."
- "There you go. She says that she is very proud of you, and that you don't need much help from her, but she's there."
  (I wasn't sure who this was until after the reading. On the way home, my mom figured out that it had to be my great-grandmother, my mom's grandmother. She passed away when I was young, but I remembered her. My mom said that she used to cover herself up with lap shawls because she always wore dresses and her legs got cold. She also had naturally gray hair, and we actually have her child's-sized antique rocking chair in Damon's bedroom that she received on her first birthday over 100 years ago. When we got home, my mom showed me one of these lap shawls that her mother had knit for my great-grandma. I couldn't believe that she actually had one of them in my house!)
- "She's showing me a shelf. She's actually getting up out of the rocking

chair with a screwdriver and tightening the screws on this shelf. I think this is a warning to check for loose screws on some type a shelf."

"I just put a shelf up in my son's room. I'll check it out." (*After we got home, I checked the shelf on the wall in Damon's room and it was fine. However, the top shelf on Damon's changing table (which had three shelves on it) was dangerously loose, and could have resulted in a fall if he had been placed on it in that condition. Wow!*)

- "There's also a cat here that just wants you to know that it is here."

  "That's cool." (*At the time I wasn't sure which cat she meant, because my family had lots of cats. But on the way home, I realized that it had to be Shadow, Darren's and my cat. I had recently had another experience where Shadow made her presence on the other side known, so I knew that this mention of her validated my last experience.*)

- "Did you have any questions you wanted to ask me?"

  (I had been hoping for Darren to come through, so I asked) *"Is there anyone else there that you can get for me?" She closed her eyes, re-opened them after a few seconds, and said:*

- "There is a brother figure here, around your age. He's like a brother."

  "Why does everyone get him as my brother? If it is who I think it is, another medium thought he was my brother too."

- "It's not your brother?"

  "No, but let's see what he says, then I'll know who it is."

- "He's standing next to you, embracing you with a long-stemmed yellow rose."

  "What does that symbolize to you?"

- "Love, unless it means something more to you. This man must have been very playful because now he's sitting next to you, trying to nudge you off of your chair."

  "Yes, that is true, it sounds like him."

- "Now he's doing something I've never seen before, maybe you'll know what it means. He's taking his t-shirt and pulling it up over his head so that his face is showing through the opening and he's doing this with his arms." (Holds her arms up like a football goalpost).

  I start laughing out loud, and say, "This is my late husband. He is doing an imitation of The Great Cornholio from Beavis and Butthead. It is an inside joke we shared. I even have a picture of him doing this."

(I couldn't believe it!)

- "I have no idea what that is, but as long as it makes sense to you. So, this is your husband? I'm sorry, you're so young. This wasn't your little boy's father, right?" (Referring to Trevor who was at the booth with me earlier). *"No, I have remarried."*

- "There is a lot of love here from him. Now, he's blowing bubbles shaped like little hearts all around you." She starts to get choked up. "I'll leave you with that okay?"

*****

Our time had been up a few minutes earlier, so I thanked her, gave her a hug, and took one of her business cards. I had the biggest smile on my face as I went to find my mom to relay what had just happened. This was completely unplanned and unexpected, yet it was one of the most precise messages I had received yet.

Leave it to Darren to choose Cornholio as the way to make himself known to me. There was no question that it was him. I couldn't believe how much information came through in such a short time. I felt so peaceful the rest of the day. After we got home, I began to receive even more validations of the accuracy of this reading. It made sense to my mom and me that my great-grandmother would come through because not only do we have her rocking chair, but my mom has some framed black and white pictures of her as a young woman in her bedroom, and we also have her china set in a box in our garage, along with a china pitcher in one of our bathrooms that was once hers. As I mentioned during the reading, upon returning home, I immediately discovered the loose shelf on Damon's changing table and quickly tightened it, which was the first validated message from the reading. Then, a few days later, the fun began.

The electric train that my great-grandma made reference to during the reading began to go on by itself! Now, in order to start the train, you need to push a button on the remote control, or push a button on the train's engine. There is no mistaking it when it is on because it says, "All aboard!" and makes authentic train sounds and whistles. The first time this happened, my mom and I had been out running errands with the boys, and when we walked in the house, the train was going. We hadn't been playing with it before we left so we thought it was a bit odd.

The second time, my mom was in Damon's room putting him down for a nap, and Trevor was in my room with me, when I heard, "All aboard!" I went in the

218

living room, and again the train had apparently started by itself, since my mom was still in Damon's room. I began to wonder how this was happening, and then I began to suspect that it was my great-grandma turning it on to validate her comment during the reading. If my mom hadn't been there to witness this stuff herself, she probably would have thought I was losing my marbles, but she couldn't explain it either.

The third time, my in-laws were in town and my mother-in-law was sitting next to the train, and I was in the next room when I heard, "All aboard!" "Who turned on the train?" my mother-in-law asked. I tried not to laugh as I answered, "It just goes on by itself sometimes." I just left it at that for the time being. I wasn't sure how she'd react if I told her my theory.

Then, the fourth time, my mom was going to visit my sister in Chicago, and I was nervous about being left alone with the two boys for the first time. I called my sister to let her know that mom made her flight on time, and I also told her about the train incidents. A short time after I hung up the phone, I heard, "All aboard!" I smiled and relaxed a bit. I knew now that I wasn't alone after all. Unfortunately, Damon decided that it was his mission to de-rail the train every ten minutes, so we had to take it down for a while. About a year after the first set of incidents with the train, we had moved into our new home and since Damon liked trains so much, we decided to try to put up the electric train again hoping that Damon, almost two-years-old, wouldn't take it apart. He was pretty good at first, so we left it up for a few weeks. During this time, my in-laws were in town visiting again. One night, I heard Trevor, now five, over the baby monitor at 5:00 a.m., laughing and carrying on. I went downstairs into his room to see what was going on, and he just kept giggling and looking up at the ceiling as though he were playing with someone. I wondered if he could see a spirit that I couldn't see. A few minutes later, the train started by itself again.

I didn't hear it go on myself, but when Trevor finally went back to sleep about an hour later, I went back upstairs and my mother-in-law was awake and asked me who turned the train on at 5:30. She had gone downstairs to turn it off. I told her it was a long story, and that I'd explain it later, which I finally did. She and my father-in-law are very spiritual, and really enjoyed the story. I knew it was my great-grandmother again because my mom and I had just been looking at pictures of her and talking about her earlier that day. It was amazing. What a wonderful string of events to validate my reading with Vickie.

Also, the message in the reading regarding the cat wanting to let me know that it was there was also validated after I got home. However, it will make more sense to read it in the appropriate chapter, The Touch Lamp. The point is that my short, fifteen minute reading turned out to be very powerful and accurate, and it was great to receive the extra confirmations long after the reading took place. Vickie was definitely the real deal.

Fast forward five months from the initial reading to March, 2003. Our new house was going to be finished in a few weeks, and my mom and I were going to go check out some local landscapers at the Home and Garden Show at the Reno- Sparks Convention Center. We found out when we arrived that there was also another Psychic Fair going on. Apparently, they have them twice a year, and we just happened to go there both times for other reasons. Go figure!

My mom said she wanted to go see if the woman who was playing the cool New-Age music last time we were there was back because she wanted to buy her CD. Of course, I had no problem with that. I decided that while we were there, I would see if Vickie was back, and maybe I'd sign up for another reading. She was there, but had a two-hour waiting list this time. Word must have been getting around on how good she was. I put my name on the list, and we decided to go to the Home Show first, and then come back for my reading.

I sat down with Vickie and told her that I had a reading with her at the last Psychic Fair, that the messages were right-on, and that I had a lot of validations after I got home. I told her briefly about my great-grandmother, and the train starting by itself. She was looking at me as if she was trying to place me, and then said that she didn't remember the reading but she was glad to hear about the validations. She asked if I wanted to ask for someone specific, or to just see who comes through. I said to just see who comes through. She held my hands in hers, closed her eyes and began:

- "Well, right away, the great-grandmother is here again, she's standing behind you on the left, and she is just acknowledging that you were talking about her here and in your home. She was the one starting the train she says. She is a very bright, strong energy; and you also have a man standing directly behind you."

    "How old is he?" I asked. Suddenly, Vickie squeezed my hands, opened her eyes, and excitedly blurted out:

- "I remember you now! This is your husband…he's doing that thing with his shirt again, pulled over his face to let me know that it is him. He's using it as his calling card."

"No way, that's hilarious!" He was doing Cornholio from Beavis and Butthead again. Vickie looked at me funny again and said:

- "I remember you now. You look different though."

  "I had long hair last time I saw you. I recently cut off about a foot of hair."

- "That's probably why I couldn't place you. Ok, let's talk to your husband. Your husband is here. He's showing me books. He's sitting on a swing, reading a book and giving me the thumbs up. Do you know what that means? Are you studying or something?"

  "No, but I wrote a book."

- "He is saying yes, it is your book, and he's turning it around, and your picture is on the back cover. He says that he is very touched by what you wrote about him in the book. He says that he was with you while you were writing it, and that he is very pleased with it."

  "Really? Ask him if I should still try to get it published." (I was getting tired of all the rejection letters and was about to give up trying.)

- "He's showing me the scan bar on the book, so that tells me that it will be published. He says that it was helpful for you to put it on paper, but that it will help others too, because they've been through it as well. It is also a good drama. I also see you signing books at a book signing. He's also showing me a stack of the books, like they will be ordering a lot of them."

  "Wow. Is this going to happen soon, or down the road some time?"

- "As soon as you said that, I saw speed, which means in a short time period."

  "I better get busy then."

- "He says that there is something missing. You need to add something to the middle and to the end of the book."

  "I have a few things I'm thinking of adding."

- "He says to tell you that you are the best. You are the greatest. He loves you so much; I can see it all around you, all the way down to your fingertips. I normally don't do this, but he wants me to ask you to close your eyes, and see if you can feel it."

  (I do as she asks, and I can feel a slight tingling sensation up my arms and on the back of my neck; and tears start to fall.)

- "Do you feel it?"

  "Yeah, I think so."

- "He's sending you love, and wants you to know that spirit never dies. The

personality, who we are, doesn't die. He says that you already know that."
   "I do."

- "He says that he lets you know that he's around in lots of ways; some subtle, some not so subtle."
   "Yes, this is very true." (Much more on this later.)
- "He says that he knows how special he is to you."
   "He will always be special."
- "I'll leave you with that, okay?"
   "Thank you so much."

*****

Our time was up so soon. I couldn't believe it; Cornholio came through again! I knew that it was really Darren, and what he said about my book meant the world to me. It motivated me to get moving on it. I had been so busy with our move, the new house, and my two kids that the book had taken the back seat.

I took this as my sign that it was time. If only finding a publisher was that easy. I had just about given up the idea that my book was going to be published, when another medium brings it up again. Just having Darren mention it again made me feel as if I needed to find a way.

We were walking back to the car and I felt absolutely peaceful. This connection to Darren that day was totally unplanned, and I felt so blessed to have had the experience. As if this reading in and of itself wasn't great enough, I got another validation on the way home. As we were driving home, I changed the station on the radio and heard, *"The boys are back in town…"* My mom and I looked at each other, laughed, and said in unison "Cornholio."

My Reading with Psychic Theresa Peacock

*"Discoveries are often made by not following instructions;
by going off the main road; by trying the untried.*

—Frank Tyger

In between the last reading with Vickie that I just described, and my next reading with Vickie, six months later, some pretty amazing things were going on in my life. I am going to change the subject briefly, but it will all come together and make sense. I am going to be writing another book devoted to this subject in the future so I don't want to divulge too much. Basically, my five-year-old son Trevor had been diagnosed with mild autism, or PDD-NOS (Pervasive Developmental Disorder, Not Otherwise Specified), or Developmental Delays, depending on who you asked, at the age of three. As you can imagine, we were all devastated.

We did not accept any of these diagnoses and felt they were inaccurate. He was developing ahead of schedule for two years and then between the second and third year, he began to regress. I knew that there was something else going on with him and was determined to figure out what it was and help him.

All of these diagnoses are based on observation. Usually there are delays in speech, social interaction and unusual responses to sensory input. I had been researching everything I could on the subject and looking into alternative therapies, as the medical community had nothing to offer. We had done Auditory Integration Training (AIT) with Trevor a month earlier which involves listening to filtered music to desensitize his extremely hyper-acute hearing and were seeing big improvements in his speech and behavior; and I wanted to continue on this healing path.

I decided to treat myself on my birthday and have a reading with a local Reno psychic named Theresa Peacock, who had her own radio show as well as her own place of business. I was impressed with what I had heard on her radio show and thought that maybe she would be able to give me some insight on how to help my son, and answer a few other things. I had Trevor with me when I made my appointment with Theresa a few days before my birthday, and scheduled my reading on my actual birthday, August 28, 2003. Theresa was much younger than I had pictured her to be from her raspy radio voice. She was small and thin with long brown hair, and a cute laugh. I was excited to see what was going to come through during my reading.

Theresa uses Tarot cards in her readings and I had always thought that Tarot was just the luck of the draw, but her interpretation of the first four cards I chose were right on the money, and I knew that we were off to a good start. Part of the interpretation of one of these cards was that I had just been through hell (losing Darren). When I later went to explain to Theresa what the card meant to me, I started to get teary-eyed, then apologized saying, "I can't believe I'm still not over it." She gave me the best advice I had ever received and taught me a big lesson.

She said, "Honey, we never get over anything. We work through it; we walk through it daily. You'll never get over your husband- so stop expecting that you'll get over it, it's unrealistic. There is always going to be that void. There's always going to be the 'what ifs,' the 'what could be,' the 'what would we be doing today.' That's a way of celebrating what he gave to you, dear. So we are to celebrate. Don't pick yourself apart because you're not over it- you're never going to get over it. Give yourself permission to not get over it- it's okay. A lot of people in the grieving process tell you that you should be at this stage or that stage. No! That is a very personal thing, and however long it takes you to get through it, which could literally be the rest of your life- know that you will get through it, you will walk through it, and you will gain strength and a sense of purpose that maybe you hadn't recognized before."

It was so refreshing to hear that. We are so conditioned to think that you should just forget about people who are no longer here and "get over it." And then, like me, feel guilty for showing any emotion. I liked her way of thinking. Okay, now we get to the good stuff. This was the best birthday present I could have ever asked for. The following excerpt from the reading is in the same format as the other readings. I mentioned to her that I had written a story that was going to be published about my son's progress with AIT and Theresa said:

- "With your son, have you checked his diet, dear?"
  "He has a horrible diet, why?"
- "How old is he?"
  "Five."
- "He might not even have autism; they're saying it's something more, actually. Check his diet, change his diet, maybe get the gluten out of his diet. Strip it,

strip it completely.

> *"I can't believe you just said the word gluten. I actually tried the gluten-free diet for a week and he wouldn't eat any of the food." (Gluten is the protein in wheat.)*

- "Right, because he's craving all the bad stuff because it is all he knows. So, yeah, he'll get hungry, honey. He'll get hungry and when this is all there is, then he'll start eating it."

> *"Okay."*

- "And also, have you got him into some motor skills thing, like jumping on a trampoline?"

> *"We just bought him a big trampoline for his birthday last month and he loves it!"*

- "Good, because he needs this kind of exercise, because I think its called *the vestibular* is off, and he needs those motor skill exercises to get that back in line. That's what's out of balance.

> *"Yes." (The vestibular system is the sense of balance and movement.)*

- "I'm not getting autism; I think it might just be diet related and vestibular. *(I told her a little bit about the theories about how a lot of children are who are diagnosed with late-onset autism, as Trevor was, are actually allergic or intolerant of gluten and/or casein (the protein in milk). These proteins are not broken down in their bodies properly and become an opiate, basically drugging them, causing symptoms that mimic autism.)*

- "Yes, he's addicted to it sweetie, he's addicted to the bread, and he's got to let it go so he can heal. And that's okay that he's addicted to it. It would be best to just strip it completely, but you can do it gradually. Then you're going to notice the difference, and then he's going to notice the difference, and then he won't want it anymore."

> *"He is starting to eat other foods that are good for him, besides bread products and pasta."*

- "So just start limiting how much gets in and when he recognizes how he feels, he's not going to want to go back to those things. It's going to be like, "No, thanks, that's making me sick. I don't want that."

> *"Wow, this is amazing. I guess I gave up too soon."*

- "You need to get disciplined and start cooking. You can make gluten-free bread. You have to experiment. You have to let him get hungry enough to start eating properly."

> *"I have such a hard time even saying that he's autistic because I'm not sure that he is."*

- "Honey, I'm not sure that he is either, but I think it's more vestibular and diet. They're so quick to label autism- that way they can just label it and go from there. A lot of those kids are not autistic at all; they have vestibular problems, gluten problems, and allergy problems that are going unchecked. Experts are saying, "Oh, its just autism," when it's not autism at all. Again, I'm not getting autism with your son. I don't really think there is autism, I think it all is diet, vestibular and food allergies- they are all related. And the little guys coming in now are all too sensitive."

> *(I started to say something, and she cut in...)*

- "He's hearing spirits; he's clairaudient. So the music thing (AIT) was a very good thing and it will keep him balanced, but it is very important to get him into communicating fully so he can start communicating what he is hearing. You can help him recognize that yes, you are hearing this, but you have every right to turn it off."

> *"I had a feeling that he was. He's even said my late husband's name before."*

- "He hears him."

> *(We continued to talk, but this was the big ooh! moment.)*

*****

I was so blown away by the mere fact that Theresa even knew what gluten was, much less all the details she provided. I decided to follow up on this incredible lead, to try the diet again, and also have him tested for a few other things that are often related that I had been reading about. I knew I was on to something. I had some lab tests performed, and I took Trevor to see an integrated medicine doctor who used homeopathy, and also used non-invasive electrodermal screening for allergy testing and for other types of testing. I was shocked at the findings. We found out that he had an overgrowth of yeast in his gastrointestinal tract (caused from overuse of antibiotics to treat recurrent ear infections), parasites (which thrive in a yeasty environment), mercury (from vaccines), vaccine damage, along with an allergy to gluten and casein. (He is also allergic to 50 other things; including various foods, food additives and preservatives, chemicals, animals, pollens, plants and trees, that we later learned by doing further allergy testing.)

As a mother, I felt extremely guilty that I hadn't figured this out sooner. I blamed myself, and felt that I had hurt my own child in an effort to protect him by following the recommended vaccination schedule, which I feel triggered a lot of his problems. I started to detoxify and treat him homeopathically for all of these things, began a strict gluten/casein free diet, did an allergy elimination technique using acupressure and eliminated other known allergens from his environment. Now, he is doing great, but that is another story.

More Readings from Vickie Gay

"I believe that dreams are more powerful than facts,
that hope always triumphs over experience,
that laughter is the only cure for grief.
And I believe that love is stronger than death."

—From the movie "The Crow"

Okay, now we will get back to Vickie. After our last reading, I began working some more on this book since Darren brought it up in our last reading. One day, I was at a health food store and happened to see a local newspaper advertising the Psychic Fair on its cover, which was to be held that weekend. I couldn't believe how quickly time had passed since the last one. I picked up a copy, and brought it home. Inside was an article about Vickie, and I noticed that she now had a website. I went to her website and e-mailed her, telling her that I wanted to stop by the Fair and give her a copy of the chapters that I added to my book in which I mention her, and to schedule another reading. She e-mailed me back and remembered me right away this time (thanks to Cornholio) and we set up a time for my reading.

One week before this next reading, I found out that Trevor had numerous health problems. I began talking to Darren everyday, asking for his help. I wanted to know that Trevor was going to be okay, and that what I was doing was going to help him. All I wanted to get out of the reading with Vickie was to have Darren tell me something about Trevor that would comfort me in this time of uncertainty.

I went to the Psychic Fair alone this time. I found Vickie, and we hugged hello. I gave her the chapters from my book and we chatted for a few minutes before we did my reading. Luckily, this time I had my tape recorder, so it is more exact than going by memory. The following is an excerpt from our reading on October 19, 2003. Vickie said:

- "I see your husband coming in, and he's easy to spot because he does that Beavis thing. He's all excited and he's skipping circles around you. He's doing the little hearts, the little bubbles. I see his face through the shirt. Do you want to ask him something? He's listening."

(I paused, not wanting to give away what I was hoping he would tell me on his own, so that I would know that he heard me when I was asking for his help all week.) I said, "I'm leaving it open. I asked him to come today to tell me something."

- "He's just looking at you, and he's showing me a little boy."

  (I start crying already.) "I wanted to ask him about my son."

- "He's showing me a little boy and I see him holding him. I see his arm around you, he's standing next to you with his hand on your shoulder, and he's pulling you close to him. He says he can do stuff over there and he's manipulating everything that he can, and he's showing me the little boy again. He'll take care of him. He'll take care of the little boy."

  (I'm sobbing so hard, I can't speak.)

- "Okay, he's just looking at you through that hole in his shirt and again, he gets back by you. He says it's okay, it's going to be okay."

  "I needed to hear that."

- "Now he's showing me a crossing over, and he's caught pets that have crossed over. It's like they bounce over there and he catches them. So he's got them with him. I think you just needed to hear that again."

  (I'm sure he was referring to Shadow again.)

- "He says he's all over the place; he's everywhere. He doesn't only come to you. He says that he not only helps you, but he manipulates things for you. He says that you're the love of his life. That's something that should be automatic. It's natural; it's normal, that's the way it should be."

  "Wow!"

- "And I see him rocking the little boy, but he's kind of big."

  "Yeah, he's five."

- "But he holds him like he is his own."

  "Really?"

- "I feel like you wrote your book from the heart, but I feel like you're going to write some more. It may not be along those lines, but there is more material you're going to write."

  "Yes."

- "I think Darren enjoys that. He likes the writing part. I don't know if it is because the book was about him, but he also enjoys the writing. I don't think he was much of a writer. It's like he can pop the ideas in there for you.

He's got a lot of ideas."

"I get inspired."

- "That would be the right word. It may be a series of books that go from one to the other. Because once you get the first one out, people already know you, and it keeps on going. I read this one, now I'll read this one."

"I'm working on some things."

- "He just sends you a lot of love. He's got his arms around your shoulders. He's more centered now. He loves you very much. He loves you so much." "What is wrong with your son? Is he ill?"

(I explain to her about our recent medical findings with Trevor, and how the message from Theresa was the key to get me on that path to help him.)

- "Darren is definitely working with you. He's got the little boy, and he's looking out after him. Maybe that's why you're on the path; but he's there too."

"I just feel so guilty. Why didn't I figure this out earlier? I could kick myself."

- "Don't feel like that; and your husband doesn't send that kind of feeling either. You figured it out, and kept on it. If anything, you should be glad that you figured it out, because now you can reverse it."

"I hope so."

*****

This reading gave me so much comfort, because it let me know that Darren is not only helping me, he's helping my children, who mean the world to me. Also, I had been desperately asking for Darren's help all week, and for him to say that he had the little boy and that everything was going to be okay, let me know that I was on the right path to help Trevor; and best of all, I was being guided by Darren as to how to help him. It just fueled my fire to keep going in the same direction and to not give up.

Then the coolest thing started happening that very night. Darren began going to Vickie at her home to give me messages, and she welcomed him. She says she is a spirit magnet, and they often come to her during meditation and other times. The next morning I had an e-mail from Vickie saying that although she was very tired, Darren talked her into reading the pages from my book, and then he requested that she ask me to change one thing in the book. I couldn't believe it! Not only was he coming to her at home, but he was doing it in order to edit my book!

Vickie received a few more messages from Darren over the next month. One of them was a security warning not to pass my book around to other widows yet on the same day that I went to mail a copy to someone I had recently met. It didn't go out, thanks to the mailman being late that day. I had to go back to the post office to rescue it after receiving Vickie's e-mail. I figured Darren wouldn't have warned me without reason. Vickie had no idea that I was mailing it that day. It was amazing. It showed me that there are no coincidences.

Then Darren gave Vickie a message on his mom's birthday that I really needed to hear again. She said, "I see your husband in spirit…he shows himself with his shirt over his head to identify himself. Very seriously, he pulls his shirt in the normal position and says he is there for your son." It had been a month since our last reading and it had become my mission to help my child and I really needed that extra confirmation that he was still helping me. However, I e-mailed Vickie back and told her that the e-mail brought tears to my eyes, which she mistakenly thought that it meant it had upset me, and she asked Darren to stop, which he did.

About a month and a half later, at a New Year's Psychic Fair, I brought two friends to have a reading with Vickie, and before we got started, Vickie said that she had a story to tell me. She said that she has a daughter who is married for the second time and has a daughter from her first marriage, and a new baby with her current husband. Her first husband was still very much in love with Vickie's daughter and never let her go. Well, about a month earlier, in December, her daughter's first husband was killed in a car accident, and that *Darren* was there to help him cross over! Vickie helped Darren contact me, so in turn; he was there to help Vickie and her family when her daughter's first husband crossed over. I was blown away! It made sense that Darren would do that, not only to return the favor to Vickie, but because he and Vickie's ex-son-in-law both died young and in an auto accident. Now I feel that Vickie and I are even more connected.

Along with my friends, I had a short reading myself. It was mainly my great-grandmother again, telling me that she likes how I decorated Damon's room (we had just put some Thomas the Tank Engine bedding and accessories in there), and that she plays with my baby a lot. It was good to hear that she was watching over him. Darren was helping Trevor, and my great-grandma was with Damon.

She also said that she helps me maintain my "sparkle," and said to say hello to my mom, and that she comes to her a lot. My mom was happy to receive that message. Darren came in for a few minutes, doing the Beavis thing to identify himself, and didn't say very much because there was an audience. He did say one thing that was very heartwarming. Vickie relayed the message, "He loves you very much, he loves your whole family; including your husband. To him, if Matt does well, and things go well, then Darren's doing well." When I got home, I told Matt about it, and although he thought it was kind of weird to hear that my late husband loved him, it also made him feel good.

After our reading at the Psychic Fair, I explained to her in an e-mail that when I said that it brought tears to my eyes after hearing from Darren, that they were tears of joy. I inherited the wussy gene from my mom, and I cry during commercials and soap operas, I told her. After that, she felt better about relaying Darren's messages to me, especially after he assisted her former son-in-law in his crossing. Then he gave her another message to give to me. She said that at the Fair, he held back because my friends were there and were able to hear everything, and he likes to talk to me in private.

Vickie also relayed the following message which really got to me: "Darren loves the book; especially the part about the touch lamp. He is so excited to be able to communicate with Laura. He loves the children very much and watches over the whole family. Darren loves you forever and he will not sit still through your moments here on the Earth plane. A pact is a pact; it's made coming in, and when going out it's double. Darren wants you to feel the love. It is so beautiful. Both Laura and Darren have changed. Both have grown. Darren's spirit rescued you. Knowing he is there, you realized your strength."

*****

In conclusion, the validations that I received during all of the readings mentioned in this section from the various spirit messengers I have met have profoundly changed my life and everything I had formerly believed about life and death. These incredibly gifted people helped me heal my grief and propelled me further along on my own spiritual journey. It took me five years to process my grief before I was ready to have this type of experience, but as they say, when the student is ready, the teacher appears.

I knew that seeing a medium was not a substitute for the grief process, but that it could be a valuable part of it. Widowhood and mediumship naturally go hand in hand, and in my opinion, is the best form of grief therapy. By first researching mediumship, I had an idea of what to expect. I've never liked surprises, so for me to be willing to pursue this type of connection at all, I had to be prepared.

Before Darren's death, all I knew about communicating with the dead was what I saw on TV, or in the movies, like Whoopi Goldberg's character in the movie *"Ghost."* Even after I'd read about other people's experiences, I wasn't fully convinced that they were real. Even though I had personally met some of the people who were in these books that I read, I thought that maybe these stories had all been made up just to sell books. To erase all shadow of doubt, I needed my own authentic experience. I've realized that going to see a medium is a very courageous way to confront your grief, and I applaud anyone brave enough to step outside the box and think for themselves.

I admit that I was very apprehensive about going to see a medium for the first time, and was a bit frightened by it. I guess it was the fear of the unknown coupled with the fears that my religious upbringing planted in my mind that communicating with the dead was bad. Now I know why they were so threatened; it proves that all of the church's dogma is a bunch of hooey. There is nothing scary or evil about it in the least. It is very joyous, healing and is all about love.

During my first reading with Brian, I cried years of pent-up tears. Now when I get messages from departed loved ones during a reading, if I do cry, they are tears of joy, not pain. A shift has taken place. I have gone from a place of desperation to a place of contentment. It took me a few years of having readings to get to this peaceful place, but I remember quite well how it felt going for the first time. I have been given more than enough evidence in the form of personal validations during these readings to go beyond *hoping* that we survive death to *knowing* that we survive death. Now that I know the truth; that there is no death, I can truly live.

Direct After-Death Communication

"Belief consists of accepting the affirmations of the soul;
unbelief, in denying them."

—*Ralph Waldo Emerson*

So far, all of the examples of after-death communication in this part of the book were possible with the assistance of a medium. I've often heard the mediums themselves say that you don't need a medium to contact those on the other side. Some of the more famous ones even have books and do seminars on how to learn to do it yourself. We all have the God-given ability, but are not taught how to tap into it. Before Darren died, I'd already suspected that it was possible for the dead to contact us directly, without the help of a medium, because of the experiences that trusted friends and family members had shared with me. I discussed some of them in the chapter called "The Paranormal." There are so many ways for spirits to contact us *directly*, and in the years since Darren died I've experienced many of them personally. I've already mentioned quite a few of them throughout the book.

For instance, the rainbow sightings that my mom and I shared were signs that we were certain came from Darren. Now, you might say: What's so special about a rainbow? Well, the timing was not random; the pieces fit for me. When I saw rainbows after forgiving Dave, and again after talking to his wife, Kristine, it was a sunny day with not a cloud in the sky. Not exactly conditions for a giant circular rainbow to appear around the sun- twice, mind you.

Also, the rainbow connection made sense for me because I had told God that I would look for a rainbow as a sign from Darren. There was also the double rainbow we saw driving up to my grandfather's funeral, shortly after Darren's death. There was one rainbow for Darren, and one for my grandpa. And I also saw one when Matt and I moved to California. I cried when I saw it, and even took a picture. To me, it meant that Darren was supporting me in what I was doing.

These signs were symbolic, but I intuitively knew that they were a special gift for me, and I acknowledged them as such. I also mentioned in the music section how I would always hear two particular songs that reminded me of Darren on the radio at special moments. I also had friends who had the same experience with their own meaningful songs. I have also talked to other grieving people about this and it seems to be a common phenomenon. My friend Brenda even told me a heartwarming story where the very moment her beloved pet parakeet died in her hands, a song came on the radio that reminded her of her late grandfather, and she intuitively knew that this was his way of letting her know that her "pudgy-bird" was safe with him. This is another subtle way of knowing that our loved ones in spirit are still around us in our times of need.

Any of the six senses can be involved in after-death phenomena. Seeing an apparition of them, hearing their voice, smelling something that reminds you of them, tasting something associated with them, feeling them touch you or lay next to you. Those are the familiar five senses. The sixth sense is clairsentience, or clear sensing. Sensing, or feeling the departed person's presence is a very common occurrence. For example, I described how I felt Darren's presence in the delivery room while giving birth to my first son, Trevor. Energetically, I felt him in the room.

For some, they are able to acknowledge the presence of a spirit by a certain smell. For example, my old college roommate, Kimberly called me and was very excited. She told me that she was driving in her car, crying and upset over a recent breakup, and she started talking to Darren out loud. She asked him to help her out and send her a decent guy. At that moment, she swore that she smelled his cologne. Which cologne? I asked. Drakkar, she replied. This was his favorite, and the one he wore during college when she knew him. This story warmed my heart, knowing that Darren was also helping my friends.

Another example using three different ways to communicate happened to my mom. I had a reading with Vickie Gay, and before our reading, Vickie excused herself to go use the restroom. She returned to the room laughing and explained that Darren came to her in the bathroom and told her to hurry up and get out there. Then he told her that he was just kidding, and to take her time. When our reading started, he came through right away, and immediately brought through my mom's mom, who had passed on three months earlier. She said that she has been trying to get my mom's attention to let her know she's around; she said she even nibbled on my mom's ear and she just didn't pay attention to her.

I shared this information with my mom, along with the message that her mom loves her very much. After my reading, my grandma made more attempts to let my mom know she was around. Five days later, my mom woke up and was lying in bed awake, but with her eyes closed. Suddenly, she saw a bright light from behind her closed eyes. When she opened her eyes, she noticed that the light on her ceiling fan had gone on by itself. The remote was on her bookshelf next to her bed. She came out of her room to tell me what happened. I told her that Darren must have shown her how to turn lights on, since that was one of the ways he got my attention. I suggested that her mom was trying to get her attention as she mentioned in my reading. I told her to challenge grandma to do something else.

A short time later, my mom was taking a bath after everyone had gone to bed, and the next morning, she asked me who knocked on the bathroom door during her bath. I told her no one did; we were all in bed sleeping. She said that someone knocked on the bathroom door three times. I told her it was probably grandma again, trying to get her attention. This made her feel good to think that her mom was around.

Shortly after this episode, my mom was watching TV in her room, when she smelled burnt toast. She went upstairs to see who was burning toast at midnight, and everyone was sleeping. The same thing happened a few days later. After telling me what happened, she realized that her parents used to make very well done toast, and distinctly remembered the house smelling like burnt toast. So, she associated the smell of burnt toast to her parents. To me, this was a sign to let her know that they were together in the afterlife.

Also during this time, every time she got up in the middle of the night to go to the bathroom, the computer next to the bathroom lit up (the screensaver went off). It never did this any other time. She thought about her mom every time this happened. So, she experienced seeing a light go on that was manipulated by spirit, heard knocking on the door, smelled something associated with her departed parents, and witnessed physical phenomenon with the computer. I'd say my grandma finally got her attention. These were all wonderful gifts of love, which she acknowledged as such.

There are so many other ways that our departed loved ones can give us signs and let us know that they have survived death, and are still with us. You first need to be aware of the different ways that spirits can give us these signs, and not have your own agenda by limiting the ways they can let you know that they are around. Then, you just have to ask for the signs, look for them, and when you get them, recognize them for what they truly are instead of thinking that they are merely a figment of your overactive imagination. We put the limits on what they can do. The next two chapters include stories of the most common ways that Darren communicated with me directly after he died.

Dream Visits

"Trust in dreams, for in them is hidden the gate to eternity."

—Kahlil Gibran

I had always been fascinated by dreams. I even did a report on dreams for a psychology class in college. I read a lot of books about dream interpretation, even goofy Sigmund Freud's theories of what dreams mean. When I wrote the report, I concluded that dreams were mainly our subconscious mind at work while we slept, and the content of our dreams were things we had recently thought about during waking hours. Basically, I thought that they meant nothing. Now, I believe that dreams are a way to process and release emotional pain, and even a place where we can visit loved ones on the other side.

Many mediums- among them, John Edward and Sylvia Browne- affirm that while we are in a dream state, or even meditating, we can visit our loved ones on the other side. This is possible through astral travel, where your spirit body temporarily leaves your physical body. Our departed loved ones can also visit us in our dreams. The dream state is a real and safe place for spirits to visit us and comfort us. (Let's face it, most of us would freak out if we saw them appear in our kitchen!) In our dream state, our energy vibration is closer to those in spirit. You can distinguish a dream from a visit because your senses are involved. You can clearly see them, smell them, hear their voice, and touch them. The visit won't fade from your memory the way a dream would. When you wake up, you feel like you were actually with your loved one, because you were.

When Darren first died, I was already aware of the possibility of dream visits from my old roommate from college whose late brother came to her in a dream visit and told her specifics of his car accident and gave her comfort. Also, shortly after Darren's death, my friend Laura, who owned the modeling agency, told me of a story in which her late father came to her in a dream visit. He told her that he wasn't supposed to be there, but wanted to let her know that he was okay. She knew it was him, and was comforted.

When I began the long grieving process, I considered killing myself to be with

Darren. A dream visit from him stopped me. I describe this visit in detail in the chapter on depression. Since then, I, along with a few others close to me have had what we consider to be visits from Darren in our dreams.

Shortly after Darren's death, two of my best friends had what they considered to be dream visits, with messages for me from Darren. My friend Moe, who went to college with Darren and me, had a dream that was so real and vivid that she gets emotional talking about it to this day. In the dream, she saw a bright white light, and Darren came walking through the light toward her, dressed all in white. He told her that he was okay now, and that he hadn't felt any pain when he died. He also asked her to be there to comfort and support me, but not to worry because I would be okay. I was strong, he told her. Moe woke up, crying and confused because the dream had been so intense and vivid. She even wrote it down, so she would remember everything. She said it was the most realistic dream she had ever had, and she knew it was Darren coming to her with a message to comfort me. At the time, this was a very important message for me to hear, because I kept reliving the accident in my mind and was tormented by the thought of the physical suffering I imagined Darren must have gone through. His message to Moe gave me a lot of peace.

My friend Brenda also had a vivid dream visit from Darren. He had a message for me, he said, but he couldn't tell me himself, so Brenda needed to relay it to me for him. The message was for me not to go back to work at the restaurant where I used to work. When Brenda told me about the dream, she didn't know that I had been contemplating it. Initially, I thought that Darren meant that the restaurant wasn't a good environment for me, because I'd have to serve alcohol. But later, in a reading with Sherry, she told me that Darren had hand-picked Matt for me, and that he had planned the way Matt and I met. Was this dream part of the plan? If I had been working at the restaurant, I wouldn't have been at the trade show, or met Matt. Could Darren have gone to Brenda in her dream to prevent me from being in the wrong place at the wrong time, unable to meet my future husband?

I have had plenty of dreams in which Darren just briefly appears. These dreams are wonderful because I can see him clearly and hear his familiar voice. Just when I fear I may be forgetting him, I realize in my dreams that my spirit hasn't forgotten. These types of dreams feel more like my subconscious sorting out my feelings and the reality of my situation. I've also had dreams in which Darren is missing. He's not dead, but no one can find him. In other dreams, Darren returned after I had moved on with my life; and I had to go back to him, because he wasn't really dead, and we were still married. These were dreams that played on my fear that his death was all a big mistake. Part of me still hadn't accepted his death.

There was one particular dream that really stuck with me, that I felt was a true visit. In this very vivid dream, I was married to Matt, and we had two children. (This dream was years before we were married and had two kids.) Matt and I were living in the home that Darren and I had built (representing me living in the past.) We were playing with our kids in the family room and the doorbell rang. When I opened the door, I saw Darren standing there, just as I remembered him. He said he was back, and that he wanted me to come back to him. I turned around to look at Matt and the children (representing my future). In that instant, I knew the answer. I told Darren I didn't want to live in the past anymore and that I was happy now. I chose to stay with Matt and the children. He just smiled at me, winked, and walked away.

I was alarmed when I woke up because I thought it had really happened. I saw Darren clearly, his hair and clothing were just as I remembered, and so was his voice. The dream unfolded in logical order, not scattered like other dreams that I've had. I realized afterward that I was okay with letting Darren go and moving on with my life with Matt; and so was Darren. I could let go of any guilty feelings of moving on with my life. This dream visit was such a blessing as it silently helped me heal and move on while I slept.

Darren's mom had the most incredible dream visit. It wasn't so much the content of the dream that was so remarkable; it was the timing of it, and the validation that came later. Until this dream visit, the most memorable one that she'd had occurred shortly after Darren's death. In the dream, he was a little boy. He said nothing, but just stood in front of her wearing a jacket with a big pin on the lapel that said "I'm sorry." The severity of her pain prevented her from even dreaming about her son.

The day after my first reading with Sherry, in which Darren had been so emotional while talking about his mom, I couldn't wait to call her to tell her what had happened. She answered the phone, and said, "Oh my gosh, Laura, it's so weird that you called me today, because I've just had the most realistic dream I've ever had about Darren. I saw him, smelled him, and felt him when I hugged him; and I told him over and over that I loved him. I woke up crying tears of joy. Then I cried harder because I realized that he wasn't really here, and it was only a dream." "It was real," I told her, "And maybe you'll understand why you had it after I tell you what happened to me yesterday." I told her everything that Darren said during my reading, and we both cried the whole time. She was so happy, and thanked me for sharing it with her. Darren had come to her in a dream the very night of my reading.

That was incredible! I explained why I believed her dream was really a visit from Darren, and I know she felt comforted.

The validation came during a later reading with Sherry. When Darren came through, I asked him if he had really come through to his mom in her dream. He confirmed that he had visited her for several reasons: first, he wanted to comfort her; but also, he wanted his mom and me to connect what he does in each of our lives to say, "I'm here." The dream visit was not a figment of her imagination, Sherry explained. She's not making it up. She felt something, and she didn't know that you were having a connected reading with her son. This was Darren's way of saying, "Look at how we all are one." That's why it happened. Darren's mom was excited and happy when I told her about this validation. She knew the truth, and that's all that mattered.

These incidents were most memorable because they happened early on; when dreams were the only way I knew I could still visit Darren. Now, I dream of him often, and they don't startle, frighten, or upset me like they once did. Now I look forward to my dream state, and even invite Darren to come and visit me in my dreams. I am surprised at how often he is there.

I was going back to Chicago for the first time in years, and was going to be visiting Darren's mom, whom I hadn't seen in five years. I couldn't wait to see her. The morning before I left, I had an amazing dream visit from Darren. In the dream, I was standing in front of a mirror looking at myself, and trying to make a mental connection to Darren. Suddenly, I started to hear his familiar voice. I telepathically said to him, "I can hear you, I can hear you." Looking in the mirror, I could see him appear behind me, transparent at first, but then becoming clearer as I said in my mind, "I can see you, I can see you." I turned around, and he was really there. He looked perfect, his hair looked immaculate (he was worse than a girl, primping his hair), and he was wearing a jean jacket that he used to own with a leather collar. I used to love this jacket on him, and had forgotten about it. Then, he motioned for me to follow him, which I did. He stopped, and opened his arms, inviting me in. I ran to him with open arms, giving him a huge hug. I told him how much I missed him. It felt so good to hold him again. Then, I woke up, feeling like he was right there with me. I just stayed in bed for a while and savored the moment. When I saw Darren's mom in Chicago, I told her about my dream, and she cried.

It is such a great comfort to be able to hear Darren's voice, feel him holding me, and see his familiar face in my dreams. It is a wonderful feeling to know that in our dream state, we can visit our departed loved ones, and also receive messages from the dreams of others close to us. The spirits of those we love are as close as our dreams.

The Touch Lamp

"Faith is like electricity. You can't see it, but you can see the light."

—*Source Unknown*

At the beginning of my loss, except for my occasional rainbow signs, and a few vivid dreams, I didn't have the consistent contact from Darren that I wished for. I wanted to be sure that he hadn't forgotten about me, and I kept praying for a sign so I would know that he heard me when I talked to him. Then, I read a great book called *Hello from Heaven*, by Bill and Judy Guggenheim. It's a collection of true stories about people who have been contacted directly by their departed loved ones. There were stories ranging from people seeing full apparitions, or hearing their loved ones voice, to people smelling their loved one's cologne, or noticing electrical disturbances, as well as more subtle signs... like rainbows and butterflies. After I read this book I suddenly realized that I had been receiving a particular sign from Darren for quite a while, I just hadn't made the connection.

In 1998, shortly before Trevor was born, my mom came to live with us in California. (My parents split up in 1993). She would be our live-in nanny when I went back to work. I simply didn't trust anyone else but family to take care of my children, and we felt blessed that a veteran mom, who had raised five children of her own, was willing to help us out. When she moved, she brought a lot of things with her that we tried to make room for in our house. One of these items was a "touch lamp," the kind that turns on and off by touch only. It had four settings: low, medium, high, and off. Every touch changed the setting.

We put the lamp on a small table in Trevor's room, next to his rocking chair. Since it wasn't connected to a wall switch, you had to physically touch it to operate it. Shortly after Trevor was born, we noticed that after we had put him to bed for the night, with just a nightlight on, the touch lamp would turn on in the middle of the night apparently by itself. At first we were all baffled. One of us would go into Trevor's room at night to check on him or to go get him up in the morning, and the touch lamp would be lit up on the low setting. We each thought that one of the others was doing it.

One morning, after finding the light on again, I asked my mom if the lamp had ever lit up by itself when she lived in Milwaukee. "No," she said. "In all of the eight years that I've had it, it never did that. But I have noticed it being on in Trevor's room, and I thought you and Matt were leaving it on for some strange reason." "No," I told her. "No one has been in there all night, and I doubt that a baby who can't even crawl yet could climb out of his crib to turn it on, and sneak back into bed." "I don't know what to tell you," she said. It was a puzzle.

Matt thought that the light was shorting out, or that there was a problem with the outlet. This mysterious light went on every now and then for about a year before I came up with a new theory. In *Hello from Heaven* there were numerous accounts of spirits manipulating lights and electronic equipment. Stories of spiritually altered lights, computers, telephones and pagers were mentioned in the book. Apparently it's easy for spirits to do this because their energy vibration is higher than ours, closer to the vibration of electrical things.

So, based on these stories, I began to suspect that maybe Darren was playing with the touch lamp to get my attention. One night, Matt returned to our room after checking on Trevor and asked, "Who keeps turning that light on in Trevor's room?" When I suggested that it was a spirit, he laughed and said, "Yeah, sure it is." "I'm serious," I said, "Spirits can do that." For a while, every time the light went on by itself, we joked that "our ghost" was back.

After a while, I noticed that the touch lamp would come on during significant times in my life, most notably, the morning after I called to forgive Dave. I also saw the giant circular rainbow that day. There was just too much synchronicity going on for me not to take notice. Then, the day after I talked to Kristine, the light was on again in the morning, and I saw another circular rainbow, identical to the first. This could not be a coincidence! It also started lighting up on days that I associated with Darren: his birthday, his death day, our wedding anniversary, Valentine's Day. I had to find out if it was him doing this.

I decided I needed to challenge Darren. One night, while rocking Trevor to sleep, I was talking to Darren (as I often did), and said "Okay, Darren, if this is really you turning on the light in Trevor's room, please do it tonight, so I know for sure that you're with me. Please, I'm begging you; turn it on again tonight if it has really been you doing it." The next morning Matt looked in on Trevor before going to work. He came back into our bedroom and said, "That light is on in Trevor's room again!" I sat up in bed and said, "What?!" Matt was surprised to see me move so quickly in the morning. After I told him why it was so significant, that I had asked for it to come on, he began to believe my theory; but I think it was creepy for him to think that my late husband was in our house, fiddling with a touch lamp.

After Kristine and I resumed our friendship and began talking on a regular basis, I realized that we shared many of the same spiritual beliefs. She got goose bumps when I told her about the touch lamp and my theory behind it. Kristine believed me, and said she thought it was so cool. During one conversation, I went upstairs for an emergency diaper change, and said I'd call her right back. When I reached Trevor's room, the touch lamp was on. It wasn't lit up just an hour before when I was in there changing him. It had gone on while I was telling Kristine about the lamp. I quickly changed Trevor, called Kristine back, and said "You're not going to believe this... but I went up to change Trevor's diaper in his room, and the light was on." She squealed, and said, "Hi Darren, you little stinker."

Another significant incident occurred with the touch lamp that was yet another confirmation that it was Darren manipulating the light. Ever since Trevor was a baby he would occasionally start laughing uncontrollably for no apparent reason while on his back on the changing table or in my arms, facing up in the rocking chair. He would look toward the ceiling or next to me (not at me), and just start cracking up, as though he were seeing something or someone that was making him laugh. I'd even look behind or above myself, trying to discover the source of his laughter, but there was never anything there. "Trevor," I'd ask, "What's so funny? What are you laughing at?" He'd just keep laughing. I just thought all babies did this.

As he got older, he'd sometimes look toward the ceiling, laugh, and then start babbling and making hand gestures, as though he were having a conversation with someone on the ceiling. It was amusing to watch, but I always thought that perhaps he could see Darren, and was playing with him. It was only in his bedroom that this happened.

One night, I was rocking Trevor to sleep and he was looking up toward the ceiling, laughing uncontrollably as he had many times before. He was a little over two-years-old, and his vocabulary was limited to mainly one-syllable words or to repeating the same syllable twice. For example, his buddy Elmo (from "*Sesame Street*") he called "Mo-Mo." With his stuffed Elmo in his hand, Trevor was playing "peek-a-boo" with whatever he saw above me. I kept looking up as he laughed and babbled and continued his game, but I saw nothing. This went on for at least ten minutes. "What's so funny?" I kept asking. "What are you laughing at? Who's up there?" Then, as clear as he could be, he said "Darren," with his "r's" sounding like a "w," - more like "Dawin." Chills shot up and down my spine and the hair on my arms stood up. How could he know that name? It wasn't one he was used to hearing. Silently, I thanked Darren for watching over Trevor.

The next night, while getting his pajamas on in his room, Trevor began laughing and pointing up at the ceiling, then looking at me as if to say "Don't you see what I see? I looked up and saw nothing. This time, as I rocked Trevor to sleep, I asked Darren to turn on the light if Trevor had indeed been playing with him, and if it had been his name that Trevor had spoken the night before. The touch lamp was lit up the next morning as my confirmation to what I felt in my heart to be true. I smiled when I saw it, and said "Hi Darren, I knew it was you!"

John Edward, the famous medium, author, and television host says that children and animals are more sensitive to a spirit's energy, and can see them more easily than adults can. Medium and author Sylvia Browne says in her books that children are the most psychic beings on the planet. Because they're still so fresh from the higher vibrational frequency of the other side, the vast majority of children interact with spirits as though they were "imaginary friends." These theories comforted me, and confirmed my belief that Darren was keeping watch over and playing with Trevor.

Confirmations like these motivated me to note down the times whenever the light came on. I even began asking it to go on for guidance with things happening in my life. For example, Matt and I were considering moving into a bigger house. The one we wanted was new and still under construction, so our purchase would be contingent on the sale of our house. Houses in our area were selling within a month, so we weren't worried. Three months went by, and we had two offers fall through. Our contingency expired and we decided it wasn't meant to be. We cancelled our offer on the new house and took ours off the market. It was now just before Christmas, and we didn't want to show our house with company visiting over the holidays, so we decided we'd look again in the spring.

A month went by and one day a realtor came to our door that had shown it previously. He said that a potential buyer who'd already seen the house had asked if we were still interested in selling. I told him that I'd talk to my husband and we'd also have to see if the house we were going to buy was still available. As it turned out, the house we were interested in was still available, and they'd even lowered the price considerably! Matt and I figured it was worth a shot to try and sell our house to this buyer or someone else because of the savings on the new house.

To make a long story short, the potential buyer decided to wait, so we re-listed our house the next day with our real estate agent. Twenty-four hours later, we had a showing, the house sold for the price we wanted, and we moved into our new house 30 days later! What does this have to do with the touch lamp? The day we re-listed the house, I was rocking Trevor to sleep, almost in tears, feeling confused and nervous about this whole ordeal, so I desperately pleaded to Darren. "Please, Darren, give me a sign. If moving is the right thing to do, let me know by turning on the light in the morning. I don't want to have to clean the house every day, and have people coming over for showings during the holidays. So, if this is the right thing to do, please turn on the light. I don't know what to do anymore. I need your help."

The next morning, when Matt went to get Trevor up, the light was on! "That is the sign I asked for," I told Matt. "We're going to be moving!" He was still a little bit skeptical about the whole idea of Darren turning on a light to give me a sign; but when we got an offer on the house that same day, he said, "Maybe someone is looking out for us after all." The light was also on the following morning. I just smiled, and said "Thank you, Darren." During a later reading with Sherry Lynn, Darren took full credit for the quick sale. This just validated what I knew to be true.

Since I'm on the subject of real estate, I'll skip ahead to a year and three months later. Matt had gotten a job offer in Reno, NV. After visiting the area and talking it over, we decided to make the move. The touch lamp was on as Matt and I were leaving to go on our trip to Reno, which was a good sign, but not the point I'm trying to make. Anyway, Matt had accepted the job and I was very stressed out because they wanted Matt to start in two weeks, and we hadn't even listed our house in California yet. Our realtor came over with paperwork to sign and said the house would be on the Multiple Listing Service the next day, so other realtors could show it. That night, the touch lamp went on while I had Trevor in the tub. The house would sell the next day, I prophesized to Matt and my brother Joey. Of course, they both laughed. You'll see, I thought.

The next day, a call came from our realtor's assistant around noon. There was just one more thing to add in the computer, she said, and then the house would be listed. Expect some calls, she added. Half an hour later, a realtor called and made an appointment to preview our home for a client in town from Texas. A few hours later, the Texan came to see the house himself and was calling his wife and taking pictures. The realtor brought his purchase offer to our house later that evening. We accepted, of course. No contingencies, thirty-day escrow, and the price we needed. It was only on the market for a few hours and it was sold. We didn't even have the For Sale sign in our yard yet! When the realtor left, I reminded Matt "See, I told you that the touch lamp going on last night meant that we'd sell our house today." "Wow," he said. "I guess I'll never doubt it again."

I don't want to get too redundant with touch lamp stories because there are so many of them now. But this next one was the true test of its validity. After we'd sold our first house and moved, I was concerned that Darren wouldn't find me in the new house; or worse yet, that the lamp wouldn't light up in the new house. I worried that I'd been imagining the whole thing, and that it had just been an electrical quirk, as Matt had initially suggested.

The day we moved into the new house, I made sure to set up the lamp in Trevor's room right away. I even personally drove it over to the new house. I didn't want to pack it and risk having it break. On our first night in the new house, as I rocked Trevor to sleep, I made a conscious connection to Darren to ask him for more proof. "Okay, Darren," I said. "This is the true test. We're in a new house and the touch lamp has been moved. If you're still here with us, and all of this is real and not my imagination running wild, turn it on in the morning."

The blinds hadn't been installed in Trevor's room yet, so with the sun coming in and the lamp placed in front of the window, I didn't notice if the lamp was on or not the next morning when I went to get him out of bed. I decided to give Trevor a tour of our new house. As I showed him around, I said "Here's Mommy and Daddy's room, and here is Trevor's room… and outside, you can see your doggies." As I looked out the window pointing to the dogs, the lamp was in my line of vision. I noticed, very faintly, that all three bulbs were glowing! I was so thrilled, I almost cried. I called to my mom and showed her. Darren was here! It really was him turning on the lamp. Now, I was really convinced. I felt validated.

During the next couple of weeks, Darren contacted me through the touch lamp several times to prove that he was the one doing it. One of these times was when I was taking a bath by candlelight; listening to the same CD that Darren and Dave were playing in the SUV the night that Darren died. I hadn't listened to "*The Best of Sade*" in years, because it made me sad. I started to cry when I heard "*No Ordinary Love*," a song that Darren had often said reminded him of our relationship. I had a long cry and after I finally got out of the tub, I went to check on Trevor before I went to bed, and found the touch lamp was glowing. My sadness gave way to sweetness and consolation. He really does know when I'm thinking about him, I thought.

Another instance shortly after our move was a double congratulation. I finished writing the rough draft for my book the same day that I took a home pregnancy test and found out that I was pregnant with my second child. The touch lamp was on that morning. I wondered what the reason was when I saw it was on, and at the end of the day I had my answer.

At one of Sherry's group readings, Darren came through without my asking for him. He told Sherry that he has been doing things with our lights to let me know that he's still around, and that he'll always be with me wherever I go- in my home, and in my car… everywhere. This comment validated what I already knew. However, the fact that Sherry didn't know I was concerned that Darren wouldn't find me when we moved, or my concern over the authenticity of the touch lamp, made this validation very special.

A few months later, Matt was in Trevor's room rocking him to sleep when the touch lamp went on and lit up the darkened room. He started to panic and called out to me. When I opened Trevor's door, I saw that the touch lamp was lit. "It just went on by itself," Matt said, pointing to the lamp. "Were you doing something in the other room that might have made it go on?" "No, you know why it goes on." I told him. "It's just a little thank you for being such a good daddy." I teased. I think it kind of freaked Matt out a bit. I actually felt a little jealous because the lamp never went on while I was in the room. As I walked away, I laughed to myself. It was just like Darren, the prankster, to get a kick out of messing with Matt!

The next two stories happened during and after my pregnancy with Damon, our second child. I started bleeding heavily two separate times during the first trimester of my pregnancy, and I thought I was going to lose him. The bleeding happened at night, both times. I frantically called my doctor, who, after listening to my symptoms, said that there was nothing to be done unless the bleeding got worse, or I started having contractions. He advised me to rest in bed and come in the next day for an ultrasound.

Both times, Matt and I were lying in bed holding each other, as I was crying and praying to God that I wouldn't lose the baby. On both occasions, as Matt left our room to walk down the hall and give my mom an update, he noticed that the touch lamp in Trevor's room had gone on during the crisis! I knew that my prayers had been heard, and that everything would be all right. It's funny, but that light going on was more of a reassurance to me than anything the doctor could have said.

Damon was born on October 15, 2001. Although he was a big baby (8 pounds, 10 ounces, and 21 inches long), I was able to deliver naturally again. A little side note; while I was in labor, *"Crossing Over with John Edward"* came on the TV in my hospital room. One of the nurses asked me, "Do you believe in this stuff?" Matt says, "Don't get her started." I answered, "Yes, absolutely." It was comforting to see my favorite show during the most painful experience of my life. Thanks, John!

Anyway, Damon was born at 1:40 p.m. I hadn't slept the whole night before and was exhausted. After all of my visitors had gone home so I could get some much-needed sleep, I said a prayer. I thanked God for helping me with the delivery, and for my beautiful, healthy son. Then, I talked to Darren and asked him to give me a sign that he was still with me, since I hadn't felt his presence in the delivery room as I had during Trevor's birth. And then...before I knew it, I was fast asleep.

The next morning, I called my mom at the house to check up on things. The first thing she said to me was "The touch lamp was on in Trevor's room this morning when I went in to get him up." That was the icing on the cake. I knew that Darren was there with me after all, as I know that he'll be with me in spirit for all the other important times in my life.

One last string of touch lamp stories to tell. (Save the best for last, right?) When Darren and I became engaged in 1990, we adopted Shadow, a 2-year-old cat, from the humane society. We named her Shadow because she was black, and followed me everywhere. Two years later, we got our dog, Dakota. Dakota thought it was her job to chase Shadow every time she tried to eat or use her litter box. So, poor Shadow was basically exiled to the island in the kitchen or to the top of the refrigerator for an entire year.

One day, Kristine stopped at the house to pick me and my sister up to go to the Winger/Sweetwater concert, and was admiring Shadow. "She is the sweetest cat" Kristine commented. Half jokingly I asked, "Do you want her?" "Are you kidding? I'd love to have her!" she said. I told her about how Dakota wouldn't leave Shadow alone, and she said that if I was really serious, she'd take her. Darren and I decided this would be best for Shadow (and for me as well- I'd discovered that I was allergic to her.) Kristine treated Shadow like a princess for 10 years or so; and then, because of the cat's failing health, reluctantly had her put to sleep.

Kim, who is also Kristine's friend, called to tell me about it. Feeling very sad, I asked Darren to give me a sign that Shadow had found her way to him. (I hoped that our pets also went to heaven and wanted his confirmation.) A few days later, I was lying in Trevor's bed with him, rubbing his back in the dark, when the touch lamp went on behind me! While I was in the room! I heard my mom's footsteps in the hall and excitedly called out to her. She came into his room and said that she saw the light go on too, but she thought that I had turned it on myself. "No," I told her. "It just went on by itself, and I was in the room to see it firsthand." Now there was no denying the validity of Darren's spiritual presence. As if that wasn't great enough, after my mom left the room I silently asked Darren if this meant that he had Shadow with him. As I was looking at the lamp for some sort of answer, the lights visibly dimmed! My heart filled with joy, as my eyes filled with tears. I couldn't wait to share this with Kristine.

I called Kristine the next day to tell her the story, and she couldn't stop crying and thanking me. She said that as she was driving home from the vet after putting Shadow to sleep, she had asked Darren to please be there to greet Shadow. Actually, she said she had *demanded* that he be there to greet Shadow. "He sure was." I told her. Kristine was halfway across the country, praying for a sign that Darren had Shadow with him, and both our prayers were answered through the touch lamp to let us know that he did. He had to make it extra-special by doing it while I was in the room. Knowing that our pets remain connected to us even in death gives me great peace. Dakota is no spring chicken, and as heartbroken as I'll be when it's her time to go, I know she won't be alone; Darren will be there to welcome her with open arms.

Kristine knew the significance of the touch lamp, and was crying tears of joy and was very comforted by this story. I told her that this was the first time I had ever been in the room when the touch lamp went on, and how great I thought it was. The next night, I was in Trevor's room again. (He likes me to stay with him until he falls asleep.) I was lying on my stomach with my head turned toward the nightstand with the touch lamp on it, when it went on by itself again. I smiled because I knew Darren must have been listening in on my conversation with Kristine and wanted to do it again, just to show me that he could, and to prove that I hadn't been mistaken about it the first time it happened.

The other part of this story that included both Shadow and the touch lamp was the story I referred to during the chapter on my reading with medium Vickie Gay. To refresh your memory, she told me in the reading that there was a cat there that just wanted to let me know that it was there. I knew it had to be Shadow because the previous incident with the touch lamp going on while I was in the room to let me know that Darren had Shadow with him had recently occurred. Having Vickie mention it validated that what the touch lamp told me was true, Shadow was there.

After I figured out the connection, I was excited to call Kristine and tell her about this new reference to Shadow in my reading. As I was walking down the hallway toward my bedroom to call Kristine and tell her the news, I passed Trevor's room and noticed that the touch lamp was on. He was now big enough to turn it on himself, and so was Damon, so I stopped in the hallway and yelled to my mom in the other room, asking her if anyone had been in Trevor's room and turned the touch lamp on. She said no, adding that she had just been in there, and it wasn't on. I went in my bedroom, and while I was dialing Kristine's phone number, I noticed that another touch lamp in my bedroom was also on! It was on top of a tall dresser that I could barely reach. Because I was questioning the reason for the touch lamp being on, now that the boys could have turned it on, Darren decided to turn two touch lamps on simultaneously, so there would be no question. This was a double validation.

I could write a whole book on this subject, since it has become a regular phenomenon in my house. Another notable incident with the two touch lamps on New Year's Eve. Two years in a row, both touch lamps went on simultaneously at midnight. I have fond memories of spending New Year's Eve with Darren. I actually received a videotape of us (five years after his death) from a New Year's Eve party we attended a month before he passed on. The party was a blast, and the video contained rare footage of him dancing. The dual touch lamps lighting up at midnight on New Years occurred the two years immediately following receipt of the video.

The touch lamp also went on during other family member's readings with Sherry Lynn in my house; once during my sister's reading and again during my brother Joey's reading. It went on again while I was in the room on the day of my 18-year-old second cousin's funeral. Again, as in the story with Shadow, I mentally asked Darren to turn the light on to let me know that my cousin was on the other side, and with my family. After it went on in front of me, I mentally asked if this meant that my cousin was there, and again, the lights visibly dimmed. I cried and felt such a sense of peace that I decided to share this experience in a letter with his grieving parents. I don't know how well it was received, but I did my part to relay the message.

I now know without a doubt that this is one of Darren's ways of contacting me from the other side. If I hadn't experienced it myself, I'd probably be one of those people who would say, "Yeah, sure, a dead person is turning on lights in your house." I really don't care if someone doesn't believe it, I know the truth. The touch lamp has been moved into new homes six times now and still lights up on special dates, to give me a heads up, when I pray for a sign as an answer, and sometimes just to let me know that Darren is still with me. I feel blessed to receive and recognize this ongoing wonderful connection between the two of us.

This type of spontaneous direct contact, as opposed to communication through a medium, was much more personal, and it gave me a different kind of comfort. It didn't happen regularly however, until I began asking for signs, and then believing they were real and not dismissing them as something else. Awareness and an open mind are the keys to connecting with spiritual energy. I've learned that I don't need a medium to connect to Darren on the other side. For my own healing it was important to experience both types of after-death contact. It was one thing to have a total stranger confirm the existence of the spirits of my loved ones on the other side, and quite another to personally see that proof demonstrated in my life.

My relationship with Darren did not end with his death. My views of life and death have been forever altered by these experiences and I can't imagine the emotional pain I would still be in had I not experienced them. Darren is not sitting on some cloud somewhere unreachable playing a harp, as my skewed former ideas of heaven would have had me believe. Or worse yet, in hell, as my former religion would have me believe. He is right here, wherever I am, whenever I need him, and will always be a part of me. Even though he is no longer here physically, I know he is with me and my family spiritually, helping us in oh, so many ways.

Part Seven

<u>Lessons</u>

<u>What I've Learned</u>

"If you wish to be eternally happy, know and believe you will live after death. Always remember this, for it is the truth."

—Emmanuel Swedenborg

When Darren died, I thought my life was over too. It was impossible for me to imagine anything good coming from his death. But now, over a decade later, I can look back and see how much I've grown; and can honestly say that I feel grateful for all the hard lessons I've learned. Here is a list of some of the gifts that this experience has given me:

- I've learned to appreciate life, and those that I love. You never know when it is anyone's time to go.
- I've learned that each day is a gift, maybe that's why it is called "The Present."
- I've learned to never pass up an opportunity to say "I love you," because you never know when it will be the last time.
- I've learned not to fear death. It is not the end, it is the beginning.
- I've learned that relationships with people we love don't have to end just because the person is no longer physically here.
- I've learned about my own spiritual nature, and my connection to all living things.
- I've learned that tragedy can make you a bitter person, or a better person; it's your choice.
- I've learned to be grateful for what Darren's life gave to me, not angry for what his death took from me.
- I've learned that I have the capacity to forgive what I once thought was unforgivable; and that forgiveness is the antidote of anger.
- I've learned that it's not as important what happens to you in life, but rather how you react to what happens that matters. You are in control of that part.
- I've learned that through pain, suffering, and adversity come our greatest

lessons. Think about it, what do you learn during the good times?

- I've learned to be courageous... because I had to.
- I've learned to think for myself, to speak my mind and be more assertive, instead of being the passive do-gooder that I used to be.
- I've learned to be more compassionate and sensitive to another's pain, and more tolerant of another's grief. We all grieve in our own way, and in our own time.
- I've learned not to blindly believe in what others have traditionally believed, to question everything, and to be true to what feels right to me.
- I've learned that our childhood ideals of love are unrealistic. Not all relationships are supposed to last a lifetime.
- I've rekindled my love for reading and learning, and I've became more open-minded to new ideas. When we are done learning the lessons we came here to learn, we go home.
- I've learned that the people we love are our most important assets. When you first lose someone you love, you would gladly give away all your possessions to have them back. In the grand scheme of things, money and possessions don't matter at all, only love matters. It is the only thing you can take with you.
- I've learned that we choose our parents, siblings, partners, children, and friends before we incarnate into a human body, to assist each other in learning the lessons we came here to learn. It is all perfect. Our pain is self-chosen as well. Which leads me to the following quote from *"The Prophet"* by Kahlil Gibran:

"Much of your pain is self-chosen.
It is the bitter potion by which the physician
within you heals your sick self.
Therefore trust the physician, and drink his
remedy in silence and tranquility:
For his hand, though heavy and hard, is guided
by the tender hand of the Unseen.
And the cup he brings, though it burns your lips,
has been fashioned of the clay which the Potter
has moistened with His own tears."

How I've Changed

"Your vision will become clear only when you look into your heart. Who looks outside, dreams. Who looks inside, awakens."

—Carl Jung

With the aid of time, and as a result of working through my grief, having readings with mediums, and experiencing my own direct after-death communication, I can say that I have made peace with losing Darren. This is not the same as being "over" losing Darren, which is a very unrealistic expectation. The goal of grief is not to "get over it," but instead, to be able to celebrate the life of those we've lost by talking about them and remembering them with joy, instead of pain. Grief is the price we pay for loving someone.

There are so many ways that becoming a widow and the journey that my life has taken as a result has changed me. My life and my ideas about the world have been forever altered. I have been forever altered. Being a widow will always be a part of who I am. It's not like I'll ever forget what happened. In fact, there are many uncomfortable residual effects along with the good things I have learned from this experience. For instance, when someone I love is missing or late, I get this sinking, panicky feeling. I return to that fateful day when I waited and waited, and my husband never came home. It's like a recurring nightmare. When people say goodbye, I don't automatically assume that I'll see them again.

It is also difficult for me to watch the news. For years I was desensitized to the tragedies the media serve up daily. I rarely watch the news at all anymore. It is so depressing. It is all bad news. When I do watch it, I often see myself in the faces of the people being interviewed. I hate it when the media interview a victim's loved one right after a tragedy. I see the shock and the unbelievable pain in their eyes and on their faces. It makes me want to scream at the TV, "Leave those poor people alone! Take that camera away!" The media have no respect for the grieving. I often cry when I hear about someone losing a loved one to violence or accidents. I find myself praying to God for the families, and especially for the children of the victims. I also can't watch hospital shows, violent movies, or horror movies. Death is taken so lightly, and the way grief is portrayed is not based at all in reality.

My attitude about life in general has also changed. I no longer believe that the world is a place of random violence. I believe that everything happens for a reason, and that there are no coincidences. I am also a firm believer that God does not give us more than we can handle, although in the beginning it feels as though He has overestimated us and has made a mistake. I believe that life's challenges are for our own growth. The more adversity you face, the more you learn and grow. Now, when something unexpected or disappointing happens, I don't think that I have bad luck, or a dark cloud following me. I question everything, and ask "What am I supposed to learn from this situation?" If I am honest with myself, I can usually find the answers.

One good thing that came from this tragedy is that I, as well as some of my friends, have become intolerant of drunk driving. When my friends go out, there is now a designated driver. We have all lived through the consequences of an irresponsible decision. It is naïve to think it only happens to other people. Before the accident, a lot of people I knew would go out drinking; and their idea of a designated driver was the person who was the least drunk. Not any more. A lapse in judgment can ruin lives forever. I was living proof of that.

Personally, since the accident, I've had no desire to visit clubs. I used to love going out to see bands play, and go dancing with friends; but in the whole six years that I lived in California, I did not go out to a club one time. I am such a homebody now. The old me would have loved to go out to all the Hollywood rock clubs that all my favorite hair bands got their start. But now, the idea of being in a crowded bar with a bunch of drunk or drugged up people has no appeal to me. I can listen to music at home, thank you. Darren's tragic death was a wake up call and it forced me to grow up and re-evaluate my priorities and my lifestyle.

I don't know how much of this is from maturity, or a result of my spiritual transformation, as I call it; but even subtle things like my musical tastes have changed. I used to like only rock or alternative music, and I used to say that other types of music gave me a rash. Now, I've become more melancholy at times and I'm enjoying a wider musical variety, including New Age, Native American, and Classical music. I'm still a rocker at heart, but I'm open to new sounds and my tastes are expanding.

One positive change in my life is that I believe more than ever in the power of prayer. I have also been working on gratitude and I thank God every day for the blessings in my life. I know that sometimes our prayers are not answered to our satisfaction; but I have to believe that there is a reason why certain things happen the way they do, even if I can't understand why. I have learned to accept that. Some things just aren't meant to be the way we think they should be. The plan is the plan.

Another change I've noticed in myself is that I have much more appreciation and reverence for nature and the beautiful things in this world. I see God's hand in everything. I am in awe of things that I never noticed or gave much thought to before. It's as if I am seeing the world through new eyes.

There are so many metaphors for the circle of life found in nature. I am especially fond of butterflies now. To me, they symbolize life after death. Their transformation from one form to another, from caterpillar to butterfly, perfectly symbolizes the transition from life on earth to life on the other side. Even the way the caterpillar appears to have died, and has to struggle out of the cocoon to become a beautiful, free butterfly reminds me of the grief process, and the internal transformation that I have gone through. I have lots of butterfly art in my home, and whenever I see them in nature, I think of them as a gift from Darren.

I am mostly in awe of my sons, Trevor and Damon. They are heaven-sent, and I love watching them change. I thank God for them every day. I cherish every moment I spend with them, because I know it could all change tomorrow. I even look at children differently. I've often wondered if Trevor and Damon met up with Darren in heaven before they came to earth to be my little angels. I'm sure that God has sent each of them here with a mission. No one is here by accident. I know that we don't own our children; we are just blessed to watch over them and teach them, as they in turn teach us. We chose each other, and we'll all be together again after our time here has ended. Love never dies.

In a lot of ways, I am a different person than I was before Darren's death. Certain things that were acceptable to me then, would not be acceptable to me now. I laugh at some of the choices I made back then, both personally and professionally because the person I am today would never make those same choices. I never would have dated some of the guys I did when I was younger, and I would not have chosen to model or waitress. But at the time, they fit with what was important to me. Some of those things that were so important to me back then are quite trivial to me now.

For example, I always loved to shop, and after Darren's death, I tried some Retail Therapy and I went on a few spending sprees in an effort to make myself feel better. I bought a lot of new clothes and makeup thinking that if I looked better on the outside, I'd feel better on the inside. It was only a band-aid. The adrenaline rush I felt after buying new things quickly faded away, and then I need another fix.

I know I'm not alone here. I remember one day, about a year after Darren's death, I was working at a cosmetics counter, and an older woman approached my counter with a $300.00 return from another counter that she had just bought the day before. She was too embarrassed to go to the other counter she told me. Almost in tears, she said that her husband had just died, and she tried to make herself feel better by buying all of this stuff, and then she got home and realized she had made a mistake. I told her that I completely understood, and did the return for her; even though I knew I would get in trouble later for taking such a big return from another line. I felt her pain, and had done the same thing myself.

Slowly, I realized that buying things to fill an emotional void doesn't work. You can't buy happiness. So, I gave away a lot of my old clothes to friends and family and Goodwill. It felt good to clean up the clutter in my life. Now, I am much more low-maintenance. Taking two kids with you to the mall takes most of the enjoyment out of shopping. I still enjoy getting new things, but now, I shop for clothes or other goodies when I need something or when I want to treat myself, not several days a week, like I used to. No amount of money or material possessions can make a person happy. If you want to feel rich, count all the things in your life that money can't buy.

I have even become interested in personal growth by investigating subjects such as numerology and astrology. I used to think this stuff was a joke, for entertainment purposes only. Then I began to notice that these types of books were always in the New Age section of the bookstore, my new favorite section. I also noticed that some very gifted psychics and mediums also did numerology, astrology and tarot. One day, for kicks, I ordered a numerology profile from an ad in a magazine. You need to give your full name and month, date, and year of your birth. I was expecting them to come back describing a total stranger, but I was amazed by the accuracy. This piqued my curiosity, and I took out some books from the library on numerology and astrology. I especially liked Linda Goodman's books. They are very detailed and are excellent tools for self-realization and for understanding others.

I have had numerology and tarot readings, and did my astrological chart, all with very accurate results. I have also reduced the numbers (numerology) of the birthdays of my family and friends, as well as addresses of our homes, and read about the significance of the numbers. Of course, I also looked up my friends and family members astrological signs. My mom and I got a big kick out of reading the personality descriptions of each sign. I'd make her guess who I was describing. They were all so accurate, not to mention entertaining. It gives you a little insight into what makes people tick, and even their purpose. It also showed me that there is something to this and that I still have a lot more to learn.

Tragedy forces us to look inside and confront who we are. We all know people who have had a severe trauma, and instead of being ruined by their so called misfortune, they have developed the most amazing outlook on life. I guess I'm becoming one of those people- or so I'm told. I know that I am still a work in progress, as we all are, but I am so proud of the new me who has emerged and risen up from the ashes of grief.

Through the process of writing this book, I hope to reach out to others and hopefully ease someone else's grief, and let them know they are not alone. I want to serve others by what I've learned. I never used to be that way. A new sense of compassion has blossomed within me because of my loss. Whenever you help someone else, you also help yourself. Just the thought of my story inspiring someone else, and helping them heal, fills me with pride and tears.

I'm not some spiritual guru who has all the answers to the mysteries of life. I'm your normal Midwestern girl who lived through a horrible tragedy, and through that tragedy, found my own connection to spirit and personal spiritual enlightenment. The important lessons I learned were that you can find happiness again after losing a spouse, that I am still connected to Darren, and that he is there for me whenever I need him. I have an ally on the other side, watching out for me and my family. The bond of love is eternal, that much I know.

Death is not the ending I used to think it was; and this gives me tranquility beyond measure. Even though I'm comforted by the knowledge that Darren is safe on the other side, that I will see him again some day, and that he is with me in spirit, I still cry sometimes because I miss my friend here on Earth. I still get nostalgic on special days and when I hear certain songs. But now, thinking of Darren makes me smile more often than it makes me cry.

The most important lesson I have learned is that there truly is life after death; not only for those who have passed on, but also for those left behind. I'm sure that at some point in my life, I am going to lose other loved ones. That's the way life is, we will all die one day. Knowing what I know now, I am much more equipped to handle it than I was when I lost Darren. It doesn't mean I won't have to grieve, because I will, but I will know for certain that they will be safe with other loved ones on the other side, that we are still connected, and that I will see them again. Believing these things make death a little more bearable for the living. One thought that continues to inspire me is that I know when it is my time to cross over; Darren will be there to greet me, along with my other loved ones who have gone on before me. My eyes fill with tears whenever I imagine that joyous reunion.

After all of my friends and family members read this book, I was amazed at the stories that came back to me from them. Everyone who read it either had a personal story or a story about someone that they knew who had a similar after-death experience. People don't usually discuss things like after-death contact in every day conversations; but when the ball gets rolling... look out! I've heard so many heart-warming and amazing stories, and had so many more incredible experiences of my own, that I could write another book. Maybe I will...

<u>And if I go…</u>

And if I go, while you're still here…
know that I still live on.
Vibrating to a different measure
behind a thin veil you cannot see through.

You will not see me,
so you must have faith.
I wait the time when we can soar together again,
both aware of each other.

Until then, live your life to the fullest,
and when you need me,
just whisper my name in your heart,
…I will be there.

—Colleen Hitchcock

Resources

The Mediums/Psychics I Saw

1. Psychic Medium Brian E. Hurst lives in Reseda, California, and can be reached at (818) 345-2997, or through his website, www.brianhurst.com.

2. Sherry Lynn lives in Thousand Oaks, California, and can be reached through her website, www.sherrylynn.com.

3. Holistic Therapist Ruth Kramer owns Myracle Therapeutic Center in Westlake Village, CA and can be reached at (805) 402-8020, or through her website, www.myracletherapeutic.com.

4. Psychic Medium Vickie Gay lives in Reno, NV, and can be reached at (415) 244-6321, through her website, www.vickiegay.com, or by e-mail at mail@vickiegay.com.

5. Psychic Theresa Peacock works in Reno, NV and can be reached by phone at (775) 337-8185.

Bibliography

- Altea, Rosemary, *The Eagle and the Rose* (Warner Books, 1996); and *Proud Spirit: Lessons, Insights & Healing from 'The Voice of the Spirit World* (William Morrow & Co., 1998).

- Anderson, George, and Barone, Andrew, *Lessons from the Light: Extraordinary Messages of Comfort and Hope from the Other Side* (Berkley New York, 2000); and *Walking in the Garden of Souls: George Anderson's Advice from the Hereafter, for Living in the Here and Now* (Putnam Pub Group, 2001).

- Brinkley, Dannion, *Saved by the Light: The True Story of a Man Who Died Twice and the Profound Revelations He Received* (Harper Mass Market, 1995).

- Browne, Sylvia, *The Other Side and Back: A Psychic's Guide to Our World and Beyond* (Signet, 1999); and *Life On The Other Side: A Psychic's Tour of the Afterlife* (Signet, 2000).

- Caine, Lynn, *Being a Widow* (Penguin USA, 1990).

- Eadie, Betty, *Embraced by the Light* (Bantam Books, 1992); and *The Awakening Heart: My Continuing Journey to Love* (Pocket Books, 1997).

- Edward, John, *One Last Time: A Psychic Medium Speaks to Those We Have Loved and Lost* (Berkley, 1998); *What if God Were the Sun?* (Jodere Group, 2000); *Crossing Over: The Stories Behind the Stories* (Jodere Group, 2001); and *After Life* (Princess Books, 2003).

- Feinberg, Linda Sones, *I'm Grieving as Fast as I Can: How Young Widows and Widowers Can Cope and Heal* (New Horizon Press, 1994).

- Guggenheim, Bill, and Guggenheim, Judy, *Hello from Heaven: A New Field of Research- After-Death Communication- Confirms That Life and Love are Eternal* (Bantam, 1996).

- Goodman, Linda, *Linda Goodman's Sun Signs* (Bantam Books, 1985); and *Linda Goodman's Love Signs* (Perennial, 1992).

- Goodman, Sandy, *Love Never Dies: A Mother's Journey from Loss to Love*

(Jordere Group, 2002)

- Hay, Louise, *You Can Heal Your Life* (Hay House, 1999).

- Hurst, Brian Edward, *Some Go Haunting* (Airleaf Publishing).

- Kübler-Ross, Elizabeth, M.D., *The Wheel of Life: A Memoir of Living and Dying* (Touchstone Books, 1998).

- Martin, Joel, and Romanowski, Patricia, *We Don't Die: George Anderson's Conversations With the Other Side* (G.P. Putnam's Sons, 1988); *We Are Not Forgotten: George Anderson's Messages of Love and Hope from the Other Side* (Berkley Pub Group, 1994); and *Love Beyond Life: The Healing Power of After-Death Communications* (HarperCollins; 1997).

- Mclennan, Scotty, Rev., *Finding Your Religion: When the Faith You Grew Up With Has Lost Its Meaning* (Harper San Francisco, 2000).

- Schwartz, Gary E., Ph.D., *The Afterlife Experiments: Breakthrough Scientific Evidence of Life After Death* (Pocket Books, 2002).

- Van Praagh, James, *Talking to Heaven: A Medium's Messages of Life after Death* (Dutton, 1997); *Reaching to Heaven: A Spiritual Journey Through Life and Death* (Signet, 1999); and *Healing Grief: Reclaiming Life after any Loss* (Signet, 2000).

Lightning Source UK Ltd.
Milton Keynes UK
UKOW03f0019130514

231562UK00002B/324/P